Bearing Society in Mind

DISRUPTIONS

Disruptions is a series that interrogates and analyses disruptions within and across such fields and disciplines as culture and society, media and technology, literature and philosophy, aesthetics and politics.

Bearing Society in Mind: Theories and Politics of the Social Formation, Samuel A. Chambers
Open Education: A Study in Disruption, Pauline van Mourik Broekman, Gary Hall, Ted Byfield, Shaun Hides and Simon Worthington
What Lies Between: Void Aesthetics and Postwar Politics, Matt Tierney (forthcoming)
Living Screens: Reading Melodrama in Contemporary Film and Television, Monique Rooney (forthcoming)
Word: Divine, Dissonant and Digital, Mariam Motamedi Fraser (forthcoming)
Martial Arts Studies, Paul Bowman (forthcoming)

Bearing Society in Mind

Theories and Politics of the Social Formation

Samuel A. Chambers

ROWMAN &
LITTLEFIELD
INTERNATIONAL

London • New York

Published by Rowman & Littlefield International, Ltd.
Unit A, Whitacre Mews, 26-34 Stannery Street, London SE11 4AB
www.rowmaninternational.com

Rowman & Littlefield International, Ltd. is an affiliate of Rowman & Littlefield
4501 Forbes Boulevard, Suite 200, Lanham, Maryland 20706, USA
With additional offices in Boulder, New York, Toronto (Canada), and Plymouth (UK)
www.rowman.com

British Library Cataloguing in Publication Data
A catalogue record for this book is available from the British Library

ISBN: HB 978-1-78348-022-7
PB 978-1-78348-023-4

Library of Congress Cataloging-in-Publication Data
Chambers, Samuel Allen, 1972–
Bearing society in mind : theories and politics of the social formation / Samuel A. Chambers.
pages cm. — (Disruptions)
Includes index.
ISBN 978-1-78348-022-7 (cloth : alk. paper) — ISBN 978-1-78348-023-4 (pbk. : alk. paper) — ISBN 978-1-78348-024-1 (electronic)
1. Social sciences—Philosophy. 2. Sociology—Philosophy. I. Title.
H61.15.C43 2014
301.01—dc23 2014021748

™ The paper used in this publication meets the minimum requirements of American National Standard for Information Sciences—Permanence of Paper for Printed Library Materials, ANSI/NISO Z39.48-1992.

Printed in the United States of America

To the memory of Joel Olson

Contents

Acknowledgements

This book would never have come to be were it not for my great good fortune in having Alan Finlayson as a colleague down the hall (and a friend up the street) for three delightful years. I thank Alan for his relentlessness. In navigating me toward Althusser, Alan led me to a whole new Marx. Once there, I also discovered Terrell Carver's early work on Marx. Terrell and I have been colleagues and collaborators for over a decade now, but I never expected to find myself toiling, forty years later, in the same domain as he had worked. I thank Terrell for nourishing my thinking on this project in so many ways. Finally, this text was brought to life by my students at Johns Hopkins University: from the numerous groups of intro students whose strong response to my lectures on Marx's *1857 Introduction* convinced me that there was something there, to the wonderful undergraduate seminar participants who were as excited about the long-forgotten work of Arthur Bentley as I, and further on to the dynamic and stimulating graduate seminars over the past six years in which numerous brilliant and brave students variously tackled all of the authors I address in this book, and always in the spirit of collaboration and collegiality. I am grateful to them all, but allow me to note special thanks to a few by name: Patrick Giamario, Nathan Gies, Dana Gordon, Tripp Rebrovick, and Drew Walker.

I have never been so lucky, as I have in the writing of this book, to have so many outstanding readers along the way. I offer heartfelt thanks to each of the following individuals who read parts of the manuscript at one point or another: Paul Apostolidis, Paul Bowman, Rebecca Brown, Terrell Carver, Jodi Dean, Lisa Disch, Alan Finlayson, Stuart Gray, Jairus Grove, Jonathan Hahn, Robert Hassan, Bonnie Honig, Kimberly Hutchings, Patrick Thaddeus Jackson, Isaac Kamola, George Lawson, Alex Livingston, Moya Lloyd, Nancy Luxon, Patchen Markell, Dean Mathiowetz, Davide Panagia, Anand Pandian, Smita Rahman, Tripp Rebrovick, Jemima Repo, John Seery, George Shulman, Jeremy Valentine, Drew Walker, Stephen White, and Túlio Zille. And, of course, I owe an incalculable debt to those who read the manuscript in its entirety: Rebecca Brown, Paul Bowman, Terrell Carver, Stuart Gray, Jemima Repo, George Shulman, and Drew Walker.

Some of the ideas and arguments that animate the project herein were first explored and tested at the American Political Science Association 2010 annual meeting, at the Johns Hopkins Political and Moral Thought Seminar in 2011, and at the Oxford Political Thought conference in 2014. My sincere thanks go to the organisers and all the participants at those events, especially John Marshall, Moya Lloyd, and Elizabeth Frazer. A very different version of my exploration of the case of Lance Armstrong was first published in the *Los Angeles Review of Books* (19 March 2013), and an early iteration of Chapter 4 appeared in *Time & Society* (20.2). Let me also note my genuine gratitude to Richard Katz and the department of Political Science at Johns Hopkins for financial support in the production of the book. In that context, deep thanks go to Patrick Giamario for his indefatigable work on the citation apparatus and to Nathan Gies for his peerless accomplishments on the index. All of my thinking and writing is supported and enhanced by my colleagues in political theory here at Hopkins: Jane Bennett, P. J. Brendese, Bill Connolly, and Jennifer Culbert. It has been a pleasure to work with Martina O'Sullivan at Rowman & Littlefield International, and I thank her for her support of this project and her consummate professionalism. I am thrilled that this book will help to launch Paul Bowman's *Disruptions* Series at RLI; I am proud to be a part of the series and once again grateful to Paul for his enthusiasm and support of my work.

While writing this book I was continuously sustained by colleagues who did not necessarily engage with the text but whose friendship and support were more important than any comments or criticism could ever have been. I am very grateful to Paul Apostolidis, Anne Caldwell, Terrell Carver, Lisa Disch, Alan Finlayson, Jeanne Morefield, Holloway Sparks, and Karen Zivi. No project of this scope can be produced, certainly not by me, without the help, encouragement, and ongoing support of friends and family. The following are just a few people on whom I have depended, or simply known that I could depend, during the course of writing, revising, and producing this book: Eric Appleton, John Bies, Julian Brown, Jackie Chambers, Tim Chambers, Jane Elliot, Laurie Frankel, Stephanie Hershinow, David Hershinow, Ryan McIntyre, Paul Mariz, Akim Reinhardt, Alan Smith, and Christie Snyder.

Writing can be solitary and even isolating, yet very few of us ever really write alone. In my case, I never write without Rebecca Brown somewhere in the thinking, in the text, or in my peripheral vision on the other side of the room (also writing).

I first met Joel Olson at the same time that I first read Marx—in a graduate school reading group on *Capital* that Joel organised. At the time I didn't really understand the Marx, and there was not enough time to get to know Joel. But not long after we each finished our PhDs, Joel and I became close colleagues and then good friends. When I began this project five years ago, it centered on a distinct approach to Marx, and I knew of all my colleagues and friends Joel would be the most excited about it—since Joel, as he told me, wanted some day to write about Marx "as a rigorously *political* thinker." I sent Joel a number of long emails while I was reading intensively and beginning to draft parts of what would eventually become Chapters 2 and 3. Joel was excited by the ideas and arguments, as I knew he would be, and that early infectious enthusiasm provided a great spark to me as I tried to get this project off the ground. When, in the summer of 2010, I described to him the first draft of the first chunk of writing for the book, Joel's reply was swift: "Ooh, that sounds good; I'll look forward to reading and talking to you about it." I still find myself in shock that Joel never read a word of this book—that six months later when I finished that early chapter draft I would have forgotten to send it on to him, and that less than a year after that he would be gone. This one's for you, compañero.

Introduction

Bearing Society in Mind

How to tell the story of a (financial) crisis? Where to begin, where to stop; how to narrate or describe, much less to understand or explain a series of moments that culminate in this "crisis" event? How, even, to name the event itself? These general questions have arisen again in the face of the most recent event that large numbers have chosen to call either the "Financial Crisis of 2008" or the "Great Recession of 2008–2012." Most settle on a starting date of 2008 (or 2007), while the "end" date proves much murkier. (When does a crisis end?) And "great recession" proves popular as a general name for precisely the reason that almost no one wants to call this another "Depression," yet just about everyone wants to insist on characterising it as the worst economic crisis since the Depression. Hence the pull and repulsion of this analogy: this crisis is not like anything else other than the Depression, but it cannot be truly *like* the Depression. In any case, even if writers and commentators can agree, loosely, on a name and date, there is no such agreement to be found when it comes to how this event came about, what precipitated it, or what it means. For these very reasons, the story of the 2008 crisis has been narrated in a wide variety of ways, with distinct timelines, contrasting foci, and above all with widely divergent apportionment of blame. Indeed, wading through these narratives one is reminded of the song lyric: "if you need someone to blame / throw a rock in the air you'll hit someone guilty."

This is not another book on the 2008 crisis, and it is surely not an attempt to apportion blame or find "the cause" of the financial meltdown of 2008 and the subsequent recessions experienced across much of the globe. I start with the question of crisis in general, and with the 2008 crisis in particular, because the problem of trying to understand or explain such an event helps to focus my own inquiry here. In this book I make the case for *the theoretical importance and political necessity of the concept of the social formation*. Yet I also show that "social formation" proves to be a very particular and peculiar type of "concept," since it is not a reflection or model of the world, but rather a definite and concrete part of the world. To *theorise* the social formation means to embed one's very activity of theorising deeply within the context being studied. Put differently, knowledge of the social formation is always a part of the social formation. I articulate the political salience of the concept of the social formation in broad terms, but giving an account of the social formation is particularly important in times of crisis.

Here, then, I want to dive directly into the middle of one particular narrative of our most recent crisis. In his 2010 best seller, *The Big Short*, Michael Lewis once again writes a nonfiction work that tells its tale through fabulous and compelling characters—characters who would prove utterly farcical if Lewis had made them up, but whose amazing (but real) traits and incredible (but actual) choices and decisions grab readers and pull them through the true story that Lewis wants to narrate. Lewis is interested in the way that people with different visions of the world do not just see it differently but somehow "better" than everyone else. My own concern here is not with those particular people per se, nor with their individual *capacities* for sight. I am interested in *what* they see, in what enables that vision, and in the broader conditions that make such perception possible. In early 2005, Michael Burry, a neurologist-turned-financial-management-firm-owner, and a central character in Lewis's tale, saw something very significant.

OBJECTS OF THE SOCIAL FORMATION

> Vision then loses the religious privileges of divine reading: it is no more than a reflection of immanent necessity that ties an object or problem to its conditions of existence. (Althusser 2009 [1965]: 26)

Burry perceived two objects that are absolutely essential not only to understanding the 2008 crisis but also to grasping the meaning and importance of the social formation. Both of these objects came starkly into his view in early 2005, after he had spent months closely studying the bond market, especially the market for mortgage-backed securities (MBS) based on subprime mortgages. The first object was there for anyone to see, as it was a newly available mortgage product, a creation of the US housing boom: "*the interest-only negative amortizing adjustable-rate subprime mortgage*" (Lewis 2010: 27).[1] This is nothing other than a particular mortgage that a prospective home-buyer would be offered, but it is a very special mortgage. I think it is worth unpacking the elements that make up this financial product:

- *subprime*
  This just means that the loan product is designed for people who do not have the highest credit ratings or have otherwise been determined to be less likely to make the necessary repayments. Obviously, then, from the perspective of a lender, given that the loan is going to someone more likely to default, other features of the loan must be included so that the bank can still count on making money on the loan. Traditionally subprime loans have higher interest rates or require greater collateral, but as we will see, this is not at all the case with this particular loan.
- *adjustable rate*
  The interest rate on the loan is not fixed over the term of the loan; typically an adjustable-rate mortgage (ARM) has a fixed rate for a short period of time (sometimes called a teaser rate), after which the rate fluctuates according to market rates (or, in the case of teaser rates, which are always below-market rates, goes up).
- *interest only*
  On a traditional loan, including mortgages, the regular (usually monthly) payment is calculated to include both necessary interest payments (the cost of borrowing the money given the agreed interest rate, the amount borrowed, and the term of the loan) and principal payments. Hence the borrower makes regular interest and principal payments over a fixed term, such that at the end of the term the principal on the loan is zero. With an "interest only" mortgage, the borrower makes monthly payments that only cover the regularly accruing interest on the loan. There are no payments to principal, and the principal of the loan does not change.
- *negative amortising*
  To *amortise* is to reduce or extinguish debt. Most loans are "amortising" in the very simple sense that you pay them off. "Negative

1. Here and throughout the book, unless explicitly noted, all emphasis in quotations is in the original text.

> amortising" is thus quite close to a contradiction in terms, since it names a process not of reducing debt but of increasing it. In a "negative-amortising" mortgage, rather than making full interest payments each month, part or all of the interest costs are actually tacked on to the principal of the loan. In other words, with a "negative-amortising" loan, the principal gets larger as time goes on.

The combination of "interest only" and "negative amortising" is extremely powerful, since in practice it means that a prospective "home buyer" can be offered a mortgage with literally no monthly payments. Instead, each month the bank takes the calculated interest charges and adds them onto the principal. I put "home buyer" in quotation marks not to be glib, but because it makes little sense to say that one "owns a home" if the financial transaction one commits to in order to "buy" that home instantly puts one in negative equity—since, assuming the house is purchased at fair market value, the buyer will immediately owe more on the house than it is worth.[2] What does the existence of this object tell us about the social formation in 2005? Describing Burry's perspective, and quoting him, Lewis puts it as follows: "It wasn't hard to see what sort of person might like to

---

2. This explanation provides some context for thinking about the "foreclosure crisis" that resulted from the overall 2008 crisis. At least in the American press, the foreclosure crisis was usually discussed in dramatic and tragic terms, with "millions of Americans" at risk to "lose their homes," and losing one's home was frequently described in terms similar to homelessness—a topic otherwise rarely discussed in the mainstream American media. The collapse of the housing bubble undoubtedly led to huge losses of equity for millions of Americans, and in many cases the drop in value took people from having significant positive equity to negative equity. Even more significantly, some of those borrowers with ARMs who had to refinance after the bubble burst found they could no longer get a loan to cover what they owed, and were therefore foreclosed upon. Without downplaying the severity of these events, it seems prudent to emphasise that many Americans who were counted as "homeowners" prior to the housing crash were, in all practical terms, just people renting from the bank, and many who "lost their homes" after the crash were those who were forced to relocate from a house in which they had no equity to a house they rented. My comments here apply only very narrowly to the US context, where home mortgages traditionally call for no collateral or obligation to repay other than the house itself. This structure means that it was possible then and now in the USA for those who have negative equity, or are otherwise unable to repay their mortgage, to lose only the house itself (which, given the negative equity is not an asset to begin with) along with taking a large hit to their credit rating. In many other countries around the world, mortgage lenders can come after borrowers for full repayment of the loan, above and beyond the collateral of the house, making the depth of financial ruin in a collapsed housing market all the more serious. (However, this very loan structure also serves to dampen the run-up in housing prices.)

have such a loan: one with no income. What Burry couldn't understand was why a person who lent money would want to extend such a loan. 'What you want to watch are the lenders, not the borrowers', he said. 'The borrowers will always be willing to take a great deal for themselves. It's up to the lenders to show restraint, and when they lose it, watch out'" (Lewis 2010: 27).

In 2005 this new object, the interest-only, negative-amortising, adjustable-rate, subprime mortgage, had emerged and was circulating within the American economy, and within the broader American social formation, and when Mike Burry looked closely at this object, it told him something very important about the broader social formation—*watch out*. It told him that these mortgages were going to fail. The lenders did not care if the mortgages failed (they made money on the exchange itself), since these were so-called originate-and-sell loans, meaning that the banks that create the loan do not hold it on their books. The originating bank immediately sells the loan on to huge Wall Street investment firms who repackage hundreds such mortgages into bonds—that is, MBSs. Looking at the prospectuses of those bonds, Burry also knew that they contained more and more of those negative-amortising, interest-only, destined-to-fail mortgages, which, in turn, meant that these MBSs were also destined to fail. Of course, Burry was seeing these phenomena not through the eyes of a regulator, a politician, or a social scientist. He saw it all as a financial investor, someone in the business of making money on financial markets. Thus, when Burry looked closely at these loans and at the bonds that contained them, his first instinct was to turn toward another object.

As is the practice of financial managers, Burry wanted to take advantage of his perspicuous perspective on the markets—to gain from his very clear view of the implications that sales of interest-only, negative-amortising mortgages were growing. This desire to profit from his view of one object led Burry to a vision of the second key object in this social formation: a credit default swap (CDS) on subprime MBSs. I will unpack this object below, but I want to emphasise that the CDS on MBSs is central to the argument I want to lay out here for precisely the reason that *this object did not exist at the time Burry saw the need for it.* Burry needed a method of investing his firm's money in such a way as to make money from (what he saw as) the impending collapse of the bond market in subprime mortgages. In short, he needed to bet against MBSs, but in early 2005, there was no way to do this. As Lewis helpfully explains, at this moment in time, "the market for subprime mortgages simply had no place for people in it who took a dim view of them" (Lewis 2010: 28). In general, it proves much more complicated to bet against a bond (a debt instrument) than a stock (an equity) because there is no direct way to short a bond.[3] There are a variety of ways of betting against the bond market, but the most attractive for Burry was the object invented only a decade earlier by a JP Morgan analyst, Blythe Masters. The credit default swap is an odd financial object: it is not really a financial swap, since it does not involve the standard exchange of cash flows that define a "swap." It functions much more like an insurance policy, wherein the purchaser of the CDS pays regular premiums in exchange for a possible sum of money should a certain event take place. (The event can be any form of financial restructuring, but it is usually default on the bond.) A CDS differs from traditional insurance in two ways: 1) the purchaser of a CDS can profit from the exchange (without such profit amounting to fraud, as it would in the case of traditional insurance), and 2) the purchaser of the CDS need not have any direct connection to the underlying asset. This explains why the popular press, in an effort to succinctly describe an incredibly complex financial instrument, quickly turned to the metaphor of buying home insurance on someone else's house, in the hopes that it would burn down. Understanding CDSs and their function, Burry also understood that they could solve his problem of betting against the subprime MBS market: this was the financial instrument that Burry needed to purchase in order to leverage his own understanding of the housing and financial markets in early 2005. But in early 2005, there were no CDSs on MBSs in existence, and therefore there was no one selling them.

I want to pause the story at this moment, the moment when Mike Burry envisioned this object, the CDS on MBS, that did not yet exist. Burry himself would help bring it into existence merely through the pestering and hectoring of big Wall Street investment banks, demanding they sell him this object. And Burry was more than successful—by the end of the year he held close to $1 billion in CDSs. Yet my interest lies with what his understanding of the interest-only, negative-amortising loans and his

3. As investors and economists all know, but as many others of us do not (since there is nothing intuitive about it), to "short" a stock actually means, first, to sell a stock that you do not own, thereby equivalently borrowing the value of the stock at its current market price, while also taking on interest-payment obligations to the lender of the stock. Ostensibly, one then waits for the value of the stock to go down, so that one can ultimately buy the stock back at a lower price, thereby paying off the lender of the stock and pocketing the difference between the original value at which one sold and the current value at which one bought (minus interest to the lender for the time in between). Shorting a stock has infinite downside risk, since if the price of the stock continues to rise the obligation of the short seller can continue to go up. The "loan repayment" must come in the form of buying the borrowed shares of the stock and not in paying back the original amount borrowed. While, as I discuss below, there are numerous ways to take a "short position" (i.e., bet against) the bond market, one cannot simply and directly short a bond.

vision for the CDS on MBS tell us about the relationship between an object within the social formation and that social formation itself. Burry was well ahead of the curve, and he profited greatly from placing early and huge bets against the soon-to-be-unravelling subprime mortgage market. But Burry himself did not invent this object out of thin air; he simply saw sooner than everyone else that this object was an inevitable invention of this particular social formation. Some agents would want to bet against MBSs, and other agents would desperately need the cash flow provided by CDS premiums.[4] The CDS on MBS "belongs" to the social formation of American political and cultural economy of the first decade of the twenty-first century, in the sense that it sustains and partially constitutes that broader and larger social formation and also in the sense that that social formation produces and conditions this object.

Grasping this mutually constitutive relationship, between the object and the social formation of which it is a part, leads directly to a much deeper understanding of the importance of the social formation.[5] Put differently, to see this relation between object and formation is to begin to glimpse what is at stake in studying the social formation, historically and politically, and to

---

4. The primary agent who needed that cash flow, it turns out, was the enormous international insurance corporation called "American International Group," otherwise known across the globe as AIG. In the aftermath of the US government's bailout of AIG, the story has become thoroughly politicised and the competing accounts diverge widely. For those interested, places to start pursuing that story could include Boyd (2011) and indirectly Harvey (2010b).

5. In a significant sense, to grasp the object of a social formation *as an object of the social formation* is the deepest and most rigorous way to "grasp" (in the sense of conceptual sighting and understanding) the social formation itself. This is the idea conveyed in the quotation from Althusser that stands as an epigraph to this section. On this point, let me temporise by quoting that passage in full, the terms of which I will circle back to later in the book: "Any object or problem situated on the terrain and within the horizon, i.e. in the definite structured field of the theoretical problematic of a given theoretical discipline, is visible. We must take these words literally. The sighting is thus no longer the act of an individual subject, endowed with the faculty of 'vision' which he exercises either attentively or distractedly; the sighting is the act of its structural conditions, it is the relations of immanent reflection between the field of the problematic and *its* objects and *its* problems. Vision then loses the religious privileges of divine reading: it is no more than a reflection of immanent necessity that ties an object or problem to its conditions of existence, which lie in the conditions of production. It is literally no longer the eye (the mind's eye) of a subject which *sees* what exists in the field defined by a theoretical problematic: it is this field itself which *sees itself* in the objects or problems it defines—sighting being merely the necessary reflection of the field on its objects" (Althusser 2009: 26). In later chapters I will expand Althusser's vision metaphor to sound and other senses—to what Rancière calls the realm of the sensible, of that which can be perceived (Rancière 2006).

gain a clear sense of what is involved in giving an account of the social formation, conceptually and theoretically. I begin this project on the politics and theory of social formations with Mike Burry's perspicuous view of one object (the interest-only, negative-amortising subprime mortgage) and his vision of a second object (the CDS on MBS) as an indirect way of drawing out the crucial significance of the social formation—"indirect" because the lens of analysis focuses not on the social formation but on its objects. I take this somewhat oblique approach for the very reason that "the social formation" is not itself an "object" in any simple sense, and it surely cannot be focused upon narrowly. To pursue the cinematic metaphor, we would have to say that the camera can never "focus" on the social formation because we can never zoom or dolly out far enough; or, if we could, our angle would be so wide as to call into question the very idea of "focus."

THE WHOLE

In order to see or to grasp conceptually an object within the social formation, we must (even if only implicitly) operate with some broader sense of the social formation itself, and this means understanding it in the sense of a larger totality, a wider whole. The history of political thought provides a long line of thinkers who have tried to "think the whole" in diverse ways—from Plato to Hegel to Spinoza. I want to stress, however, that an account of the social formation cannot be derived from a transcendental philosophy; it cannot be deduced from an ontology. In developing an understanding of the social formation, it helps to call on certain philosophical resources, but there is no one single "correct" thinking of the whole that produces a definitive concept of the social formation.[6] Let me develop this point by turning to one way of thinking the whole philosophically.

In the eighth and final numbered paragraph of "The Four Great Errors," the well-known section of *Twilight of the Idols* wherein he attacks a number of the central tenets of what we might call "Western Reason," Friedrich Nietzsche interrupts his own critique to ask (of himself, of his free-spirit readers): "what alone can be *our* doctrine?" (Nietzsche 1889: VI, 8, my translation). Nietzsche then answers his question directly: "that no one *gives* man his qualities, neither God, nor society, nor his parents and ancestors *nor man himself*" (Nietzsche 1998: 32). Yet Nietzsche's immediate answer to the question, of what he

6. However, there are better and worse understandings of the whole, a point I explore in detail in Chapters 2 and 3, through discussion of both Marx's and Althusser's claims concerning the whole.

affirms, still sounds a critical note, and he goes on to conclude the paragraph with another denial of God and the doctrine of responsibility. However, in the middle of the passage Nietzsche offers a sharper vision of "our doctrine," when he writes: "A man is necessary, a man is a piece of fate, a man belongs to the whole, a man *is* in the whole; there is nothing that could judge, measure, compare, or sentence his being, for that would mean judging, measuring, comparing, or sentencing the whole. . . . *But there is nothing other than the whole!*" (Nietzsche 1889: VI, 8, my translation).

Putting aside Nietzsche's own use of italics (as he seems to throw them around so freely), the very structure of these two sentences—wherein Nietzsche sets up the second with the conclusion to the first by using the ellipsis to walk the reader slowly to the peroration—indicates the significance for Nietzsche of this last line. In German, it reads, "*Aber es gibt nichts außer dem Ganzen!*" The translation seems straightforward, yet a lot hangs on the "außer dem," which has, in popular translations, been variously rendered as "besides" or "apart from" and which I choose to give as "other than." While Nietzsche's emphasis on the importance of "the whole" cannot be doubted, at issue in the various translations is a question central to my project: How to grasp the status of the whole?[7] Does Nietzsche mean to say that the whole is all, that nothing else exists—that is, that every single *thing* is always and only *everything*? Or, is he making the milder (but perhaps still portentous) claim that no single thing can ever stand apart from a wider context, a larger whole, or a more encompassing totality?[8] I interpret the passage in this second sense, not only because I find it a more tenable, plausible, and important philosophical position (i.e., regardless of what Nietzsche thinks) but also because, taken in its entirety, the passage

7. Nietzsche's claim that there is nothing other than the whole places him within a long line of illustrious thinkers who reject atomistic views of the universe—a diverse list that includes, among others, Plato, Hegel, Marx, Burke, and Derrida. I should emphasise that not every philosophical conception of the whole is the same, nor are they all reducible to some general sense of holism. Nietzsche's understanding of the whole is quite different from Heidegger's or Hegel's, Marx's, or Althusser's. I turn to Nietzsche's account here to punctuate the point I am making in the text: an account of the social formation cannot be derived from an ontology of the whole. For this reason it helps to look at an example of "thinking the whole" (Nietzsche's) that stands at some remove from the Althusserian thinking of the whole that I will draw on in later chapters.

8. Derrida's (in)famous line relating to this issue was first translated as "there's nothing outside the text" (Derrida 1998 [1974]: 163), and then taken by numerous critics as damning evidence of Derrida's naive linguistic idealism. Derrideans, and more sober readers generally, quickly pointed out that Derrida's French, "il n'y a pas de hors-texte," would be literally translated as "there is no extra-text." The distinct meanings of these translations mirror the two different readings of Nietzsche on the whole.

suggests to me that this is indeed Nietzsche's own meaning. He says "there is nothing other than the whole," not as a bald philosophical thesis, not as a starting principle or a condition of possibility for knowledge (no reader of Nietzsche can ever underestimate his revulsion to Kant). Rather, the line appears in direct response to the notion of "judging, measuring, comparing, or sentencing the whole" (cf. Nietzsche 1968). We cannot judge or measure the whole because there is no position outside of it from which to judge or measure. Given this, we might even be tempted to render "außer dem" as "other than/to" the whole; that is, the whole has no "other." Such a reading also sheds light on Nietzsche's own emphasis earlier in the passage, an emphasis elided from many translations (e.g., Kaufmann 1977; Hollingdale 1990). Nietzsche does not simply say that "man is in the whole," in the sense of locating the human individual in a context; rather, with his original emphasis in German, Nietzsche states "man *is* in the whole." The whole, therefore, is the site of the human being's very existence—a claim that both underwrites and helps to explain Heidegger's later-developed central concepts of *Dasein* and *In-der-Welt-sein.*

While deeply concerned with "the whole," and while largely agreeing with Nietzschean and other philosophical affirmations that there is nothing outside the whole, my project here eschews the turn to ontology. I am interested less in producing a metaphysics of the whole and concerned more with developing a better historical, political, and theoretical account of the whole—a better specification of what "the whole" is and does and means. "The social formation" answers directly to this problematic. In other words, and still putting it rather generically, I would say that to give an account of the social formation is to provide a better account of the whole for the purposes of political theory. A theory of the social formation, as I understand it and develop it in this book, takes its place within philosophical accounts of the whole; it owes much to all those thinkers—from left and right Hegelians, to conservatives and Marxists—who have rejected atomistic accounts of the universe and resisted liberal accounts of society. Yet at the same time, a political theory of the social formation must be more and other than a political ontology of the whole, since a theory of the social formation must exceed and eschew the mere development of an abstract concept. It must be a historical and political *account* of the social formation that is also a theoretical grasping of the social formation.

PROBLEMATIQUE

To specify these terms, I offer in my penultimate section a series of "hypotheses" on the social formation. These are speculative theses that lay out the (contentious) terms of any theory/account of the social formation. But before I turn to those hypotheses, let me here provide a general description of what I am repeatedly calling "the social formation." First, and on the broader level of description, it seems worth repeating that unlike the specific objects that appear within it (two of which I discussed at the opening), the social formation is not itself an object in any empirical sense. To theorise the social formation, or to give an account of it, is therefore to *produce* it conceptually as an "object" of reflection. Second, it is perhaps most important to insist that the notion of the social formation already calls into question any disciplinary effort to carve the world up into discrete domains. Study of the social formation can be confined to neither the domain of "politics," nor "economics," nor "culture." (This list could be expanded almost infinitely.)

Writing amidst the crisis of 1857, and trying to give his own account of how we understand, make sense of, and respond to such a crisis, Marx insisted on the following point: "The [real] subject . . . society, must always be borne in mind" (Marx 1996a: 147). "Society" here cannot be confused with "the social domain" as a sphere that would be separate from other such spheres ("economy," for example). What Marx refers to with the simple name "society," is "the real subject" of his ongoing investigations. Elsewhere he refers, in this sense, to *the social formation*, a term that Althusser takes up as central to his own interpretation of Marx, and which I use here (both following and occasionally departing from Althusser). *Social formation* denotes the complex form in which various elements that make up our lived human world are held together. That is, *social formation* points to a combination and discontinuous overlapping of domains that we often take to be separate or separable. The name *social formation* indicates the way in which the fabric of "society"—of the social and political orders that we live in—is formed by threads that are simultaneously economic, political, and cultural. The great critical purchase in studying "the social formation" lies in the fact that such analysis focuses attention on the indissociably interconnected nature of these realms. To theorise the social formation means to see these not as distinct spaces, but as interpenetrating logics, as intermixed, porous domains that constantly interact with and infiltrate one another.[9]

9. To reject the idea of the "the political" as a unique sphere or precise domain is not to deny a certain specificity to the political. There is no specific *place* of the political, but there is a distinct *logic* of the political. I have previously tried to show how Jacques Rancière mobilises such an account of politics (Chambers 2013), and in my hypotheses, below, I propose the idea that the political thread in the social formation is one that holds the social order together. My thanks to Elizabeth Frazer for spurring me to clarify this important point.

As I have already shown above, to give an account of the social formation means to study a social order as a "whole." Crucially, however, such an account does not take the whole as a static or fixed or a-temporal structure; rather, it grasps the whole as a living, breathing, and always transmogrifying entity that can never be pinned or held in place.

To raise the question of the social formation is to broach one of the most important questions of politics, while simultaneously insisting that "questions of politics" are not reducible to a pre-given or legally delimited domain of "the political." Indeed, to ask after or inquire into the social formation means to pose multiple questions simultaneously, all of which prove to be political in an important sense. Put in a condensed language, an account of the social formation must address the questions of: how a social order is put together, what it must do to stay together, and how the work required to stay together transforms the very regime that it simultaneously maintains. Importantly, these questions are not lexically ordered: the analysis of how a social order is put together is not a purely empirical project that can be carried out prior to or in isolation from the very normative transformations of the social order that help maintain its integrity.

I will expand this particular claim in the next section, as I attempt to delineate the larger stakes of my project in the book. At this point, I want to make the following, broader argument: to theorise the social formation or study its politics means to engage with the complex form in which various elements that make up our lived human world are held together. Crucially, this claim entails another: the social formation is not a "concept" that one would "apply" (see Althusser 1969: 170). Rather than seeing it as a tool of empiricist social science, a theory of the social formation must always be understood in relation to Althusser's borrowed (and developed) notion of *problematique*. Althusser's use of "problematic" bears a number of family resemblances to better-known ideas such as Kuhn's paradigms or Foucault's epistemes, as, like them, it too indicates the context, structure, or wider conceptual field in which knowledge is produced. When introducing the term in *For Marx*, Althusser offers two important clarifications for his usage: first, that its purpose is "to designate the particular unity of a theoretical formation," and second, that he turns to the term in the first place in an effort to help him "indicate the specific difference that distinguishes two different theoretical formations" (Althusser 1969: 32). The first point is hard to miss because the term *problematic* operates as a unifying and congealing term, allowing its user to point to one "thing" (the problematic) while operating within a diverse field.

But the second point is easier to forget—and, I submit, has often been missed by readers and critics of Althusser. Althusser brings this term into his analysis for the central aim of helping to explain how Marx moved from one problematic to another—of showing how Marx's earlier writings operated within the problematic established by Feuerbach, while the later writings broke with that problematic and (potentially) established a new one. More subtly, at the very center of Althusser's entire hermeneutic for reading Marx lies the claim that Marx's early writings, while extending to themes that went well beyond Feuerbach (primarily by moving from religion to political economy), were trapped in and contained by the Feuerbachian problematic of an anthropology of "man" (Althusser 1969: 45). Therefore, according to Althusser, whatever appeared original in Marx's early writings was radically circumscribed by the fact that he still worked within a unified theoretical field that was thoroughly Feuerbachian (Althusser 1969: 46, 66–67).

Regardless of where we might stand on Althusser's broader argument about reading Marx, it is important to see here that the idea of a "Feuerbachian problematic" must not be confused with a particular concept of Feuerbach's (that Marx or any other author might, or might not, use). Like the social formation, a "problematic" is not something one can simply point to; thus, to designate it with a name is not to reduce it to an applicable concept. As Althusser insists, a theorist or writer "*thinks in it rather than thinking of it*" (Althusser 1969: 69). One works within the terms of a problematic, and to understand the problematic is to understand *how one works*. But the problematic cannot be grasped in its singularity because it is not single—it designates a unity, as Althusser says, but it is the unity of a theoretical field that cannot be condensed into a concept.

My efforts in this book to give an account of the social formation, to work through and develop theories of the social formation, must be distinguished from the sort of project in philosophy that would build up concepts for reflection or application. To put the point sharply, the social formation is nothing like John Rawls's "veil of ignorance"; these two different ideas simply operate within utterly distinct theoretical problematics.[10] Rawls's veil is not the type of concept that grasps the practices and workings of a political conjuncture; it is instead, as Rawls clearly indicates, an imaginary concept designed to mark and maintain a gap between "theory" and

10. It would be tempting to say that they operate in different "epistemological planes," but even that formulation suggests too much of a shared problematic. For a much more detailed account of the epistemological status (and attendant political stakes) of "social formation," see my discussion in Chapters 2 and 3, where I explore and defend the idea that knowledge of the social formation is a constituent element of the social formation and, therefore, that an account of the social formation requires maintaining a certain gap between "thought" and "the real."

"reality." In a more critical tone one might go on to say that the veil of ignorance is only made possible by the very problematic in which Rawls operates, but which he rarely, if ever, attempts to think. Putting Rawls aside, by briefly developing Althusser's notion of problematic, and in drawing out the similarities between it and social formation, I am able to place into starker relief the status of social formation and its distance from "concepts" that belong to a certain type of "theory." I should also make clear here, however, that social formation is not simply another term for problematic. Althusser delineates problematic as quite specifically a "theoretical formation," whereas social formations are populated by objects that are both conceptual and abstract, on the one hand, and historical and concrete, on the other.

Moreover, although the turn to Althusser's language of problematic productively clarifies what is at stake in theories and politics of the social formation, there is no need to think the idea of social formation only within the universe of Althusserian terms. While Althusser clearly had a proclivity toward developing specialised language, and while often that language can help provide a more perspicacious understanding of the social formation, I want to insist that one can engage with the theories and politics of the social formation without being required to shift into a terminologically narrow philosophical register. Indeed, one of the claims of this book is that there is no real alternative to giving an account of the social formation, since we live in hierarchical social orders—and we always will.[11] Many other thinkers and writers are thus also trying to grapple with a better understanding of the social order, and I am by no means the first to see the complex and overdetermined nature of the social formation. Other authors take different approaches (more poetic and creative, or more philosophical, or more historical), and they use different names (complexity theory, becoming, new materialism, rhetorical, discursive), but rather than make overblown claims for the uniqueness of my project here, I want to emphasise the way in which my effort to offer an account of the social formation can overlap with and complement these other projects.

THEORISING THE SOCIAL FORMATION

As I have already made clear in various ways up to this point, to "theorise" the social formation is to do political theory in a particular sort of way.

---

11. See my discussion of Jacques Rancière's understanding of police orders, in the text below.

This book does not develop a systematic and singular "theory of the social formation"; it matters that the theory referred to in the book's subtitle is plural. Not to pick on Rawls, but merely for the sake of illumination: to account theoretically for the social formation is nothing like building a theory of justice. There is no such thing as a theory of the social formation utterly abstracted from history; any "theory" of the social formation must remain tied to a historical account of the social formation, and in this book I often prefer the language of "account of" the social formation to "theory of" it. This is not to say that the work is not theoretical, but to indicate more specifically the type of theory I am doing here. In a further effort to specify the scope and terms of the project undertaken in this book, in this section I will briefly say something more about three distinct types of theoretical and critical projects from which I *distinguish* my work. These clarifications will set the stage for the next section, where I place my own cards on the table in the form of my working hypotheses on the social formation.

1. Ethical Critique

To give an account of the social formation is to eschew the temptation of ethical critique. This contention owes a lot to Marx's critical engagements with the work of utopian socialists. In those writings, Marx consistently shows that while certain socialist thinkers may have admirable goals in mind, their work is continually hamstrung by their refusal to engage with capitalism on its own terms—that is, the terms in which capitalism actually functions in the world. Instead, the utopian socialists offer a moral condemnation of the capitalist system's effects, without ever challenging the terms of capitalism itself. This tendency toward a certain sort of moral denunciation can easily be extended to the present day, where examples abound: from criticising debt policy while assuming that the financial industry generates profit sheerly by "circulating paper" (Ross 2013) to those (even those in positions of power) expressing surprise and outrage that investment banks have cornered the market on "ethanol credits."[12] Speaking more generally, whenever the effects of capitalist systems or structures are attributed to the "greed" of individual actors, we witness the refusal to analyse the logic of capital today in favour of the moral castigation of

12. In the *New York Times* article describing these events, the chairman of a New Jersey energy company, Thomas O'Malley, is quoted as follows: "They weren't designed to become a speculative item. For the life of me I can't see the justification for it." Of course, the "justification" for seeking profit should be rather obvious to a businessman like Mr. O'Malley; it's called "capitalism," and seeking profit (by speculation or any other means) turns out to be rather central to its very being (Morgenson and Gebeloff 2013).

individuals operating within those structures—individuals who may well be acting quite rationally. To develop theories of the social formation can surely be to engage in a form of critique, since the account one offers of the social order may prove to be a necessarily critical one. Yet there is a fundamental difference in approach between the effort to analyse the functioning of a social formation, and the inclination to condemn certain elements of that larger social whole.

This means, concomitantly, that giving an account of the social formation must be distinguished more broadly from a certain Kantian tradition, one that has been taken up and resignified by Foucauldians. Across a range of crucial differences, there remains a thread that ties Kantian critique to certain forms of post-Kantian critique: the general idea of "critique" as the work of the subject on itself; critique as the work a subject engages in so as to produce a general (and generalisable) ethical framework that applies beyond the self. I highlight these connections not in order to deny the importance of this strand of thought, nor to dismiss or challenge this brand of critique. I am only trying to circumscribe my own project by showing that it stands apart from this tradition. To give an account of the social formation is to do something different, something other than ethical critique.[13]

2. Normative Theory

I take a more strident relation to the currently common usage of "normative theory." While I certainly see a space for ethical critique and theories of the social formation to work alongside one another, it remains my fervent hope that each of these projects might help to crowd out the increased tendency both to describe work done in political theory (and by political theorists) as "normative" and to easily accept the distinction between two putatively distinct categories of work: normative and non-normative. This distinction usually takes the form of the dichotomy normative/empirical, but this particular form of the distinction obviously relies on the received notion that some research and writings on politics is normative and some is not normative. My polemical goal would be to call into question the very idea of normative theory, and my grounds for making such a broad-sweeping gesture are really quite simple: *there is no non-normative.*

13. One might highlight these differences in terms of a shift from the question, "Given the conditions, what can I be?" to the question, "Given the conditions, what can I *see*?" Better still, what can be seen, or heard—what is perceptible? Here, and as I will discuss both below and in later chapters, the project of giving an account of the social formation crosses with and draws from Rancière's notion of *le partage du sensible* (the distribution/partition of the sensory/sensible) (Rancière 2006). Thanks to Drew Walker for insights on this point.

My project in this book is not to develop a full-blown polemic against normative theory, but as a way of delineating the distance between my project and the very conception of "normative theory," I will briefly expand on the above claim that there is no non-normative. To develop this logic, let me start by making clear that I, perhaps like those who self-identify as "normative theorists," contend that the world is made up of normativity—of overlapping, complementing, and cross-cutting axes of normativity—and that it can often prove prudent or important to assert this fact. Moreover, coming at the issue from the other side of things, we might usefully call something "empirical" in order to designate a focus on the concrete and definite nature of the phenomenon under discussion. Put differently, there is a meaningful and practical difference between things we can see/feel/touch/taste/hear and entities that are logical, abstract, ideological, or conceptual; it would be naive to deny those differences. At this point, however, we come to a crucial juncture in the logic: to admit a distinction between the empirical and the non-empirical *does not entail* acceptance of the distinction between the normative and the non-normative. That some things are empirical and some are not simply does not mean that the empirical is "non-normative" or that the non-empirical coincides with some autonomous "normative realm." The category of the non-normative cannot be established merely by showing the validity of the adjective "empirical" (i.e., based on observation and experience). Finally, I contend that it is the presumption of the validity of the normative/non-normative dichotomy—which I am here showing to be bogus—that underwrites an even more questionable dichotomy, that between empirical and normative.

It does not require all that much work to show that the establishment of the category "empirical" does not establish the category "non-normative." The reason is quite simple: *even the empirical, and sometimes especially the empirical, is thoroughly normative.* In saying this I am not making anything like an original argument: Charles Taylor, William Connolly, Sheldon Wolin, and a host of other prominent thinkers long ago argued persuasively that all "facts" are value laden (Wolin 1969; Taylor 1985; Connolly 1993 [1974]). No social scientist, no scientist, no citizen, and no mere observer can describe without also evaluating. To put it differently, to establish the empirically "given" is both to operate within and simultaneously to reproduce and alter a matrix with normative orientations and spin. Foucault powerfully condenses this argument when he formulates the notion of a "prescriptive fact" (Foucault 2005; see Luxon 2013: 235). Thus, so-called empirical work, even in the sense of work that is *empiricist* (i.e., not just based on observation and experience, but based on the untenable claim that all knowledge rests only on verifiable observation), operates within a realm of normativity. There is no non-normative.[14] To make this claim is not only to undermine radically dichotomies like normative/non-normative and empirical/normative but also to call into question the very use of "normative" as either a distinguishing or an identifying category. If there is no non-normative, then it makes little or no sense at all to use normative as a mark of distinction. It distinguishes nothing from nothing. So-called normative claims or demands are nothing more than claims or demands with an extra word added to them.[15]

In terms of giving an account of the social formation, my polemic against "normative theory" indicates that such an account must not be reduced to or confused with the sort of work that would construct a "normative order" or build an "ideal theory" model designed to measure the legitimacy of an extant social order. Within some strands of political theory today there operates a dominant distinction between ideal theory and non-ideal theory, and this maps onto a distinction between "the ideal world" and "the non-ideal world." My approach to social formations insists that there is only one world, this world.[16] And that world is always already *ordered* in a variety of ways; the task of the social and political theorist is therefore not to construct new orders but to engage with the ones already in place—to grasp how they function, to challenge their terms, to indicate possible cleavages and potential moments of transformation.

---

14. Just as I defend this claim in the context of understanding various modes of political thought, I would also circumscribe my argument there. The category of the "non-normative" has also been used as a way to think about those practices and identities that are rendered marginal or deviant vis-à-vis dominant norms. That is, heteronormativity operates in such a way as to produce "the non-normative." But here the term functions quite differently and in a way very much consistent with my argument, because to call a certain sort of sexuality "non-normative" in this sense is certainly not to suggest that it has nothing to do with normativity, but rather the opposite—the "non-normative" only makes sense as a category in relation to a broader field of normativity (Lloyd 2007; Chambers and Carver 2008). For more on this wider understanding of normativity, see my 4th hypothesis, in the text below.

15. More insidiously, although the label of "normative" has no logical bite, this does not mean it fails to register rhetorically and politically. When political theorists identify as "normative theorists," they may not logically distinguish what they do from the work of their colleagues, but rhetorically they subtly reinforce the apparent validity of the empirical/normative dichotomy. Such identifications shore up the false pretenses of empiricist social science by making it sound as if there are some folks out there who are *not* doing normative work, but somehow operating (perhaps magically) in the realm of pure, non-normative science.

16. Here I follow Nietzsche in his discourse on "how the true world became a fable" in *Twilight* (Nietzsche 1889).

3. Logics of Inversion

The question then becomes *how* to engage with those orders. Asked in another form, how does political theory approach the whole—what relation or stance does it take vis-à-vis the social formation? Elsewhere I have identified one common if not predominant approach to the social whole, as found within a wide range of post-Frankfurt School critical theory and contemporary thought. Across a variety of significant substantive differences, we are still able to pick out a certain critical rationality by which the social whole is purported to present one thing on its surface while masking another thing within its depths. This is the familiar argument for demystification or unmasking, an argumentative structure wherein a truth is discerned (or imputed) beneath the lies. Building from the work of Jacques Rancière, and in an effort to capture the broader structure and movement of this approach to the social order, I have described this as a logic of inversion (Chambers 2013: 123–56). "Inversion" works in two mirrored ways within this logic: on the one hand, the social order is approached as if it were already inverted, turned upside down so that falsehood, ignorance or ideology masquerades as common sense; on the other hand, the task of the critical theorist of inversion is to *invert* the structure of the social order by revealing the underlying truth that will dispel (demystify) all that is false and wrong.

Tired of the dead-end cynicism of this logic of inversion, much of the most important work in political theory today has rejected this logic of inversion and turned to new and creative ways to conceive of different political possibilities, perhaps even of alternative political futures (Bennett 2010; Latour 2004; Connolly 2013).[17] I, too, staunchly reject any conception of critique undergirded by unmasking or demystification, but I am perhaps more sanguine on the possibility of a renewed critical theory that might operate according to a logic other than inversion. Such a critical theory would require, I submit, a rich account of the social formation; that is, critique would not be ethical denunciation, but would operate through

17. In his recent book, William Connolly writes insightfully that "the strength of structural theory, at its best, was in identifying institutional intersections that hold a system together; its conceit, at its worst, was the claim to know in advance how resistant such intersections are to potential change" (Connolly 2013: 37). On both fronts, I concur. Connolly hedges his bets against this conceit of structural theory by moving away from it, whereas I run the risk of turning toward a certain sort of structural theory. I am interested in rethinking and renewing a more modest theory of the social formation that can leverage these insights about how structures are held together while eschewing any pretense of closure, much less prediction. Indeed, understanding the *way* a system is held together reveals the impossibility of closure or prediction.

a critical accounting of the social order. A new critical theory, that is, can only emerge in tandem with and on the basis of new theories of the social formation. A critical theory for today must be a critical theory *of the social formation.*

Hence we need a deeper and richer account of the social formation—precisely the project of this book. I carry out that project, again, not by building a linear and singular "theory of" *the* social formation, but by engaging with a variety of thinkers in distinct contexts so as to multiply *theories* and *accounts* of the social formation. I build an image of the social formation not by narrowing my focus to one object, but by adding a series of images from different perspectives so as to produce a composite—much like the social formation itself. In the final section of this Introduction I briefly summarise each of the chapters that adds to that compound and blended overall image, but first, in the next section, I lay out a series of speculative hypotheses that the book's chapters will probe and explore (if not quite test). Collectively, I'm calling these not "theses," because they are not quite arguments I seek to prove, or even polemical claims with which I seek to provoke. Rather, these are *speculative* premises or *working* hypotheses about the social formation that have an important, symmetrical relation to the substantive chapters of the book: they guide the work I do in the chapters, setting me on a certain path of exploration, and at the same time the chapters serve to try out, to modify, to rework the hypotheses. Overall, these hypotheses lay out the parameters through which I explore the theories and politics of social formations.

EIGHT HYPOTHESES ON THE SOCIAL FORMATION

To this point my description of the "theories and politics of the social formation" that animate this book has occasionally also used the language of "social order" to capture the sense of "the whole" that is my larger object of investigation and analysis. On the one hand, *social formation* and *social order* are roughly equivalent phrases for this "whole," and for this reason I sometimes use the terms interchangeably. However, on the other, each phrase gestures toward the whole in a slightly different manner and with a slightly different inflection. To distinguish between the two terms, we might say that *social order* names the general way in which the roles, institutions, norms, rules, and mechanisms are *distributed* or *patterned* in a society, whereas *social formation* points to the specific way in which that very distribution is *maintained* and *transformed*, the process by which that very pattern is preserved, altered, or reworked. It is for this reason that each of my hypotheses on the social formation is stated as a claim about or description of the social order.[18]

1. *The social order is not an aggregation of individuals, but its constituent elements include both individuals and groups.*

This first hypothesis is meant to mark a clear line between a critical theory of the social formation and any type of social contract theory liberalism (or any sort of empiricist social science). It draws this line of contrast by rejecting any account of the social order that sees society as the willful (or otherwise) construction of atomistic individuals. Individuals do not precede the social formation, and their actions do not create it. This refusal of the idea of an autonomous individual that precedes a social order has been articulated both by a long line of conservative writers (from Burke to Oakeshott) and by numerous posthumanist or poststructural thinkers. I follow them in starting with my own insistence that the social order can never be reduced to the individuals contained within it, and, as something of a corollary to this hypothesis, I follow Arthur Bentley in suggesting that the key elements of any social formation may turn out to be groups, not individuals.

2. *The social order is founded on neither contract nor consent, and it is not natural, but it is fundamentally, constitutively, political.*

This hypothesis builds on the first by specifying that consent cannot found a social order, yet it goes further than the first by refusing a common alternative to contractualist understandings of society—namely, conservative accounts that would lay claim to a "natural" social order. In so doing, this hypothesis seeks to capture the relation between the social and the political by delineating a specific understanding of the way in which a social formation is political. Thus, the hypothesis postulates what I would call "the *political* question of social order." This question must be (perhaps repeatedly) disentangled from two related, but very much distinct, questions:

18. In addition, I would note that *social order* is simply a more generic term for describing the structure or ordering of a social whole, while *social formation* is a specific concept that Althusser derives from/attributes to Marx. Thus, those chapters that focus more on Althusser and Marx (Chapters 2–4) also tend to use the language of "social formation" more frequently, while the other chapters shift more frequently to the term *social order*. The movement back and forth between these terms reflects my effort to make use of Althusser's idea of the social formation without limiting myself to the Althusserian terminology or theoretical framework.

A) The question of *political order*. In the social contract tradition we see two possible states, separated by a wide chasm: we have *either* an a-political (a-historical, etc.) state of nature *or* a political order constituted by a founding political act. Social contract theory fictionalises a natural but a-political social order so that it can naturalise (through the very state-of-nature narrative) a thoroughly political order. By presupposing/hypostatising a prior order of nature, the political order comes to be understood, paradoxically, as simultaneously both constructed and natural. That is, the exit of individuals from the state of nature (itself a non-political realm) *is* the creation of a political society or community—the production of a thoroughly political order—but the necessity of that exit is built into the very structure of the state of nature (it always has a flaw that forces "us" to flee it). In this way any question of social order is always reduced to the question of political order, since our current social formation is thought to be formed by contract/consent.

B) The question of *social order*. In certain strands of sociology or social theory, the question of "social order" stands apart from any question of politics; that is, for certain thinkers a social order can be understood as both natural and non-political, since the social order can be said to exist (naturally) outside of political forces.

Eschewing both of these approaches, a critical account of the social formation hypothesises a social order as never *not* political, so it rejects this second account outright by refusing the idea of a social realm that would somehow be separate or shielded from politics. At the same time, this hypothesis eschews the liberal option again, by refusing the notion that all social formations are formed by founding political acts. Political vectors *run through* any and every social order, but politics does not found or otherwise underlie the social formation. Politics is in, not underneath, the social order.

3. *The social order does not manifest equality—it is not a sphere of fairness or justice; a society is never "well-ordered"—but at the same time the vertical relations of power in a social order should not be called "unjust."*

This hypothesis draws on Rancière's claim that "in the social order, there can be no vacuum" (Rancière 1999: 35). In other words, the social order is always a police order, marked by vertical relations of hierarchy and domination. To hypothesise a social order that cannot be other than a police order is to resist the very idea of a "well-ordered" society that would manifest full equality and justice. However, to reject these notions is also to forsake the conception of the social formation smuggled in by so-called ideal theory; to say the social order cannot produce substantive equality is not to embrace or defend inequality. Quite the contrary, as a police order the social formation cannot properly be called "unjust" precisely because a political philosophy of justice presumes the very "vacuum" that cannot exist in the social order. The question of justice is the incorrect question to ask. As I explained above, a theory of justice approaches a social formation in the wrong way since it tries to "judge" the current social formation in relation to some ideal. But the project of grasping the social whole in its material reality is not the same as ethically "judging" it from the perspective of the ideal. None of this entails rejecting all claims to "justice," but it sharply distinguishes an account or critique of the social order, on the one hand, from an ethical condemnation of that order as "unjust," on the other.[19]

4. *The social order is neither constituted nor redeemed by a theory of norms, but it is nevertheless inextricably bound up with normativity.*

This hypothesis reformulates and expands the second one, above, yet it does so in a language better suited to engage directly with the Habermasian project. Hence the formulation takes on a polemical dimension with respect to the goals of Habermas's "discourse ethics"—goals rejected here. Instead, this hypothesis draws strongly from, and sides decidedly with, Foucault. Here I point toward a conception of normativity as produced through and built into daily practices, discourses, and infrastructures. Normativity is the very material of a social formation, but norms do not found, independently alter, or underlie a social order. Norms run through and across the social formation, like a complex and a-systematic pattern of bicycle spokes. Norms are not a ground. Clearly, then, this hypothesis eschews the Habermasian conception of discourse ethics, a project committed to the goal that philosophy can help produce a normativity that would legitimate (or redeem) the social order. The social order, as a police order, can never be a candidate for redemption.

19. The distinction I am making here draws inspiration from Marx's effort to distinguish his project from that of the socialist utopians, as I discussed briefly in the text above. Marx's critique of Proudhon hinges upon the difference between, on the one hand, Proudhon's naive, utopian, and *ethical* (mis)interpretation of Ricardo's theory, which strives for what Marx describes as "Proudhon's eternal justice," and, on the other, Marx's own further elaboration of Ricardo's own logic, which extends that logic to its breaking point (Marx 1955: 20, 22). Marx, of course, shared many of the socialist utopians' goals; similarly, I do not eschew all senses of justice. Rather than reject the project of critique I am attempting to rethink it.

5. *The social order cannot be defined ostensively; it is not a referent and it cannot simply be depicted empirically, but it is still real.*

We cannot point to or measure the social order for the simple reason that a social formation is not an "object" in that sense. The social order is subject neither to verifiability by the terms of empiricist epistemology nor to explanation through the framework of quantitative social science. We might fairly call the social order an "abstraction," but only if we also insisted, with Marx, that nothing is more real than abstractions. In Chapter 3 I engage with the terms of this hypothesis by exploring in some detail Althusser's defense of the distinction between the "real object" and the "object of knowledge." The hypothesis itself also relies on Lyotard's helpful insistence that a regime of phrases (his term for the social order, and also his translation of Wittgenstein's language games) can never be cognitively grasped (Lyotard 1988).

6. *The social order is not a totality, but it is a whole.*

This hypothesis flows directly from my discussion of "the whole" above. In his own way, Althusser offers this hypothesis as a test case for the proper way to read Marx in contradistinction to Hegel. With respect to the project of giving an account of the social formation, this whole/totality distinction matters a great deal, since we can see that many of the previous hypotheses track alongside Hegel's thought—Hegel obviously accounts for the social order in a thoroughly non-liberal manner. From Althusser's perspective, the difference between Hegel and Marx proves so meaningful because Hegel produces a non-differentiated account of the social order—a "totality" that has an essential core. In contrast, Marx's conception of the whole is open and uneven; it is "overdetermined," and therefore lacking any essential core. And when it comes to grasping the *politics* of the social formation, or to producing a *critical* account of the social order, this difference matters a great deal.

7. *The social order is not a system, but it has a systematicity.*

With this hypothesis I emphasise a pivotal if not decisive point: the social order is not a closed system, and for this reason no account of the social formation can be advanced by way of functionalist explanations or determinist analyses. This hypothesis comes at the social formation from a different angle, trying to get at a similar set of aspects as has been covered in previous hypotheses, but doing so in a different language—one that helps make particular dimensions stand out. Thus, here I gesture in a slightly different theoretical direction—toward Derridean understandings of systematicity, toward complexity theory's grasp of emergent causality, toward new materialism's thinking of agentic capacities. To shift away from a model of individual aggregation and toward "the whole" does not require a shift to fixed or static structures. Yet to say that the social order is not a system—and that an account of the social formation cannot be a crude structuralist account—does not mean that the social order does not have systematicity or structuration. No social order is either random or anarchic. Any social formation is marked by emergent (and changing) patterns, systems, norms, rules—all of which can and must be studied, grasped, challenged, and resisted within an account of the social formation.

8. *The social order is not egalitarian, but it depends upon equality—and this dependence opens it up to politics and to critique.*

The key to this hypothesis lies in careful clarification of what it means to say that the inegalitarian social order depends on something egalitarian, on some particular conception of equality. I read Rancière as offering that clarification, because I interpret him as making polemical claims that can contribute to a theory of the social formation—not as laying out an ontology of politics. However, Rancière's writings have often been taken in just this latter way, and when so understood it then proves straightforward to staunchly criticise him for his apparent naivety—a "naivety" that emerges starkly in his putative claim that inequality depends on equality. Jodi Dean has offered the strongest and most tenable critique of Rancière in this vein, showing as she does that if Rancière means to ground this claim to equality on a Davidson-esque conception of language—in which background understandings provide the grounds for any misunderstanding—then Rancière's argument falls apart precisely because language does not work that way.

To my eyes, Dean's critique of Davidson is right on target, but it misses the mark in the case of Rancière because he does not seek to ground his claim about the social order's dependence on equality in a theory of language. I take Rancière at his word when he repeatedly says he has no theory of language—and no theory of politics, for that matter. Instead, the presumption of equality that makes inequality possible is connected to Rancière's earlier work—his radical pedagogy of the (radical) equality of intelligence. He says that this "equality of intelligence" is itself the "absolute condition for all communication" (Rancière 1999: 34). But this is not because of background understandings; it is because of nothing else than the assumption of equality itself—an assumption that is made/verified every time we invoke the hierarchy and domination of the social order. In the context of insisting on the equality that makes the social formation possible, directly after contending that there is no vacuum (no substantive equality or freedom) in the social order, Rancière writes: "Politics is not, therefore, the name of nothing" (Rancière 1995: 58, my translation).[20] Insisting on this "not nothing" of politics means showing that any critical account of the social formation will also be a political theory—or turned the other way around, that political theory for today must be a critical theory of the social formation.

METHOD OF PRESENTATION

I have insisted throughout this Introduction that my approach to theories and politics of the social formation refuses the very idea of accounting for the social formation in a linear or a priori fashion: with the social formation one simply cannot start with "givens" and then build them up into a singular "theory." In taking this tack, I echo Marx's own famous reflections on the process of accounting for a capitalist social formation. In one of his many formulations of an "introduction" to *Capital*, Marx elaborated on the key difference between, on the one hand, his own "method of inquiry" over the many years that he spent studying the capitalist social formation of nineteenth-century Europe and, on the other, the "method of presentation" of his account of the social formation given in the multiple volumes of *Capital*. Marx explains:

> The [method of inquiry] has to appropriate the material in detail, to analyse its different forms of development and to track down their inner connection. Only after this work has been done can the real movement be appropriately presented. If this is done successfully, if the life of the subject-matter [the capitalist social formation] is now reflected back in the ideas, then it may appear as if we have before us an a priori construction. (Marx 1990: 102)

In Marx's case, such a clarification proved absolutely necessary, since his "method of presentation" can indeed appear a priori, linear, singular, and a-historical: the opening chapters of *Capital, Volume 1* seem to emerge from the ether, with concepts like the commodity, value, and fetishism articulated by Marx in distinctly abstract terms. I cite Marx's famous lines above not because I wish to follow him in marking a wide gap between

20. The English translation of *Disagreement* reads very differently: "Politics is thus the name of nothing" (Rancière 1999: 35). The original French has "La politique n'est ainsi le nom de rien" (Rancière 1995: 58), and I contend that Rancière chooses "n'est" for a reason—hence my translation in the text above. My thanks to Moya Lloyd and Davide Panagia for helpful discussion on this point.

inquiry and presentation but because those lines capture a sense of the social formation as impossible to grasp in a priori, abstractly theoretical terms. As Harvey puts it, commenting on this passage: "Marx's method of inquiry starts with everything that exists—with reality as it's experienced, as well as with all available descriptions of that experience by political economists, philosophers, novelists and the like" (Harvey 2010a: 8). Nonetheless, in many ways, the distinction itself serves mainly as an apology for the difficulty of the opening chapters of *Capital, Volume 1*. Marx is telling his readers, in effect: a capitalist social formation cannot be understood by way of a priori formulations or a-historical concepts, so please do not read these opening chapters, which sound precisely like the presentation of a priori concepts, in this manner.

Rather than warning readers not to misread me, I have constructed and organised the chapters in this book so as to convey, from the beginning, the idea that any account of the social formation must be an engaged one—so as to underscore my claim that there can be no singular theory of the social formation. In the chapters that follow, my main concern lies in retracing for the reader my specific efforts at grasping the social formation—of producing various accounts of it. In that sense, and using Marx's language, we might say that my method of presentation is nothing other than a reformulation, a restaging of my method of inquiry. Such a restaging entails a series of engagements with particular thinkers (with their ideas and concepts) so as to build an account of the social formation (to work through its theory and its politics), and to engage with these writings also requires taking up certain disciplinary debates and historical disputes. However, my primary aim in each encounter is not to settle disciplinary scores, nor is it merely to show how other thinkers hold (or do not hold) an account of the social formation that resonates with mine. Rather, my critical readings of these thinkers are themselves performances of what it looks like or what it means to give an account of the social formation.[21]

Just as with Marx's project, a series of concepts prove central to my work here, but unlike Marx, I do not begin the book with a presentation of those concepts. I follow this introductory chapter with a brief *intermezzo*; this section works both to *interrupt* the standard series of substantive body chapters of the book and also to *connect* the Introduction to Chapter 1. I use this space to focus tightly on two different examples—examples of thinking through and thereby in a certain sense *seeing* the social formation. Bundling

21. Relatedly, I sometimes demonstrate that particular misreadings of certain authors can be traced to the failure to interpret these thinkers with a concept of the social formation in mind. I develop this point in Chapter 4.

together the conceptual and methodological claims and explanations of this chapter, I put them to work to shine a light on two concrete cases. In a sense I am saying, "this is what the social formation looks like," but also, "this is what we see when we look for/through the social formation." In the first case, I offer an interpretation of Timothy Mitchell's recent work on what he calls "carbon democracy," a reading designed to show that, despite not using the language, Mitchell's book serves as a fine example of giving an account of the social formation. His argument about the modern history of democracy and colonialism, embedded in the history of human production and distribution and use of energy, can serve to crystallise what is at stake in giving an account of the social formation. Put succinctly, Mitchell's work relies on an implicit theory of the social formation, while at the same time it helps to develop such a theory. The second example operates at a different level: rather than read the text of a scholar, I offer an analysis of a recent example of cultural politics—the rise and fall of "Lance Armstrong." I trace the larger social formation that surrounds and supports professional road cycling, and I show the mutual interdependence of that order, on the one hand, and the figure of "Lance Armstrong," on the other. Working against the standard media narrative, I retell this familiar story, eschewing the morality tale of a fallen hero and instead focusing on the histories and structure that made a "Lance Armstrong" possible (and in certain important ways, *necessary*) in the first place. The conditions of possibility for his rise to international sports hero turn out to be the very same elements that led to (or required) his downfall.

With these concrete examples brought into view, I then shift in Chapter 1 to a critical engagement with the work of Judith Butler. Moreover, I begin with Butler not because I want to develop her account of the social formation or to build on resources from her work that I think add up to my own theory of the social formation. My first example is a negative one: through an extended engagement with specific writings of Butler over the course of her vibrant career, I argue that an account of the social formation is just what goes missing from that work. Thus, despite what I see as the deep significance of Butler's writings to both political theory and cultural politics, I offer in this chapter a strong critique of one strand of her work. I demonstrate that Butler's writings consistently lack an efficacious conception of the social formation, and that this absence costs Butler severely when it comes to her wider understanding of politics, historical change, and agency.

Specifically, I show how in Butler's 1997 text, *The Psychic Life of Power*, she reads Althusser in such a way as to actively expunge his theory of the social formation from the very texts she addresses. The elimination of an account of the social formation leads Butler to a dead end theoretically: she must substitute the psyche or a universalising ethics for her own missing account of the social formation. But worse still, in Butler's more recent works this failure to account for the social formation has led her toward a thin set of philosophical generalisations—what Bonnie Honig negatively describes as Butler's "mortalist humanism" (Honig 2010; Honig 2013). Ultimately, Butler's radical insights have been so defanged that she winds up repeating the language of liberal political philosophy, a misstep that I trace back genealogically to the key location in her work where she not only fails to develop her own account of the social formation but also goes so far as to erase it from her own sources. This critical chapter proves productive to my overall project because it highlights the political stakes of an account of the social formation, and because its negative example prepares the ground for the central conceptual and theoretical work of the entire book.

I take up that effort in Chapter 2, which is devoted to a detailed reading of Marx's *1857 Introduction* and an elaboration of its importance for theories and politics of the social formation. I open the chapter with some reflections on the status of Marx's work within the canon of political theory, suggesting that it proves quite difficult to fit any of Marx's texts into a political theory curriculum. My claim here is that despite its elliptical outline form, Marx's *1857 Introduction* may be the place to recover Marx as a theorist of politics. Perhaps only as a theorist of the social formation does Marx appear as a political theorist. I locate in that short text the core idea of the social formation that each chapter of my book amplifies, augments and continuously reworks. I read the text with the goal of illuminating Marx's powerful understanding of: 1) the social formation itself as a complex societal form that contains within it both specific practices and important abstract conceptions (with material effects), and 2) the peculiar historical development of social formations. Explicating Marx's understanding of the historical movement and transformation of social formations leads me to a number of conclusions about the epistemological status of the social formation. Based on this reading, I stake out a few key positions on the question of how we produce knowledge *about* a social formation while at the same time understanding all such knowledge as itself a *part of* the social formation.

To defend these epistemological claims, and to advance and augment this reading of Marx, I then, in Chapter 3, call on the hermeneutic suggestions of Althusser. I argue that Althusser proved a much better reader of

Marx than an originator of his own, unique "Theory."[22] In order to defend my reading of Marx and to spell out its implications, I thus resuscitate Althusser's crucial contributions to understanding Marx, specifically as they relate to the ideas contained in the *1857 Introduction.* To make this case and to delineate the key elements of my theoretical understanding of the social formation, this chapter enters into a series of significant debates over the methodological status and import of Marx's writings. Stuart Hall, above all, has taken a crucial (because ostensibly decisive) position here—one that rejects much of Althusser's reading. I engage in a detailed response to Hall, not for the sake of winning debating points but because a rejoinder to Hall is required in order to clear the way to a renewed understanding of the social formation.

Chapter 4 contains a focused and specific development of the social formation as I leverage the work from the previous chapters in order to set into motion some of the ideas on the politics of social orders already articulated. To this end I revisit a vibrant and fecund recent debate in contemporary political theory, one that has been committed to moving beyond linear conceptions of temporality and toward an understanding of politics as untimely. As much as my approach to this debate involves the "use" of the concept of the social formation—since that concept allows us, I argue, to see this debate in a different light and to bring a crucial new dimension to it—I continue to resist the idea that the social formation is a "concept that can be applied." Hence, just as my work in this chapter brings a thinking of the social formation to bear on the untimely politics literature, it also amplifies our understanding of the social formation (it augments the nascent theories of the social formation already in play in the book) by exploring the temporal dimensions of all social formations. Rather than adding the singular concept of "untimeliness" to the singular concept of "the social formation," this chapter explores the necessary temporal dimensions of any concrete account of the social formation.

Bringing an account of the social formation to bear on earlier work on radical temporality allows me to demonstrate how contemporary

---

22. My insistence on "theories of" the social formation works against and remains in tension with Althusser's putative drive to produce a singular Theory, or to privilege science over ideology in any simplistic sense. Further, as I demonstrated in the previous section, I remain consistently committed to a form of theory that is always engaged with the world, always tethered to specific historical time and place in that world. This commitment marks one of my departures from Althusser (even as I draw on his idea of a historical conjuncture in order to situate my understanding of theory) since it serves to resist the early Althusser's commitment to a grand Theory that would provide the meta-level, unifying explanation for these specific engagements (see Althusser 1969: 164–74).

political theory's important attention to time (and untimeliness) can be redirected and improved. And the key to doing so lies in thinking temporality through the social formation. Rather than conceive of temporality only within phenomenological or existential terms—as an experience of the subject—we must instead come to see that a social formation can itself be temporally marked. In exploring the temporal dimensions of the social formation, this chapter thus points both to the next and final body chapter (on groups as the constituent elements of a social formation) and to my concluding suggestions about articulating a critical account of the social formation.

Resisting any intrinsic pull toward teleology, my 5th and final chapter shifts the focus of analysis away from any sort of "general theory" of the social formation and centers instead on the question of interests and groups. This area of inquiry has perhaps been more consistently explored by the literature of American politics than by contemporary political theory, but here I rethink the understanding of the group (and "its" interests) by situating the group squarely within the social formation. The chapter offers an exploration and development of Arthur Bentley's understanding of groups, reading Bentley against those who have tried to appropriate him for the purposes of mid-twentieth-century empiricist pluralist theory. Bentley, I argue, was a much more radical pluralist than the empiricist pluralists (such as Robert Dahl and David Truman) could grasp in their impoverished references to Bentley's most famous book. Bentley's understanding of interests and groups as co-constitutive has more affinities with contemporary postfoundational political thought than it does with mid-century pluralism, but more than this, Bentley's idea of the group adds a crucial dimension to any effort to account for the social formation. Bentley's anti-empiricist, anti-foundationalist, and transactional account of politics helps us to see an irreducible idea of "the group" as the constituent element of any social formation. As he himself stresses, Bentley's idea of the group can never be equated with a reductionist account of class, but his work contributes powerfully to theories of the social formation since it offers an important resource for resisting any sort of individual/structure dichotomy in approaching the study of social orders.

Bentley's "groups" are the very stuff of the social formation. Making this argument in Chapter 5 leads me to a few final remarks, in the Coda, concerning the multiple relationships between three overlapping entities: theories of the social formation, political theory, and critical theory. As I discussed earlier in this Introduction, the social formation is never a unified or singular totality but is instead always an overlapping, discontinuous, and overdetermined whole. For this reason, an account of the social formation can never be merely an effort to understand or reconcile ourselves to a given social formation in its positivity. Quite the opposite: an account of the social formation must always be, in some sense, a critical account. I thus end the book with a brief discussion that fleshes out this logic and suggests the central importance of theories of the social formation to the work of political theory itself.

Intermezzo

In the Introduction I have claimed that an account of the social formation must always be a definite account of a concrete historical conjuncture; I have insisted that the concept of the social formation is not something drawn up "in theory" and then "applied" to so-called practice. Despite these contentions, by their very nature as introductory formulations, my discussion of the social formation in the preceding chapter remains somewhat diffuse and reflective. Before turning again, in Chapter 1, to another engagement with theories of the social formation (or the absence thereof), I want here to interrupt that narrative. The goal is simple yet crucial: to show directly the stakes of giving an account of the social formation by offering two concrete examples of such accounts. The examples serve to demonstrate how "giving an account of the social formation" differs from other approaches (e.g., understanding history, offering causal social scientific explanation, or narrating a journalistic story). My analyses here thus indicate how such an account lets us see the definite cases in a distinct light: new objects emerge and different political stakes become legible.

I offer two non-parallel examples here. In the first, I operate at the level of textual analysis, as I read Timothy Mitchell's recent work *through the lens* of the social formation. The point is to show that Mitchell's project can be understood to operate *as an account* of the social formation, and such an understanding draws to light the greatest strengths of the project. I am therefore using Mitchell's research and writing as an illustration of my case *for* the social formation, but at the same time I am augmenting his work by indicating its power *as* an account of the social formation. The second example works quite differently; in it, I offer my own description of the social order (and thereby my own piece of an account of the social formation), analysing, through the terms of the social formation, a recent and well-known example from popular culture. To think the case of Lance Armstrong through the problematic of the social formation means to rethink decisively both the terms of the case and their political implications. This shift entails a different orientation to Armstrong as individual, eschewing the tempting characterisation of him as hero/anti-hero, and trying instead to see the larger social formation that makes that very representation not just possible but, in a crucial sense, which I will explain below, *necessary*. The different levels at which these examples operate help to clarify the specific contours of the idea of the social formation. Above all, these examples give me an opportunity to emphasise the political salience of giving an account of the social formation.

"CARBON DEMOCRACY"

I read Timothy Mitchell's recent work as offering a richly historical account of the social formation. To show how, it is worth repeating two important points about the social formation that were crystalised in the example of Michael Burry from my Introduction: first, a social formation both produces and is made possible by the "objects" within it, and new or changed social formations produce *new objects*; second, the concept of the social formation holds particular potency in moments of crisis, because these are times when new objects emerge and when the social order itself sometimes changes significantly. Mitchell's book is set squarely in a moment of crisis; indeed, it centers on a dual crisis, that of democracy and that of energy. And Mitchell's technique for helping his readers to rethink these crises is to name a new object that he thinks captures them both (and captures them at their intersection). As Mitchell formulates the point, his is not a book about "democracy and oil"; it is, instead, "a book about democracy *as* oil" (Mitchell 2011: 4). To think democracy *as* oil is to think a whole new object: *carbon democracy*.

That sentence in which Mitchell names this object sounds straightforward enough, but in the little phrase "democracy *as* oil" Mitchell declares—or so I here contend—not just a new understanding of the relation between carbon and democracy, but a whole new understanding (both historical and theoretical) of democracy itself. Mitchell argues that we cannot understand the rise of modern democracy apart from the discovery/development/exploitation first of coal reserves and then of oil, and for Mitchell the different forms that carbon takes (first as coal, and then, historically, as oil) point to radically different potentialities for democratic politics. For Mitchell, carbon and democracy are not separable variables; it is not a question, for example, of understanding how profits from oil "impact" the possibilities for the emergence and sustenance of democratic institutions (Mitchell 2011: 5). Rather, Mitchell shows that democracy only first emerges (much less flourishes) within a social formation overdetermined by the dominance of coal as a primary energy source.

The key to democratic transformations lay in the nature of coal production and consumption: just as an extremely large portion of the population grew more dependent on coal for their energy *use*, so did a much smaller portion of the population become responsible for, and take over a certain control of, energy *production* and *distribution* (Mitchell 2011: 18). This transformation to carbon energy proved central to democratic revolutions, according to Mitchell, not because of solidarity or "class consciousness" of workers, but because of the very precariousness of this new system of energy production and distribution. What we would come to call *democratic* power emerged not mainly from ideals of freedom or communications among workers, "but from the extraordinary quantities of carbon energy that could be used to assemble political agency, by employing the ability to slow, disrupt or cut off its supply" (Mitchell 2011: 19). Mitchell goes on to document, in great detail, the historical connections between democratic transformations and the political agency of coal workers.

But his point is not just that there were material preconditions necessary for the emergence of what we know today as "democratic" institutions. At times he makes it clear that he is arguing for a distinct understanding of democracy. He does so, first, by showing that in its liberal guise, democracy often functions as a way to co-opt a certain kind of "popular consent" so as to blunt claims for radical equality (Mitchell 2011: 9). Moreover, he insists that the movement toward "democracy" (i.e., the movement of democratisation) centers on transformations in the social formation that render the resources of energy and capital highly vulnerable to the political action of (certain) workers. He concludes, "Democratisation has generally *depended on engineering such forms of vulnerability*" (Mitchell 2011: 146, emphasis added). On my reading of Mitchell's book, "carbon democracy" names three different entities:

1. The specific form of democracy's emergence within a social formation heavily marked by coal as the primary energy source. In this

context, the threat (and sometimes execution of threats) to thwart and sabotage the extraction and distribution of coal led to dramatic increases in the rights and equalities of workers and everyday citizens; from this structure emerged what we today often call *modern democracy*. In other words, the precarity of carbon made possible the increasing health and security of workers.

2. The specific form of democracy's neoliberal transformation within a social formation structured by oil as the primary energy source. In this changed context, stores of energy (and capital) prove far less vulnerable than they did within the coal regime, and in this time period we see the erosion of workers' rights and dramatic increases in socio-economic inequality. The *decreased* vulnerability of carbon made workers *more* vulnerable.
3. The broader, conceptual notion of conceiving democracy not as a universalisable set of institutional forms, or as a set of transcendental rights, but always as a concretely embodied set of practices, inextricably linked to the social formation.

Mitchell himself does not necessarily highlight this third notion or mark it as distinct, but I find it a crucial element of his text, since with it Mitchell suggests that the idea of "carbon democracy" requires a thorough rethinking of democracy itself. While there can be no doubt that historical analysis and concrete political explanation drive Mitchell's project, I claim that his work almost always implies, and often relies upon, the sort of conceptual framework that I develop in this book. Put differently, Mitchell's argument for "carbon democracy" presupposes, just as it also develops and draws out, a wider theory of the social formation. My putative summary of Mitchell is therefore something more than that, since I have portrayed Mitchell's project as one very much bound up with questions of the social formation. As I will discuss in Chapter 2 (in the context of Marx's thought), often the presentation of a system, a theory, or history is itself a re-presentation—the creation of something new. In this light, I would draw attention to the close focus that Mitchell's text gives to the object—that is, carbon democracy. As I argued in my discussion of particular objects of the social formation of the Great Recession, to understand a social formation one must be able to grasp the objects that both produce it and make it possible, and Mitchell does just this in centering his entire book on one main object, carbon. And as the form that carbon takes changes, as it transforms, as it were, from coal to oil, the social formation changes as well.

Yet Mitchell makes it quite clear, as I do here, that to focus on the object is not to allow that object to determine the social formation (much less to determine politics). And this leads to perhaps the most important, illuminating connection between Mitchell's project and mine. Both early and late in his book—in places where he clarifies how his approach centers on material, technological transformations while still eschewing any sort of technological determinism—Mitchell actually describes in his own language, what I am here calling the social formation. Early on, Mitchell insists that carbon cannot "determine" any particular political form, since "the carbon itself must be transformed, beginning with the work done by those who bring it out of the ground" (Mitchell 2011: 7). Later, he elaborates on this point in a formulation that gets at a number of central elements in the idea of the social formation:

> We have always inhabited a mixed world, made up of imbroglios of the technical, the natural and the human. As the kinds of controversies we face clearly show, our world is an entanglement of technical, natural and human elements. Any technical apparatus or social process combines different kinds of materials and forces, involving various combinations of human cognition, mechanical power, chance, stored memory, self-acting mechanisms, organic matter and more. In introducing technical innovations, or using energy in novel ways, or developing alternative sources of power, we are not subjecting "society" to some new external influence, or conversely using social forces to alter an external reality called "nature." We are reorganising socio-technical worlds, in which what we call social, natural and technical processes are present at every point. (Mitchell 2011: 239)

This extended quote not only captures the sense of the social formation but also complements and extends my general claim about Mitchell's work, and the reason I invoke it here: carbon democracy names the historical social formation in which democracy becomes possible based on a certain human relationship to, and political and technological development of, first coal and then oil.

At the same time, however, the above quote demands a degree of clarification; in a sense it calls on me to distinguish social formation from other concepts with which it might have a family resemblance. I say this because various readers of the above quote from Mitchell might see in it not a description of the social formation, but a Deleuzean account of assemblages (Deleuze and Guattari 1987), or a Latourian description of the relation between nature and the social (Latour 2005), or a new materialist gloss on the interconnection between people and things (Bennett 2010). As I suggested in the Introduction, I aim to affirm the overlaps between social formation and other ways of theorising the whole. Yet at the same time, I also insist on an important set of differences, or at least on a certain emphasis that is central to the concept of the social formation but that may not be present in these other ideas. Let me highlight two central, distinguishing elements. First, the effort to give an account of the social formation always remains an attempt to think of the social formation *as a whole*. Unlike certain Deleuzean approaches that would focus on a *particular* rhizome or fractal or flow, to theorise the social formation means to retain the important sense of the broader structure—to always be *bearing society in mind*—rather than to isolate one particular element within that structure.[1] Second, and relatedly, this means that an account of the social formation is always a rooted historical account. Analysis of the social formation emerges only from a particular political conjuncture, and it takes that conjuncture to be a historical product.

Adding these points together, we can say that to think the social formation today means to think a social formation overdetermined by (neo)liberal capitalism. Thus, in the Mitchell quote above, the "imbroglio of the technical, the natural and the human" is not just any intermixture of elements, not just any assemblage. It is, in Mitchell's case, a particular set of very specific and very potent intermixtures of the human and the technical: as Mitchell shows, the connection between the human and the material in coal-based carbon democracy led to radically different political effects than the very different connection between the human and the material in an oil-based carbon democracy. Thus, Mitchell's goal—and mine in reading him for his account of the social formation—is not to make the general philosophical point that the human and the technical are interconnected, but rather to give a definite historical analysis of *how* they are interconnected (and with what effects). To focus only on particular assemblages in isolation from the wider structure (as some, but surely not all Deleuzeans do) would be to miss precisely what is at stake in an analysis of social formations.

The political salience of giving an account of a social formation depends upon not just identifying interconnections, but seeing the historical transformation of a social formation. Mitchell's work provides such a powerful example because his project is exactly to retell the story of the emergence and transformation of modern democracy. He does so not only by showing the connection between social and political forms, on the one hand, and material forms, on the other, but also by tracking the changes made to those social and political forms when the material interconnections are altered.

1. In making these claims, I mean to suggest neither that all Deleuzean analysis is narrow or overly focused on the particular nor that my own project returns to an "arboreal" model. My point is simply that in trying always to bear in mind the whole, an account of the social formation differs in general terms from a Deleuzean project.

As I stressed, this is not technological determinism, but it is materialist history, which as I have shown here, cannot be easily encapsulated by or conflated with new materialist ontology.

"LANCE ARMSTRONG"

This second example involves my own direct reading of historical events, my own re-articulation of the social order, and this example shifts the levels of analysis since it turns from the wide historical account given by Mitchell (one that tries to take in the entirety of the social formation) to a focused present-day analysis (one that looks at one specific area of the social order). Most of all, this case also proves distinct because it centers not on a specific new object of the social formation but on a particular subject position.[2] In saying this I am first of all drawing on a point discussed in the Introduction: the social formation is not itself a simple object that could be

2. The language of "subject position" has long been out of fashion, and is therefore, perhaps, most commonly understood within the terms of its standard critique. That is, "subject position" is often associated with a generic and simplistic "structuralist account" by which vibrant human subjects are reduced to "positions," fixed locations within the given material/economic structure. This idea of subject positions as locations-determined-by-structures is even, and often, linked to Althusser (see Faigley 2002: 139), despite the fact that Althusser's essay containing the famous discussion of interpellation does not mention "subject positions" at all (Althusser 1971). The term was perhaps most prominently mobilised by Laclau and Mouffe in *Hegemony and Socialist Strategy* (1985) in order to indicate the proliferation of "points of antagonism" within the class struggle and to designate the diversity of locations within the social order in which workers found themselves—particularly given the rising power of identity politics and the new social movements (Laclau and Mouffe 1985: 11, 20 ff.). Their notion of "subject positions" has been repeatedly challenged, but never more prominently than by Slavoj Žižek, who mobilises a forceful critique of "subject positions" in the service of advocating a Lacanian idea of the subject (as lack) that comes "before" any historical conflict or structural ordering of roles (Žižek 1990: 250–54; cf. Bowman 2006). My own approach consistently resists Žižek's Lacanian turn to the ahistorical or the transcendental, but for this reason, my use of "subject position" owes more to Foucault than to Laclau and Mouffe. Foucault's early work defended the notion of "discursive practices" as precisely *historical* practices; Foucault rejected the idea of discourse as the pure expression of a subject (somehow standing outside of history), and instead insisted that discursive practices contained various positions from which speech could be enunciated. A "subject position" is therefore a location within a social order; yet, as I argue here, the position cannot be fixed or fully determined by that order since analysis of the social formation demonstrates how and to what extent certain positions maintain that order in the first place (Foucault 1972; Chambers 2003). It is in this way, as I explain below in the text, that subject positions are necessary to the social order.

observed directly in its totality, and this means that the social formation is not available for manipulation by the political agent or for comprehension by the philosophical subject. In much the same way that any social formation determines and requires its objects—those objects are the conditions of (im)possibility for the social order itself—so too it determines and requires various subject positions. One way of capturing the notion that the location of a subject position within the social order is both "required" and "determined" by the social formation is to say that such a subject position is *necessary* to/for the social formation.

In calling a subject position "necessary," I am specifying the nature of my analysis in a number of ways. First, the idea of necessity sharply distinguishes my analysis from any sort of determinist account (whether materialist, technological, or other). A determinist analysis would explain a subject or subject position as an obligatory and expected "product" of the social formation; it might thereby see the subject position as a necessary *outcome* of the development of the social order. However, it could not grasp the necessity of that subject position *to* the social order; it would easily emphasise the way the subject position is made possible by the social formation, but it would thereby underestimate the ways in which the social formation itself depends upon that subject position. Below I flesh out this general account in more specific terms, but first I need to turn my attention to the particular case at hand.

Here, then, I will attend to the following subject position: the cycling champion as international sports hero, the Tour de France winner as American sports icon, the victor in a bike race as a "world champion" who is also a marketing and advertising superstar. Lance Armstrong is the name of a particular individual, but "Lance Armstrong" also refers to this particular subject position, one produced by, and one productive of, a particular (late-capitalist, media-saturated, sports-hungry) social formation. "Armstrong" thus names this powerful and important figure, one that is required in the social formation and necessary to it, and in a way "Lance Armstrong" is made possible not just by what Armstrong the man did, but by all sorts of broader forces that entailed "him."

To understand "Lance Armstrong" as a structural location within the social order means, first, to reinterpret the case of Armstrong, to take a certain distance from other narratives—this includes Armstrong's own telling of his tale (in his earlier book, in his later confession) as well as the standard media narration of the Armstrong story (Armstrong and Jenkins 2001; Armstrong 2013). Here, then, I want to *situate* Armstrong within the social order—thereby offering an account of the social formation—while at the same time using the case of Armstrong to throw into relief a few of the central elements of that order, thus making possible a keener understanding of how the larger social formation is held together. Armstrong both exemplified and shaped the social formation of which he was a part, and this social formation, in turn, helped to form and constitute him as not only "professional cyclist" but also "celebrity," "survivor," and "international superstar." In the analysis below, then, I move back and forth between, on the one hand, specific domains within the social order (cycling rules and culture, doping and testing regimes, corporate sponsorship and celebrity culture), and, on the other, a wider account of the social formation that binds together these related but disparate elements.

The standard account of Armstrong proves straightforward, and is very well known, although it certainly also takes on a particular flavor in an American context—one in which European professional road cycling is only accessed *through* Armstrong. This context stands in strong contrast to an understanding of Armstrong from a European perspective, in which Armstrong himself is only understood *through* a certain culture of European cycling. Yet the perspective of the major American media outlets, and from your "average American," includes very little background knowledge or awareness of professional cycling—and what familiarity has emerged over the last two decades has been connected to, and mediated by, the towering celebrity figure of Armstrong, who within this vision was never just a cyclist, but always also a cancer survivor, a hero. Given all this, the story about Armstrong as told in popular culture, especially during the time of my writing (2013), seems quite straightforward: he cheated (and lied to cover up his cheating) and therefore was not the athletic champion and great man we thought him to be. There can, of course, be no doubt that Armstrong clearly violated the formal rules of international cycling by taking performance-enhancing drugs during all of his Tour de France victories.

My point is not that this media frame distorts—every frame distorts to the extent that it captures some elements and excludes others—but that it tells us little to nothing about the social formation at stake in these historical events. The spotlight it shines on Armstrong the individual only occludes a wider view of the social order in which Armstrong exists, and it may completely eclipse any analysis of the social formation that makes a "Lance Armstrong" possible and necessary in the first place. An account of the social formation will almost always need to move beyond powerful partisan and media frames—those that would reduce an issue to a single set of pro/con positions, or explain phenomena by way of a single set of causal variables. The social formation at stake and in play with respect to the Armstrong affair proves to be far deeper, wider, and more politically significant than that media story could ever hope to convey.

To approach any particular media story or cultural event in terms of the social formation means to begin by giving an account of that social order so as to identify key structural features. Here are a few central ones. First, in the late 1980s and then into the 1990s, advances in doping dramatically outpaced advances in testing, such that by the late 1990s (the Armstrong era) the advantages of taking erythropoietin (EPO), testosterone, and then later, blood transfusions far outweighed the apparent risks of getting caught. In this time period the rules were lax and the testing system was easy to game, such that the chances of getting caught, while real, proved quite small. At the same time, the advantage created by doping had gone up dramatically, with benefits estimated at anywhere from a 5 percent to 15 percent increase in performance (Hamilton and Coyle 2012: 4).[3] And this boost in potential power output applies to the world's best cyclists, not to the average person—a huge impact at the margin. Given this context, it is perhaps unsurprising that from 1991 to 2010 almost every rider who initially placed in the top ten in the Tour de France has, at some point in his career, either confessed to doping, been accused of doping, or failed a drug test. Greg LeMond, in 1990, and (at the time of my writing) the winners since 2012 appear to be truly "clean." Focusing, however, on the twenty years in between leads directly to this conclusion: understood internally to this context there is truly no such thing as a "clean" winner of the Tour. This is certainly not to say that "everyone was doping," as there were many riders (perhaps even the majority) who rode clean, but the very structure of the race during these years was such that no one who

3. Coyle gives a range of "10% to 15%" for the boost in performance, and a variety of other sources claim something similar, with no one that I have read who writes about professional cycling suggesting a number lower than 5 percent. After Armstrong was stripped of his titles, in 2012 a group of Dutch researchers published a review article in the *British Journal of Clinical Pharmacology* that caused much controversy for its suggestion that EPO has no verifiable performance benefits (Heuberger et al. 2013). Their review of the existing clinical studies and trials does show that no one has yet *scientifically proved*, through such a study, that EPO boosts performance for elite cyclists. However, the main reason for this is surely that no one has conducted a study of the effects of EPO on elite cyclists. The media was quick to report on this article with the frame "EPO has no effects," often then going so far as to conclude that all the dopers in cycling are therefore proven to be not just cheaters, but idiots who cheated for no reason. Yet as a number of more sober responses showed, while we have no clinical study that proves the effectiveness of EPO for elite cyclists, the medical evidence available to us, along with basic logic, would still seem to auger in favour of a very real performance impact. It is also worth noting that while certainly not clinical, the closest we might come to such a study of EPO is the evidence of twenty years of Tours de France in which no one *not* taking EPO won.

came out on top did so while riding clean. To win the Tour (or even to have a reasonable chance of winning the Tour) was to dope.[4]

Moreover, this recent twenty-year period is not an anomaly. Far from it: the history of doping in professional cycling stretches back from the Armstrong era to periods in the 1960s and 1970s when the most important champions, the undisputed cycling heroes of this time period, were not only caught doping but also responded by *defending doping* (Strickland 2013; see also Wikipedia, "Doping at the Tour de France"). If we move back even earlier in history, we see that in the first half of the twentieth century, doping was simply a legal and accepted norm; it did not even require a defence. As many commentators have mentioned, doping and bike racing have, in a sense, always gone together. To pick any single rider and judge him guilty or innocent of doping is to misunderstand the very nature of cycling. Yet to say this is not to exculpate Armstrong or any other rider. Rather, the actions and choices of those riders must be considered from the wider perspective of the social formation, and this means to ask not whether doping was right or wrong, but why cycling "needed" riders that doped.

Here I must stress that to theorise the social formation is not simply to historicise. While some sense of history helps to draw out the multiple dimensions of any social order, the social formation at stake in the Armstrong story is not determined or fixed by a certain history of cycling (or of a history of cycling and drug use). To give an account of the social formation that makes "Lance Armstrong" possible—or to describe the social formation that makes "Lance Armstrong" necessary—is not the same thing as merely articulating a "culture of cycling." There is not a "social formation of cycling" since the social formation is much larger than the culture of cycling, and that larger social formation involves elements, objects, flows, and fields of forces that far exceed cycling per se—and which may at first seem to have nothing directly to do with cycling.

Even though the history of cycling matters, other features of the social order also have central, and in certain ways much more significant, roles to play. Hence, to give a rich account of this social formation requires connecting the history of cycling to many other elements. Perhaps most prominent should be the rise in multinational corporate sponsorship of professional racing: the "Armstrong era" overflowed not just with dope but also with money. Armstrong's long list of sponsors included such

4. Derrida makes a related point about the concept of drugs—one that, in another context, I would reinterpret in light of the social formation: "The concept of drugs supposes an instituted and an institutional definition: a history is required, and a culture, conventions, evaluations, norms" (Derrida 1995: 229).

mega-corporations as Oakley sunglasses and Trek bicycles, both brands that grew enormously during the years that they sponsored Armstrong. This is not to mention Nike. The money flowing into professional cycling on an unprecedented scale dovetails with the first-ever effort by the American press to treat cycling, particularly the Tour de France, as a legitimate, major sport (and event). Lance Armstrong was the first American cyclist to become a household name, to become not just a great cyclist to those who knew cycling, but a sports hero on par with the likes of Jordan, Gretzky, Woods, and numerous National Football League stars.

In his live television interview/confession in 2013, given to the American television icon Oprah Winfrey, Armstrong speculated that the day his corporate sponsors all dropped him was "a $75 million day" in terms of future earnings losses. To grasp the fact that one single cyclist could this quickly lose this much in sponsorship money is to gain a clearer vision of the size and scale of the entanglement between the sport of cycling and capital. What overall value of corporate profits is now connected to professional cycling? If professional cycling is now indelibly tied to the circulation and valorisation of capital, then we also have to consider the extent to which that circulation of capital itself depends not just on the existence of "sport," but on the existence, production, and continued reproduction of "sports heroes." The list of names above with which I associated Armstrong—those are figures that make sports the big business it now is globally (see Albergotti and O'Connell 2013).

Let me put this point in direct terms: the media interest in both the celebration of Armstrong as hero and the denigration of Armstrong as cheater is a constitutive element of the social formation. The media do not stand outside the social formation and report on it; their representations are a part of the formation in question.[5] This crucial point raises a related question: How is the representation of "Lance Armstrong" not just possible but also, in certain ways, necessary—that is, required by the very social formation that his subject position helps to create? The media representations of Armstrong themselves remain entangled with the interests of corporate capital, and, more to the point, those media frames help to obscure what otherwise might be seen as the central importance of the corporate dimension. Media narratives about Armstrong as a "cheater" help to uphold ideas about

5. This central point relates to the broader idea about understanding the whole, and it concerns how one tacks back and forth between the wider social formation and the specific objects or subjects within it. Alan Finlayson puts it this way: "Everything about the whole is implicated in the specific instance and the instance helps to sustain the order of the whole" (A. Finlayson, personal communication).

natural talent and fair play. Both are linked to fundamental liberal ideas about individual merit and equal opportunity, ideas that also inform the sense of fair competition that underwrites capitalist logic. Here we begin to see how the question of "cheating" and of "fairness" are not just narrow questions weighing Armstrong's putative "guilt"; they are questions fundamental to a larger social order.

And this point helps to explain some of the cognitive dissonance with respect to "cheating" in professional cycling. It was obvious from early on that for those actually participating in professional cycling at the highest levels, the question "did Armstrong cheat?" made little sense at all. Doping—and in Armstrong's era, evading the doping regime—was and has been a constitutive part of professional cycling. It is only when we gain a more perspicacious view of these broader structures that we can make some sense out of cyclists' claims—made not just by Armstrong but by many other riders—that they genuinely did not understand their actions as cheating. In his interview with Winfrey, Armstrong pointed out that to cheat means to gain an unfair edge over one's opponents. And it is plain that those who doped had a gigantic advantage over those who did not. Nonetheless, it is also true that in the Armstrong era so many riders doped that it created a pervasive sense that what we would otherwise call "cheating" is precisely what would *level* the playing field. Armstrong said just this to Winfrey, echoing Tyler Hamilton's declaration that he saw the choices as "cheat" or "go home" (Hamilton and Coyle 2012: 253). Hamilton's own coauthor, Daniel Coyle, purports to reject the idea that cheating levels the playing field: "in fact, it does the reverse." But Coyle's logic proves curious and significant, since his explanation for why cheating is unfair reads as follows: "Widespread cheating rewards the few who have the best information, the most money, and the highest risk tolerance" (Coyle 2012). But to my ears this does not sound like much of an indictment of doping, even if doping is cheating. After all, today's neoliberal ideology of entrepreneurship tells us on a daily basis that those with "the best information, the most money, and the highest risk tolerance" are precisely the ones *who are supposed to be rewarded.* If those are the ones that cheating benefits, then the regime of cheating is no different from the social order of neoliberalism itself.[6]

6. If one still remains somewhat within the media's narrative of accountability, then the problem in Armstrong's case was not *that* he doped, but *how* he doped. To read accounts by other riders is to see that Armstrong's crime was not taking EPO, testosterone, and blood transfusions; many riders did those things. He was despised for the way in which he attacked, bullied, dominated, and sometimes destroyed the lives of those around him, including his fellow riders. It is in this sense that Armstrong seemed most honest,

The question "did Armstrong cheat?" actually makes much more sense, logically, when understood in terms of upholding certain ideological notions of fairness and equality—the very ones that we often propagate through sport but which, as I have suggested above, also operate as central principles of liberalism and capitalism. To uphold these vaunted notions of fairness and individual achievement, the possibilities for "Armstrong" are narrowed to two choices: he can be a superhuman warrior who overcomes the most difficult of life's challenges (testicular cancer that had spread to his brain) while also having incomparable natural talent (many news stories on Armstrong, when he was at his peak, suggested his cardiovascular system made him peerless); or he can be a fraud, a liar, and above all, a *cheat.* This binary directly explains the way the media turned on Armstrong, but it also elucidates an element of professional cycling that the media largely failed to mention, either before or after his downfall. Omertà, the code of silence that operates with respect to doping in cycling, has been but a footnote to this story as told in the mainstream press. Yet there can be no doubt that prior to the first unravelling of Armstrong's "web of lies" with Floyd Landis's 2010 email to US Cycling authorities, omertà helped to sustain the subject position of "Armstrong" as the sports star and cycling hero. The vision of Armstrong that was circulated by the media, by Armstrong's Livestrong Foundation, by Nike, by Oakley and all the rest—that image could have been obliterated at any moment by the numerous cyclists, doctors, and team members who knew about Armstrong's doping. Omertà was a central element in the social formation, and the media's failure to mention omertà itself helped to sustain that formation, along with Armstrong's location within it. In other words, to point to omertà as a code of silence around doping is already to indicate the centrality of doping to professional cycling, and therefore, in order to maintain the ideals of natural ability and fair achievement, cyclists must obviously not mention doping (through omertà) while the media must not mention omertà. Omertà is the glue that has helped hold this order together, an order that has not just been marked by doping, but deeply structured by it.[7]

---

most genuine, in his interview with Winfrey: when he confessed to acting in the above ways. Armstrong's greatest offense was not that he doped but that he used his power and his resources to allow him to play by a different set of rules. Indeed, Armstrong took the leveraging of his power even to the point of staging a dramatic comeback from retirement in 2009, at a time in which his stigmatised and disgraced former teammates (Landis and Hamilton) were not allowed to race at all. And this last act likely led to his downfall, since it pushed some of those "inside the peloton" to turn against him.

7. Even after USADA stripped Armstrong of all his titles, only a very few professional riders spoke out against Armstrong; most had no comment at all, but a significant number

Of course there were those, not inside the peloton but close to it, who challenged the subject position of "Armstrong" almost from the beginning. Armstrong's earliest, loudest critics were those who felt they knew all along, and with certainty, that Armstrong, like so many other top cyclists, was doping (and they were right). These critics were often less concerned to prove the guilt of Armstrong (as the mainstream media later was) than to challenge and change the very structure and practices of cycling—to contest the arrangement of this social order. To read them in their best light,[8] we could say that the case of Armstrong was important to them because of what it told us not about Armstrong the man, but about the broader systems and practices that make up professional cycling. Interpreted generously, we can say that these critics' concern for the sport of cycling led them to challenge Armstrong *as* a subject position that illustrated but also maintained a toxic and corrupt set of structures. Hence, whether individuals like David Walsh saw it this way or not, we can still read his critical narrative as evidence that "Lance Armstrong" was a necessary requirement of this social formation (Walsh 2007).

Let me specify what it means to call "Lance Armstrong" *necessary* to or for today's social formation. My redescription of the story of Armstrong—rethought, that is, in the broader context of the multiple areas of the social order of which he was a part—does not conclude that "Armstrong" was somehow *inevitable.* Nor would I claim that the subject position at stake here proves derivative or epiphenomenal. Rather than "explaining away" Armstrong, as somehow "caused" (in linear fashion) by "deeper" processes, my analysis here demonstrates instead the constitutive and essential relation of Armstrong to a set of wider political practices and historical transformations. To say Armstrong is "necessary" to this social formation is certainly to *connect* him to the social order, to delineate his location within it, but it is by no means to *reduce* him to that social order. The claim

defended Armstrong and repeated his own mantras about never testing positive. Omertà seems to have been broken only by those who were subpoenaed by USADA or who were already convicted of doping and banned from the sport (those already on the outside of the peloton, so to speak). Omertà remains a powerful force in this social formation, even after Armstrong's ban, and the mainstream media remains largely silent about omertà.

8. I recognise that not all critics of Armstrong operated in this manner; certainly some were advancing their own self-interest in various ways, but to go against the dominant narrative by speaking out against Armstrong was already to reduce significantly one's chances of personal benefit. Regardless of personal intentions, these early critics can be read as pointing away from Lance Armstrong the man and pointing toward "Lance Armstrong" the subject position—and thus toward the social formation that sustained him (and vice versa).

of "necessity" points toward the significance of Armstrong *for* that social order: "Armstrong" makes possible and sustains this arrangement of the social order just as much (though such a comparison is surely not quantifiable) as the social order sustains his subject position—that is, sustains "him" as subject position.

This prominent emphasis on, and particular inflection of, "necessity" also distinguishes my account from what we might call an "ordinary cultural analysis." With this phrase I gesture toward a common type of analysis in which capitalist commodification, advertising, and public relations activity is all cited as quasi-causal evidence for a widely observed phenomena, and especially for the actions of celebrities.[9] The central point of such so-called cultural analysis is almost always to make narrow sense of "celebrity culture" or "sports culture" in terms that tie a celebrity figure back to the culture that spawned him or her. Cultural analysis of this sort thus hinges upon tethering the sports star or celebrity to the culture, typically in order to make that figure a "symptom" of a broader culture (itself likely portrayed as "diseased"). But to say that the figure in question is necessary for/to the wider social order is to interrupt this easily digestible narrative and to call into question this sort of cultural analysis. The subject position within a social formation is never merely a symptom, but is instead just as much productive of the social formation as the other way around. There can therefore be no question of ignoring subject positions in order to "go to the root" of the problem, as it were, since a social formation is an overdetermined, complex whole; it has no roots. As I will argue in the chapters that follow, the social formation can only be analysed in terms of its uneven and often contradictory complexity.

Armstrong cannot be explained away, since, indeed, his disappearance would transform the social formation for which he is necessary. Unless it can support and sustain "Lance Armstrong," the social formation will change. To grasp the significance of this claim, however, I must also emphasise the point I made above: under the terms of the current social order, "Lance Armstrong" can be *either* the hero or the anti-hero; he must scale the greatest heights or he must fall to the lowest depths. Among a spate of new books all currently appearing in the wake of Armstrong's confession, the last part of the title of one captures this point nicely: "the Greatest

---

9. This is not to say that the work of "Cultural Studies" as a discipline (or anti-discipline) should be confused with or eclipsed by the type of reductive "cultural analysis" I mention in the text above. Nor am I the first to suggest a more subtle and complex relation between celebrity figures and the larger social order; for one prominent example, see the work of Paul Bowman on Bruce Lee (Bowman 2010; Bowman 2013).

Sports Conspiracy Ever" (Albergotti and O'Connell 2013). The framing of Armstrong as "worst person ever" only helps to sustain the subject position "Lance Armstrong" in such a way as to maintain the current social formation in which athletes become superstars as part of billion-dollar businesses. Can there be an alternative to this binary? In response, I would pose this rhetorical question: What if Lance Armstrong were not "Lance Armstrong"? To question this subject position might also mean to question the current social order. In this light, one can reconsider Armstrong's confession to Winfrey: by speaking not to internal investigators but to a wider outside world, and in speaking about the actual practices and processes of professional cycling, Armstrong's confession had the potential to bring to light certain elements of the social formation itself—hence my emphasis on his reference to a "$75 million day."[10] Indeed, one can read Armstrong's confessions in a general sense as his own attempt to reject the subject position of "Lance Armstrong"—since he can no longer play the hero role that he once happily took up, yet he refuses the anti-hero role that the social formation would now assign him.

❖ ❖

My reading of Mitchell and my analysis of Armstrong both provide specific and more fleshed-out instances of what it means to think with and through the social formation, of what a definite account of the social formation looks like. These examples illustrate how theories of the social formation might operate: in terms of rereading concrete historical and political analyses through the lens of the social formation, and with respect to doing cultural and political analysis directly. These cases also indicate a range of possible emphasis in giving an account of social formations: from the "object" of the social formation in the Mitchell example (also echoed in the Introduction's treatment of Michael Burry's vision of new objects) to the subject position of "Lance Armstrong." I advance these interpretations here, in the space between my Introduction and my first substantive body chapter, so that readers who now move on to a series of engagements with

10. Armstrong's strong push for a Truth and Reconciliation Commission (TRC) *could* be a space for investigating the internal workings of professional cycling and their connection to forces of media and capital. I do not doubt that it could also turn out to provide a PR opportunity for precisely the strongest corporate interests. There are no guarantees about what a TRC might mean in practice, but Armstrong's call for one is an effort to look at cycling and doping through a wider frame than "Lance Armstrong," and that broader vision would be the first step toward transforming the social formation.

theories of the social formation will already (and continually) have available to them this sense of the politics of social formations. Following Marx, I make the effort to always be "bearing society in mind" even when I am critically engaging with the work of a particular theorist (as I do in the next chapter), or when I am attempting to develop complex epistemologies and concepts (as I do in Chapters 2 and 3).

1

Subjectivation, the Social, and a (Missing) Account of the Social Formation

Cornel West has recently called Judith Butler "the leading social theorist of our generation" (West 2011: 92), and while I agree completely with the spirit of West's claim, I must, at the risk of sounding pedantic, dissent from the specific content of his laudatory description. Doubtless Butler takes her place today as one of the foremost theorists and public intellectuals; her work is widely recognised as helping to reshape a number of fields across the humanities; and she speaks with a powerful voice to a variety of national and international political contexts. Nonetheless, I contend that precisely a social theory—or better, a richer account of the social formation—is lacking in Butler's work. In order to defend this claim and to show why it matters, the core of this chapter examines the location in Butler's corpus where, I argue, she expunges a conception of the social formation from her very own sources, thereby calling more conspicuous attention to its absence in her own work. I also articulate the significance of this move in relation to her broader intellectual trajectory, particularly in terms of her post-2001[1] writings. I read Butler with the working hypothesis that her

1. Although there is surely nothing definitive or fixed about it, I use the year 2001 as an inflection point in the trajectory of Butler's published works for at least two reasons. First, at the time of my writing in 2013, the year 2001 splits the time period of Butler's published works almost perfectly in half, since (if we leave out the publication of her dissertation as a book, which Butler herself often seems eager to do) Butler's first important chapters and articles, pre-*Gender Trouble*, appeared in 1989, giving us twelve

putative turn to ethics has little to do with the questions of moral philosophy per se. Rather, while something is missing in Butler's early work, that something is not ethics, but rather an account of the social formation.

Butler's early fascination (indeed, at times, a fixation) with the problem of subject formation produces, within *The Psychic Life of Power*, a series of blindspots concerning the larger question of society, of the social whole. Butler's intense focus on producing a "theory of subjection" leads her to purge a viable account of the social formation from the very texts she draws from. This subtraction of the social formation in Butler's reading helps to explain her explicit efforts in recent works to offer an account of "the social"—an account, I argue, that merely falls back on a liberal, aggregative model (one that Butler would otherwise eschew).[2]

This chapter focuses on a close engagement with Butler's self-named "theory of subjection." Butler derives that theory from her readings of Freud, Foucault, Lacan, and Althusser, but here I center my analysis

years until 2001 and twelve years after. Second, Butler published two books in 2000, both of which remain clearly caught up in debates coming out of her work in the 1990s, while her first book after 2001, *Precarious Life* (2004a), just as clearly responds not to the terms of those earlier debates but to the events of 9/11 and after. This periodising remains tentative and nominalist, and will likely shift and disintegrate in the future, but at the current moment it offers a helpful way to think about the "turn" in Butler's work since 2001.

2. Taking a wider view, I am raising the question of how Butler could go from being a "radical constructivist feminist" to a "mortalist humanist." These phrases not only name and describe Butler's work (at a particular moment in time) but also shade into lines of criticism. The first term (my own) captures the stakes of the critique of Butler mounted by Seyla Benhabib and others in response to Butler's early and highly impactful work (Benhabib 1995). The latter is Bonnie Honig's description of Butler's recent project. This chapter does not provide a historical reconstruction of the path that Butler has taken over the past twenty-five years. Instead, it analyses in depth one moment in this broad movement so as to offer a more indirect response to the question I have posed here. *The Psychic Life of Power* proves to be the key text; its argument contains Butler's misstep—her move down a path that leads her to moral philosophy and mortalism and away from her earlier, concrete engagements with political theory. An alternative manner of understanding Butler's "turn"—one that I do not pursue here, but which is complementary to and resonates with the one I do advance—would be to grasp it as a shift away from concrete political critique (focused on specific political conjunctures) and toward a moral theory whose critical edge always reduces to an ethical plaint. This turn would be subject to the same critique that Marx offered, especially in "Poverty of Philosophy," of the French utopian socialists (Marx 1955). As I mentioned in my Introduction, utopian socialists fail to advance a critical understanding of capitalism, the basis of which might form a real challenge to capitalism. Instead, they offer no more than a meta-level ethical protest against capitalism. In this context, see Bennett and Shapiro (2002), Brown (2001), Butler and Connolly (2000).

specifically on Butler's readings of Hegel and Althusser. I demonstrate that Butler's appropriation of Hegel frames and limits her encounter with Althusser: ultimately Butler gives us what we might call a "Hegelianised Althusser," one stripped of the rich understanding of the social formation that Althusser himself was trying to delineate—the one that I will explore in various ways over the four chapters that follow this one. Butler's focus on desire and the theory of subject gives her no way to grasp or make sense of the social formation that provides the conditions of possibility for all subjects. I close by suggesting that Butler's ontology of vulnerability and finitude, as it emerges in her most recent writings, serves the purpose of *standing in for* a more rigorous account of the social formation. And this substitution, I suggest, proves to be a poor one, since it reduces Butler's work to the terms of liberal political philosophy.[3]

OUTWORK: THE TURN TO PHILOSOPHY

Each of Butler's first three books begins with a preface.[4] Compared to proper introductions (which may or may not follow the preface, when the book contains one), prefaces tend to provide more indirect or oblique

3. Overall, then, the function of this chapter is not merely to offer an example of a "missing account" of the social formation, but rather to track quite specifically, in Butler's work, the particular effects of attempting (on her part) to answer certain political questions and respond to particular theoretical problems without an account of the social formation.

4. Tom Boland has devoted most of an entire article to the explication of Butler's prefaces, but his concerns prove quite distinct from my own: Boland looks for an expression of Butler's subjectivity (and asks what such expressions might tell us about the nature of critique), while I remain focused on the genre of the texts themselves (Boland 2007). As I explain in the text, the prefaces of Butler's early works orient those books toward a set of concrete political engagements, and I am therefore much less interested in what the prefaces might tell us about Butler's subjectivity, and much more focused on the structure of Butler's texts and the type of narrative they take up and participate in. "Outwork," my section heading, is Barbara Johnson's translation of Derrida's preface-deconstructing-the-preface to *Dissemination*, which he titled "Hors livre, préfaces." As prior to and before, yet still somehow essential to the text, the preface has always followed the Derridean logic of supplementarity. The preface is (in)essential to the book. In his (non)preface, Derrida reads Hegel on the distinction between prefaces and introductions, where Hegel invokes the same set of differences between them that I mark below in my own text. For Hegel, the personal, historical, and transitory nature of the preface ought to make them utterly superfluous to the logic of the book, but, as Derrida shows (and somehow even Hegel knows), the book can never do without them (Derrida 1981a: 17; Hegel 2010; Johnson 1981: xxxii; cf. Dinan 2010).

entries into the body of a text; they often avoid offering anything like a comprehensive overview of the text, and they frequently eschew any effort to sum up the main arguments or synthesise its lines of logic. Prefaces almost always prove to be shorter than introductions, and unlike the latter, prefaces almost never conclude by offering the reader summaries of the chapters to come. Finally, perhaps most important for my purpose here, prefaces are more situated, and more personal, than introductions. If ever one were to spot the personality or identity of the author, if ever one were to discern the real stakes of the text for that author, such revelations would be found in the preface. Many of these elements emerge clearly in the preface to Butler's first major book, *Gender Trouble*, a work that opens with a very precise specification of the location and stakes of the argument. Butler does not hide the site and target of her arguments: she names them with the first three words of the book, "contemporary feminist debates" (Butler 1999 [1990]: xxix). Something similar can be said for *Bodies That Matter*, Butler's follow-up to *Gender Trouble*, a text that begins in the first person—"I began writing this book"—and continues with a clear articulation of the issue at stake, "the materiality of the body" (Butler 1993: viii).[5] Indeed, this opening paragraph has a very personal timbre, as Butler describes the tone that critics have taken with her in their questions and challenges to her work in *Gender Trouble*. Butler repeats this type of gesture in numerous other prefaces across her wide body of work (see Butler 1999; Butler 2004a).

I start by speaking about the nature of the preface, and Butler's use of it, in order to mark a contrast that might otherwise be hard to glimpse. *The Psychic Life of Power* (hereon *PLP*) lacks a preface or any other personalising apparatus.[6] Its introduction begins with these words: "As a form of power, subjection is paradoxical" (Butler 1997b: 1). This sentence places readers of the book onto philosophical terrain. Butler's first two major books contained subtitles that situated them squarely within the terms of feminist politics and feminist debate, whereas *PLP*'s subtitle is the broadly abstract "theories of subjection." It is not just that this book asks more sweeping questions than Butler's first two but that Butler herself seeks to shift the work of this book out of the fields (the confines?) of feminist

5. In the text I leave out a discussion of Butler's first book, based on her dissertation, *Subjects of Desire*. Butler has never disavowed that text, but she has taken a certain distance from it, suggesting it was published too early, a decision based more on career pressures than on intellectual choices. But even this text, clearly a philosophical dissertation, starts with a preface, and in the opening lines Butler quotes Tennessee Williams's Blanche Dubois (Butler 1987).

6. *PLP* and *Excitable Speech* were published almost simultaneously, appearing within two months of each other in the spring of 1997; neither contains a preface.

theory and politics and onto the stage of the discipline of philosophy. This book specifically focuses on questions of theory; it draws from and directs itself toward philosophers.[7] All of this matters to me because to see what is at stake in *PLP*, and to see it as a part of the development of Butler's thought, it helps very much to mark the genre (i.e., the discipline of philosophy) in which it is written. In *PLP* Butler retains a singular focus on questions about the philosophical category of the subject, about the process of subjection, and above all about the workings of power in relation to the subject. I frame my reading of this text in terms of this issue of genre, because the turn to a discourse of philosophy in *PLP* highlights the absence in Butler's work (in all her writings up to this point, but magnified in this particular text) of a richer account not just of "the social" as a virtual space of plurality, but of society, of the political order—of the social formation.

As I have already shown in my Introduction, the differences between an account of "the social" or a social theory, on the one hand, and a conception of the social formation, on the other, cannot be delineated by way of an abstract, analytic set of definitions of each entity. I aim to bring these distinctions into sharper relief by way of my reading of Butler's texts for their failure to account for the social formation, and I do not wish to preempt that discussion here by trying to define terms. Nevertheless, to elucidate the stakes of the argument, I can, by expanding on my 2nd hypothesis, offer a more polemical formulation of the gap between the two: the social formation is itself a political form, a politicised structure, whereas "the social" may well be a sphere separate from "the political" domain. We understand that "society" or "the social realm" (or *Gesellschaft*) can easily be seen as a virtual domain, a space in which individuals interact with one another. Hegel offers this sort of account of the social in terms of a dyadic relationship of recognition, and social contract theory depends on understanding "society" as formed by the consent of free and equal individuals. The social formation, on the other hand, points toward the always specific yet constantly shifting arrangement of practices; "social formation" names the simultaneously lateral and vertical arrangement of relationships between diverse activities. Butler has clearly maintained a constant concern with the signifying and resignifying of particular practices from within the realm of "the social." But an understanding of the social formation focuses on the way that such practices are structured from without, as part of an overall system.

---

7. *PLP* also speaks to psychoanalysis, but I contend that this fact does not distinguish the book from Butler's two previous works, which also engage with the language and literature of psychoanalysis. Rather, the marked difference in tone or style with *PLP* manifests in its commitment to a general and generalising language of theory.

While I do not attend in detail to Butler's most famous early texts, *Gender Trouble* and *Bodies That Matter*, I claim that like the later texts that I will discuss in more detail below, those early works contain no developed conception of the social formation. Butler's early writings do indeed use the word *social* quite frequently. Often the word functions simply as a modifier—for example, *social context*, *social power*, and *social norms* (Butler 1999: 20 and ff.). More frequently, *social* appears within a chain of terms such as *cultural*, *historical*, or *political*, all of which function as contrasts to terms such as *natural* or *prediscursive*; here Butler makes her well-known arguments about how to understand the distinction between sex and gender as itself a product of historical discursive practices (Butler 1999; see Chambers 2007). Above all, Butler's earlier arguments always work against the idea of a "presocial" (Butler 1999: 38; Butler 1993: 202). As with her more recent books, and as I will discuss in my final section below, Butler's early works use the word *social* mainly as a descriptor to indicate relationality, to mark contextuality, and to suggest a basic sense of plurality. Overall, Butler has no interest in developing a social theory in these early books, much less in offering an account of the social formation.[8]

To defend my claim that *PLP* lacks an account or understanding of the social formation puts me in something like the position of trying to prove the negative. However, I must make clear here that my aim is not to fault Butler for not having a "theory of . . . " anything, not even the social formation. The form of critical theory that I subscribe to, and to which I think Butler subscribes as well, does not require a thinker to have a "theory of" every concept that they discuss, nor does the failure to have a "theory of X" indicate, on its own, anything at all about their work.[9] Indeed, important critical work today proceeds by eschewing the very notion of producing more "theories of . . . " (Rancière 2009; Chambers 2013). Thus, my charge against Butler is distinctly different. Unlike much of Butler's work, especially her early work, in *PLP* Butler attempts to develop just such a "theory of"; in this case, as the book's subtitle makes clear, a "theory of subjection." And in order to create her own theory of subjection, Butler erases elements, concepts, and articulations of the social formation that are present in the authors she herself is reading. Put differently, just because Althusser has a concept of the social formation does not mean that Butler *must* do

8. Late in *Bodies That Matter* Butler does use the phrase *social formation*, but she does so only briefly and narrowly, and strictly within the terms of discussing Žižek's arguments—such that the concept, in this context, clearly seems to be his, not Butler's (Butler 1993: 202).

9. Thanks to Bonnie Honig for helpful clarification of this crucial point.

so as well, but in her reading of Althusser she expunges his account of the social formation—and it is this erasure that has significant implications for Butler's work, and for any effort to understand politics and history. I focus on *PLP* here because in that text the absence of a concept of the social formation becomes palpably visible, and has meaningful effects. Hence, in the remainder of this section I offer a broad overview of the main argument in Butler's book, and then, in the section that follows, I work closely through two of the key interpretive/philosophical readings that she uses to support this argument.

Butler's central (philosophical) claim in *PLP* can be delineated both with and without the proper (philosophical) names. Starting with Foucault, Butler moves toward Freud, with particular readings of Hegel, Nietzsche, and Althusser designed to help her on the journey. To start with Foucault means to begin with the claim that the process of subject formation always proves double: to form a subject capable of exercising power (the capacity of agency itself) is always simultaneously to *subject* to power.[10] "Subjection"

10. Butler refers to this process as "subjectivation," and she specifies this term as her translation of Foucault's *assujettissement*. I set aside here a group of complicating and at times confusing circumstances surrounding both this particular choice and Butler's general usage of, and references to, *assujettissement* over the years. Butler makes no note of the fact that Foucault actually uses *two* distinct terms, during the course of his career, to name the twofold process of subject formation. Early on, Foucault takes up the term that Butler uses consistently throughout *PLP*, but in his later writings he introduces a new term, and he does so intentionally—that is, to mark a distinction with his earlier work. That new term is *subjectivation*, the very same word whose English cognate Butler gives as a translation of Foucault's earlier French term. For these reasons, both of Butler's decisions—first, to use the English term *subjectivation*, and then to describe this as a translation of Foucault's *assujettissement*—prove problematic in light of the fact that "subjectivation" is the best translation of Foucault's later term, *subjectivation*. Milchman and Rosenberg make a strong case for "subjectification" as the optimal choice to translate *assujettissement*. More importantly, they argue convincingly for the crucial distinction between *assujettissement* and *subjectivation*, a distinction that is collapsed in Butler's writings (Milchman and Rosenberg 2007: 55–56). Moreover, this elision of the difference cannot be isolated to *PLP*, as Butler repeats it seven years later in *Giving an Account of Oneself* when she refers to a "mode of subjectivation" in relation to *assujettissement* (Butler 2005: 17). A more minor point, but perhaps telling: throughout *PLP* Butler misspells *assujettissement as assujetissement* (Butler 1997b: 5ff.). The explanation, it would seem, for this persistent error comes from an earlier article on Althusser where Butler ostensibly provides Althusser's own French, but here too she spells the word wrong. Here is Butler's quote, including her brackets: "The school teaches 'know-how' (skills) [des 'savoir-faire'] . . . in forms which ensure subjection to the ruling ideology [l'assujetissement à l'idéologie dominante]" (Butler 1995: 140; quoting Althusser 1971: 128, Butler's quote excludes a long parenthetical remark in Althusser's original). In the original French (1970) Althusser has the word

connotes both "becoming-subject" and "being subordinated to or dominated by." Thus, we see subject formation as a vexed and complex process of *turning*: the subject turns in response to power, but the subject only comes to be *through* the turning, and power only really flows *through* the turning. We might think of this process as a very odd sort of dance between power (the music) and the subject (the dancer); hence, the (solo) dancer only comes into being by responding to the music (there is no dancer prior to the music), operating to some extent autonomously yet still somehow always subject to the terms of the music, while the music itself only plays when the dancer dances (there is no music without the dancer). Now, to move toward Freud, for Butler, means insisting on something much more than a contingent connection between the subject and power; it is to indicate the "passionate attachment" of the subject to the very power that forms him/her/it. And for Butler this means an attachment not only to the agency made possible by subjection but also to the subordination at the heart of subjection (Butler 1997b: 6). The psyche (or the psychic) is one name for this stubborn tie that binds the subject to the power of domination.[11]

Thus Butler wants to go beyond—or better, to somehow go *inside*—the dance, so as to find out what links the dancer to the music, not just as a mutual condition of possibility (neither exists without the other) but as a fundamental and unbreakable link that somehow transcends any particular dance. What persists before or after the music? What makes the dance possible? Butler offers various responses to this question (e.g., guilt, or the Spinozan *conatus*[12]), but the general answer always remains the same—

spelled correctly, but here we see where the error may have first cropped up for Butler—in incorrectly transcribing Althusser's French. Strangely, in *Giving an Account* Butler again gives the French and again gets the spelling wrong, but this time differently, as she writes "*assujettisement*" (Butler 2005: 17). I spell all this out for the sake of neither digression nor nitpicking. Quite the contrary, these issues matter because Butler's collapsing of distinct permutations of subjectivation is directly related to her failure to grasp the social formation. Foucault switches terms precisely because he alters his account of the historical transformation of power/knowledge regimes (another name, I would suggest, for social formations), but in collapsing that distinction Butler departs from Foucault's historical account and moves closer to a general philosophical account of subjectivity—the very project named in the subtitle of *PLP*.

11. In this context, see Drew Walker's reading of the "sorry bind" as a key feature in so much of Butler's thinking (Walker 2013).

12. Butler's odd insistence on the supposed universality of the Spinozan desire to persist in one's being—"odd" not only in its apparently trans-historical nature but also insofar as Butler wrongly attributes a commitment to this force to authors such as Nietzsche who had explicitly rejected it—has been roundly criticised by readers of *PLP* (Lloyd 2007; Chambers and Carver 2008).

namely, the psyche. In just her second paragraph Butler poses the central and overriding question of the book: "What is the psychic form that power takes?" (Butler 1997b: 2). But the question proves to be loaded, since to ask *what psychic form* power takes is to presume that power does indeed take psychic shape. It is to presume that a full account of the process of subject formation cannot be given without the psyche. Butler's formulation of this point is pregnant with particular meaning and significant implications for her overall project: "an account of subjection, it seems, must be traced in terms of psychic life" (Butler 1997b: 18). Given this framing logic, Butler "naturally" (my quotation marks) devotes this book to tracing that psychic form, to showing within particular readings of nineteenth- and twentieth-century philosophers how power might "take psychic form." In each case it will be a matter of showing how there is something more to the relationship between power and the subject, something sticky that makes power and the subject whirl around one another and get the twofold process of subjection underway.

My primary interest lies less with this general argument that Butler positions "between Freud and Foucault," and more with the *movement* away from Foucault (clearly Butler's starting point) and with the important use of Hegel and Althusser in helping Butler to carry out this shift. While "between Freud and Foucault" points to the general location of Butler's "theory of subjection," it can be shown that the reading of these other thinkers does the bulk of the work. And it is in Butler's apparent engagement with Althusser, as framed by her interpretation of Hegel, that we can start to feel the presence of the absence of the social formation. That is, in order to trace the psychic form of power, Butler must simultaneously *read out* of Althusser (and Nietzsche) the very account of the social formation that otherwise proves so central to his project. In the following sections I will track the movement that Butler takes away from Foucault as she works through Althusser, while also making my own case for the palpable absence of an account of social order in Butler's reading—and all of this despite the clear presence of those accounts in the actual texts of Althusser (and Nietzsche as well).[13]

---

13. What follows leaves out any detailed treatment of Butler's point of departure—that is, her reading of Foucault designed to demonstrate the need to diverge from his account of subjectivation in the first place. I have analysed this argument at some length elsewhere (Chambers 2003). Space constraints mean I must also excise a detailed engagement with Butler's reading of Nietzsche, where she makes a similar but differently inflected set of moves as those she takes with Althusser. For more on Butler's reading of Nietzsche in *PLP*, see note 22 in this chapter.

HEGELIANISING ALTHUSSER

Butler's academic career begins with her dissertation on Hegel, but significantly, in her first two major books (*Gender Trouble* and *Bodies That Matter*), Hegel plays almost no role whatsoever. As I have noted above, this may be because both of those books are more situated political encounters. In any case, with *PLP* Butler returns not only to Hegel but also to the beginning with Hegel, as Butler places her reading of Hegel at the foundation of the book (in the first substantive chapter). Butler's exegesis of Hegel's *Phenomenology of Spirit* targets the section on "unhappy consciousness." This concept, Butler will stress, starkly expresses the key dimension of "self-subjection" that makes up a part of any and all forms of subjection. Butler uncovers this dimension through a close reading of the ever-famous, and infinitely read, lord and bondsman section of the *Phenomenology*. I will not rehearse the details of that subtle and sophisticated reading here. What matters most to me is not the substance of Butler's reading of the lord and bondsman passages, but the very structure, the shape, and the form of this, one of the most famous passages in the history of philosophy. The story of "the Lord" and "the Bondsman" is a story of Subjects (with a capital *S*) relating to one another. The philosophical narrative says little to nothing about context, about institutions, about the history that brought about these subject categories (clearly categories of feudalism) in the first place. For Hegel the lord and bondsman are not social creatures, enmeshed in social context; they are figures that help account, philosophically, for subjectivity itself. The subjectivity that is established, interrupted, and reconstituted in the lord and bondsman narrative never interrogates the material conditions that might underlie or be intertwined with the process of recognition that Hegel delineates, and in a certain sense—that is, subject to the terms of Hegel's discourse—such conditions ought not be investigated since these subjects are not historical subjects but philosophical subjects. Butler's reading of Hegel's famous passages always proceeds by descriptions of the actions and reactions, feelings, emotions, and senses, of the two main *characters* in a philosophical tale of subjectivity. One can see clearly why Butler would start here in an effort to write on "theories of subjection," and at the same time one can easily note that there is no social formation here, no political order.

I offer this possibly obvious reflection not as a criticism of either Hegel or Butler's reading of Hegel, but rather as a frame for making sense of Butler's interpretation of Althusser. Butler leaves nothing obvious out of her elucidation of Hegel, but the same cannot be said for her exegesis of Althusser. Butler approaches Althusser as if he, like Hegel, were describing relations among abstract philosophical subjects. For Butler, Althusser's "theory of interpellation" is clearly a "theory of subjection," one that illuminates the twofold process of subject formation by establishing an abstract relation between language and the subject. Indeed, Butler highlights and foregrounds the role of "language" to such a strong degree that a reader unfamiliar with Althusser's own texts might mis-recognise the Marxist Althusser as a philosopher of language (in dialogue with J. L. Austin). Hence she opens her chapter on Althusser with the following: "Althusser's *doctrine* of interpellation . . . offer[s] a way to account for a subject who comes into being as a *consequence* of language" (Butler 1997b: 106, my emphasis). Butler reads Althusser as symmetrical with Hegel: where Hegel has two subjects (lord and bondsman) relating to one another through a process of recognition, Althusser has two subjects (passerby and policeman) relating to one another through hailing.

Given this relatively empty framework—one that only contains subjects and a power relation between them—Butler must provide, in her account of Althusser, an explanation for *why* the subject responds to the hail. She sees this as the fundamental limitation or stumbling block with Althusser's own account. She writes: "Significantly, Althusser does not offer a clue as to why the individual turns around" (Butler 1997b: 5). For just this reason, Althusser's account of interpellation provides Butler with the perfect example for her argument that we must move away from a Foucauldian account of subjection as somehow produced only by disciplinary power itself. Precisely what we need, for Butler, is to answer this missing question in Althusser: the subject turns to respond to the hail, and in turning becomes a subject while also being subjected to power. But why does the subject turn at all? Butler's answer is guilt: "Subject formation . . . take[s] place only on the acceptance of guilt, so that there is no 'I' who might ascribe a place to itself, who might be announced in speech, without first *a self-attribution of guilt*" (Butler 1997b: 107, my emphasis). The subject—who is not a subject before he turns—turns because he is a guilty subject.

In a move that anticipates her post-2001 work on precarious lives—and her development of a position that has been called "constitutive vulnerability"[14] or "mortalist humanism"[15]—Butler rereads the Althusserian

14. George Shulman has developed perhaps the most subtle critique of Butler's post-2001 writings (Shulman 2011a; Shulman 2011b). He starts where I do here (and as I have previously argued) by rejecting the idea that Butler has simply turned from politics to ethics (Shulman 2011a; Chambers and Carver 2008). He goes on to identify carefully the problem he sees in these works: it is not a matter of eschewing politics directly but of turning to a kind of transcendental formalism that unwittingly "occludes politics." And he then proceeds to articulate the need for a different sort of response: the "answer" is not a new philosophical position, but rather a different understanding (most of all, a mediated and material one) of precarity and vulnerability themselves.

15. I see my analysis here as a complement to Honig's critique of Butler's "mortalist" position (Honig 2013; see also Honig 2010). Honig shows that Butler's articulation of

scene of interpellation in such a way as to identify (or construct) a set of universal features, what she calls "an openness or vulnerability to the law," that precede the very response to that law (Butler 1997b: 108). Butler's answer to why we respond to the call of the law is that we are somehow always already subject to its terms, vulnerable to its force. Our vulnerability "before the law" appears in the form of a guilt that precedes the law. "Guilt," Butler contends, "is prior to knowledge of the law," and guilt therefore constitutes a "prior *desire for* the law" (Butler 1997b: 108, my emphasis). Why do we turn when we hear the call of the law? Because we already want to turn; because we desire the law; because the call of the law triggers the guilt we already possess.[16]

I have called this a "rereading" of Althusser, but perhaps that description proves overly nominalist. In chapter 4 of *PLP* it is difficult to discern exactly where Althusser leaves off and Butler begins. Butler mainly writes as if she is reading, synthesising, and interpreting Althusser. Hence one might easily presume that the notion of "guilt" plays a central role in Althusser's account of subjectivation.[17] At the same time, Butler does suggest in her introduction (and as I quote above) that Althusser fails to provide any answer as to why the subject, who is hailed, turns. And for this reason one might instead assume that Butler seeks to supplement Althusser's account with her own concept of guilt (which she borrows from Freudian thought). However, neither sense is really quite right. The reasons prove multiple: first, contrary to Butler's explicit claim, Althusser poses to himself the very question of why the individual turns, and he goes on to give a response. As Drew Walker puts it, contra Butler, "*Althusser has an answer*" (Walker

---

"precarious lives" can clearly be understood as another version of a philosophy of human finitude. In turn, I am showing how such a philosophy might develop from the position Butler takes up earlier, in *PLP*, when she erases an account of the social formation. Without a concept of the social order, all that remains are general philosophical statements about the subject (e.g., concerning its finitude).

16. Butler never considers the extent to which "guilt" has a very particular, and specifically Judeo-Christian, history. Rather than bring guilt to bear on her analysis as itself a product of history, she implicitly conceptualises guilt as lying outside of history.

17. Butler has something of a history of advancing interpretations of authors that appear, on the surface, to be straightforward readings of their text, but that actually prove to be heavily inflected by and infused with another set of arguments or texts (that themselves often go uncited). For example, *Excitable Speech* introduces readers to a J. L. Austin who has already been deconstructed by Derrida (Butler 1997a). Similarly, the Althusser we meet in *PLP* has already been supplemented by Freud and Lacan; the same holds true both in Butler's earlier version of this chapter on Althusser (Butler 1997b; cf. Butler 1995) and in the discussion of Althusser in *Excitable Speech*, which largely mirrors the one here in *PLP*, but lacks the emphasis on guilt (Butler 1997a: 30–35).

2010: 3). Second, Althusser's answer excludes the very idea of guilt or bad conscience. Althusser makes both of these moves at the very center of the brief passages on the scene of interpellation, the passages that Butler suggests she is reading in her account but which she never cites.[18] Let me unpack these claims by turning to Althusser's actual text.

I should begin by emphasising a point that Butler elides: the famous *scene of interpellation*—Butler's term, not Althusser's[19]—appears quite late in Althusser's long essay on the particular question of ideology, and as part of a broad discussion of Marx's and Marxist conceptions of the social formation. Althusser's own project is quite different from Butler's: he wants to ask how the material conditions of production are themselves *reproduced* (Althusser 1971: 124). What is the status, the structure, and the dynamics of power within a social order such that it can recreate the conditions for material production? (This is Althusser's way of asking the question of the social formation.) Althusser contends that the reproduction of the conditions of production cannot come about without the workings of ideology, and it is for this reason that, very near the end of the essay, he advances a few speculative theses toward a theory of ideology. In this context Althusser seeks to show that we cannot understand any concept of "ideology" without first grasping it as fully material, as embedded within practices *that are themselves embedded within the material structures of a social formation.* I use italics here to try to capture Althusser's own emphasis in an essay marked by heavy usage of italics in the original. Thus, in the page just before the account of interpellation, Althusser claims that whenever we try to deal with a "single subject"—*apparently* isolated, in much the way the subject is for Butler throughout *PLP*—we must always remember that "the existence of the ideas of his belief is material *in that his ideas are his material actions inserted into material practices governed by material rituals which are themselves defined by the material ideological apparatus from which derive the ideas of that subject*" (Althusser 1971: 158).

Althusser's so-called scene of interpellation (again, Butler's phrase) appears almost directly after this argument, and I would insist that Althusser's thesis about interpellation, that "ideology interpellates individuals as subjects," must be understood as situated in exactly this context (Althusser

18. Both in the entirety of this chapter in *PLP* and also in the entirety of Butler's earlier article on Althusser (Butler 1995) on which the chapter was based, Butler provides the following references: three total citations of Althusser's essay, only one of them substantive, and zero citations of the key, famous passages on hailing and ideology.

19. In *Excitable Speech* Butler calls it a "linguistic scene" (Butler 1997a: 30).

1971: 160). Althusser refines the general thesis into the more focused claim that ideology hails "concrete individuals as concrete subjects" (Althusser 1971: 162). I read this line as echoing and emphasising the fact that ideology only functions (and interpellation is a function of ideology in Althusser's account) in concrete cases. It is in this light that Althusser says we might "imagine" the workings of ideology along the lines of "everyday" hailing, by the police or by anyone else. In response to "hey, you there!" a concrete individual responds, turns around, and in so turning becomes (what he/she already is) a concrete subject. Butler would have us believe that Althusser has nothing to say about *why* the individual turns: "Althusser does not offer a clue" (Butler 1997b: 5). But Althusser offers much more than a clue to the question Butler wants to pose, since he himself raises the same question, and then answers it. And he does so at the exact center of the discussion of the "scene of interpellation," the scene that Butler is putatively reading throughout chapter 4 of *PLP*. I say "putatively" since, again, Butler never quotes from these passages nor even cites them at any place in her text. Had she done so, she would have found Althusser asking her own question for her. Althusser says that the individual will turn around, will make, in response to the call, a 180-degree "physical conversion." He continues:

> Why?
>
> Because he has recognized that the hail was "really" addressed to him, and that "it was *really him* who was hailed" (and not someone else). Experience shows that the practical telecommunication of hailings is such that they hardly ever miss their man: verbal call or whistle, the one hailed always recognizes that it is really him who is being hailed. And yet it is a strange phenomenon, and one which cannot be explained solely by "guilt feelings," despite the large numbers who "have something on their consciences." (Althusser 1971: 163)

There is a great deal to unpack in this passage, particularly as it relates to Butler's project—both in *PLP* and more broadly. Althusser explains the "reflexivity" of the individual/subject not in terms of any inherent internal dimension or capacity of that subject, but rather in relation to the overall scene of ideological hailing. Put differently, for Althusser, the social formation itself provides an account of why the subject turns. He responds to the call because he hears it as a call, and as a call *for him.* For Althusser, hailings work—they almost never miss their mark—because ideology works. (I might say that hailings work because the social formation "works.") After the famous passage with the policeman and the passerby, Althusser goes on to argue that the temporality of the logic in the example is all wrong, since it presumes that there is *first* a hailing and *then* a response. However, there really is no such succession: "Ideology has always-already interpellated individuals as subjects" (Althusser 1971: 164). The "individual" is, in fact, the abstract idea, since in practice, in reality—that is, in ideology—we always find concrete subjects.[20]

It is in this sense that I read Althusser as demonstrating that the turn, the reflexivity of the subject, comes about strictly in terms of the social formation itself and without recourse to an interior psyche or *conatus* that would offer a separate, causal explanation for *why* the subject turns. When we understand the scene of interpellation as taking place within a concrete social formation, we then see that the response to the call happens "naturally" (i.e., thoroughly ideologically). For Butler, of course, Althusser's explanation for "why the individual/subject turns" will seem inadequate; it may not sound like an explanation at all, since one might hear Althusser's answer as, "It just works." Nonetheless, the apparent hollowness of this answer is not intrinsic to the Althusserian account but is rather a product of Butler's *hollowing out* of Althusser's thick, detailed, and lengthy argument. Butler has taken away the account of the social formation that Althusser offers in the more than thirty pages that precede the famous "scene of interpellation." Hence, she reads that scene as an abstract account of two entities (policeman and passerby) relating to one another within a field of power. And when taken in that way, the account lacks an explanation for how subjective reflexivity comes about.[21]

The culmination of this series of logical moves gives us the Hegelianised "Althusser" that appears in *PLP*—an Althusser shorn of his account of

20. A slightly different reading of *PLP* might rightly emphasise that Butler's primary concern lies with the problem of resistance (this is true in her reading here of Althusser, but also in her readings of Freud and Foucault) and not with a theory of the psyche per se. Butler turns to the psyche (and attendant conceptions of guilt) because she feels that a theory of resistance *requires* such a supplement. In other words, in the face of the Althusserian account of the concrete subject, Butler might still worry about that subject's capacity to *resist* the call of ideology. In the text below I suggest that such a worry on Butler's part proves misplaced: resistance need not reside in some trans-historical capacity of the subject since the historicity of the social formation makes agency possible. My argument thereby blurs the difference in emphasis (psyche/resistance) by suggesting that Butler's turn to the psyche might never have been needed.

21. Certain elements of my critique of Butler can actually be found in Butler's own response (within this same chapter) to Mladen Dolar's reading of Althusser (Dolar 1993). Butler's insistence, contra Dolar, that Althusser grasps ideology in its materiality and through its practices, can be read as a gesture toward the very concept of the social formation that Butler herself otherwise excludes (Butler 1997b: 125). Put differently, Butler sounds much more Althusserian when challenging Dolar than when she (Butler) reads Althusser directly.

the social formation.[22] Thus we see in Butler's book that without that account, Althusser has little to offer. Yet in jettisoning Althusser's account of the social formation, Butler strips any concept of social order out of her own theory of subjection. Ultimately, a philosophically abstract theory of subjection, one disconnected from any historico-political conjuncture, is not worth very much: it tells us something thin and vague about a relation between so-called subjects and so-called power, but it fails to grasp that individuals in the world always take up subject positions in the world, and these always exist within a concrete social formation.

Therefore the "scene of interpellation" that Butler describes turns out to be Butler's own scene, a product of her philosophical discourse, not Althusser's. Into that scene, Butler injects a description and theory of guilt, a story of a bad conscience that precedes the hailing and therefore allows the hailing to work. For Butler, *guilt serves as a substitute for the social formation*; she must project guilt into the philosophical narrative she offers for no other reason than the fact that she had already removed the social formation from that narrative. However, I must emphasise what Althusser states directly in the passage above, in the only place in the entire text that he mentions the word *guilt*: Althusser directly rejects Butler's narrative, and he refuses the psychoanalytic supplement. Interpellation, for Althusser, has nothing whatsoever to do with guilt or bad conscience. One is therefore led to ask why Butler turned to Althusser in the first place.

SUBJECTIVATION WITHOUT THE PSYCHE; OR, "GUILT FREE" SUBJECTIVATION

The turn to guilt gives Butler's argument within *PLP* a real consistency, since it links up the reading of Althusser with her work on/in psychoanalysis;

22. In her reading of Nietzsche in *PLP*, Butler makes a similar set of dehistoricising moves, though perhaps in this case they prove more egregious. First, because as a philologist and genealogist, Nietzsche proves more resistant to being transformed into a philosopher. Second, Butler focuses her reading of Nietzsche on the topic of "bad conscience," and she therefore, as might be expected, cites Nietzsche's famous lines from Essay II of the *Genealogy*, where Nietzsche offers "his own theory on the origin of 'bad conscience'." While Butler reads Nietzsche's lines about instincts turning inward ("the internalization of man"), she somehow manages to skip over Nietzsche's own explanation, which can best be summed up as "the rise of the social"—that is, the emergence of customs, norms, laws, state institutions, and city structures that prevent the "noble warrior" from venting his instincts externally (Nietzsche 2006: II, 16). Butler instead suggests that instincts are internalised not because of external forces but because of the "joy taken in persecuting oneself" (Butler 1997b: 75).

it renders the engagement with Althusser's text consistent with Butler's move away from Freud. Perhaps most of all, Butler's reconstruction of the so-called Althusserian "doctrine" of interpellation bridges the enormous—some would say, unbridgeable—gap between Hegel and Althusser. At the heart of Althusser's political and theoretical project, and across the range of his writings, lies his emphasis on the fundamental *difference* between a Hegelian understanding of the social "totality" and a Marxist conception of the social "whole" (Althusser 1976: 181).[23] Althusser defends the seemingly semantic distinction because it points to a fundamental difference between, on the one hand, understanding a totality as containing an "essence" or core that would always remain the same, or, on the other, grasping the whole as complex, overlapping, discontinuous, and yet still "structured in dominance" (Althusser 1976: 181). "The social formation" is a name that Althusser borrows from Marx but emphasises in a way that Marx did not: it allows him to highlight and leverage the difference between a thin, idealist concept of society and a thick, rich, materialist conception (contained in my 6th hypothesis). He writes:

> For Hegel, society, like history, is made up of circles within circles, of spheres within spheres. Dominating his whole conception is the idea of the expressive totality, in which all the elements are total parts, each expressing the internal unity of the totality which is only ever, in all its complexity, the objectification-alienation of a simple principle. (Althusser 1976: 182)

Hegel's philosophy cannot account for the social formation as formed by contradictions that are not necessarily resolved in the march of history toward its inevitable *telos*. Marx offers a concept of the social formation that has no essence, no core; society is held together by material practices that contain contradictions and tensions. What marks any particular social formation is not its "essence" or core idea, but relations of complexity and unevenness. According to Althusser, the social formation "holds together" not through simple and pure contradiction (Hegel) but through

---

23. No other distinction matters more for Althusser, and thus the entirety of his work retains a strong rejection of Hegel. Butler can overcome this rejection only by undoing the distinction between the Hegelian totality and the Marxist whole, and she can achieve this only by stripping Althusser of his account of the social formation. In this context it also seems prudent to note that, particularly in North America and the UK, Althusser has been consistently misread as a thinker primarily focused on a very different distinction, that between science and ideology. In Chapter 4 I suggest that this emphasis proves entirely misplaced, and that it likely derives from the significantly different contexts for understanding the concept of "science"—that is, social science behavioralism in the USA and Canguilhemian history of science in France.

"overdetermination and contradiction" (Marx). I will expound upon this important claim in the chapters that follow; for now it suffices to emphasise some of its implications. At the least, drawing this distinction allows Althusser to advance a very different reading of Engels's potentially determinist account of "determination in the last instance," since, according to Althusser, the "last instance" is surely not the "first instance," not a causal ground or fundamental overarching principle, but a structure of domination maintained only in and through historical practices and structures (Althusser 1969: 111–13).[24]

We can see, then, that this concept of a social formation provides the context for what appears (wrongly, I am arguing) in Butler's account to be Althusser's attenuated answer to why the individual/subject responds to the hail. The figure Althusser describes is not an "abstract" individual who only becomes a subject after the turn. Althusser depicts a figure who

---

24. As an avowed "anti-humanist" it proves simple, too simple, to take Althusser for a determinist. In order to see the importance of the social formation, one must distinctly mark Althusser's distance from determinism. Put differently, if the Althusserian social formation were reducible to determinism, then we might need/want Butler's account of "the social." Yet Althusser is so much at pains to reject determinism that he attaches an entire appendix to his essay on "overdetermination," in which he takes Engels to task for the latter's misunderstanding of the idea of "determination in the last instance" (Althusser 1969; see also Althusser 1971). This slippery phrase is the English translation of Althusser's "détermination en dernière instance" (Althusser 1970), which appears to be Althusser's own translation of Engels's German, "in letzter Instanz bestimmende Moment" (Marx and Engels 1974: 463, 464, two instances). That is, the source in Engels is a letter to Joseph Bloch in the autumn of 1890, but the key phrase, *in letzter Instanz bestimmende Moment*, is translated into English not with Althusser's phrasing, but as either "the ultimately determining element" (Engels 1972; cf. Engels 1968) or "in the final analysis" (Marx and Engels 2002: 34–35). In German, the phrase *in letzter Instanz bestimmende Moment* perhaps gained traction from the publication of Bloch's book, *Revolution der Weltpolitik* (Bloch 1938), where he quotes at length from Engels's letter (see Shamir 1997: 11). The English phrase *determination in the last instance* may therefore have come into wide circulation more through Althusser's translation/paraphrase of Engels (into French and then into English) than from a direct translation of Engels's German. On that latter front, while *bestimmen* has often been translated into English as "determining," Carver has argued that *bestimmen* is a weaker verb, meaning to delimit, to define, to constrain (T. Carver, personal communication). Pushing in a similar direction, while Althusser affirms a certain understanding of the phrase, he interprets it in the most thoroughly anti-determinist manner possible. The appendix to Althusser's famous essay on overdetermination attributes any residual determinism to Engels's misunderstanding of Marx. Put (too) simply: Engels was always too much of a Hegelian for Althusser, never fully grasping the radical difference between the Marxist whole and the Hegelian totality that Althusser himself insists upon. Hence, overdetermination is anything but determinism (Althusser 1971: 117–28; see Engels 1968; Engels 1972).

is always already interpellated by ideology—a concrete subject, situated within a social formation, itself structured in dominance. This means that the individual is always already a subject *of* a particular social formation—a "lord" in feudalism, a "worker" in capitalism, or a "mother" in the family. When I pose a question in class and a student responds by raising her hand, the response should be explained, for Althusser, not through an internal investigation of the individual's conscience, but by the structure of the ideological apparatus, the *dispositif* in which the call and response occur: the "professor-subject" asks a question, and the "student-subject" responds to this call.

Althusser's discussion of hailing provides readers with a political account of subjectivation and/or a historical account of subject formation and subjection, but it does not really provide what Butler hopes to offer—namely, a philosophical "theory of subjection."[25] In other words, Althusser's work on interpellation does not fit the frame that Butler builds and works with throughout *PLP*. (Here we see clearly why and how the genre of philosophy matters in this book.) Having started with Hegel and then worked through Freud, Butler reads what she calls Althusser's "doctrine" of interpellation as very much a "philosophy" of interpellation. But to do so she must Hegelianise Althusser, strip away his own rich understanding of the social formation, and in its place substitute a psychic account of guilt, or desire to persist in one's being.

The extent of this misreading can be highlighted by a quick comparison with another usage of, and reference to, Althusser within the context of political theory. Anne Norton mentions Althusser frequently in her work *95 Theses on Politics, Culture, and Method* and, like Butler, Norton refers almost exclusively to Althusser's conception of interpellation. Early on, however, Norton emphasises her preference for "hailing" over the more trendy "interpellation," and I would stress the possible divergence in connotations here: the term *hailing* sounds more concretely political, while the term *interpellation* resonates more with a general philosophy. Norton does

25. Carver's recent reconstruction of "The German Ideology" manuscripts (of Marx and Engels) produces a powerful rethinking of these pages, one that subtly teases out the differences in *approach* and *effects* of a political and historical analysis, in contrast with a philosophical analysis. Carver shows how Engels's original draft was frequently edited and revised by Marx to push the argument away from the laying down of philosophical truths and the proclaiming of trans-historical principles toward a historical analysis that always proceeds by developing "*political* points through and through" (Carver 2014). In the main text here I am showing something like the reverse phenomena, as Butler rereads Althusser's thoroughly political and consistently historical arguments *as if* they were declarations of philosophical principles.

not propose a broad or incisive reading of Althusser, but it is the straightforward nature of her references to Althusser that help me make my point about Butler's reading—and concomitantly about the stakes of the social formation for an account of political subjectivation. Norton's succinct and direct sentences capture the flavor of Althusser's own presentation: "You are called by a name, and you answer to it. One is hailed as a man or woman, black or white" (Norton 2004: 53).

Norton's work in political theory always remains in dialogue with that of anthropologists, feminists, and colonial historians. She has little interest in a philosophical account of hailing; rather, she remains powerfully focused on the historico-political workings of social orders, across time and place. Hence, one of her overall "theses" in the book can best be grasped in light of Althusserian interpellation—yet understood in a thoroughly non-Butlerian way. Norton's thirtieth thesis reads, "Every political institution calls for identities." Norton explains the concept of "call" in terms that make perfect sense in the context of Althusser's understandings of interpellation and the social formation: "Institutions call up and constitute not only the identities of those who act in and as the institution but also of those the institution acts upon" (Norton 2004: 56). Here Norton captures an obvious point from Althusser's account, but one that Butler seems completely to miss: the process of interpellation that goes on within ideology, and thus within the social formation, applies to *all* individuals/subjects within the social formation. Thus, in Althusser's all-too-famous example, ideology interpellates the passerby as a subject who responds to the call of the police officer, but at the very same time, ideology also interpellates the police officer subject as he who calls to the passerby.

Here, then, we see a very different rendering of Althusserian interpellation. Norton's reference to Althusser emphasises one of my broader points against Butler's major argument in *PLP* (and elsewhere), a point that can be succinctly formulated as follows: *an account of subjectivation does not require a psychic dimension*. One can conceptualise the twofold process of subject formation using the context of history and the logic of politics. The psyche or the *conatus* only becomes necessary within a *philosophical* account—that is, only if the historical and political contexts have been peeled away. Yet if one seeks a rich and rigorous account of subjectivation, one need not make the philosophical turn in the first place. Norton's text cites a deep archive of sources for this project, works that show historically how subject formation comes about. One famous example referenced by Norton is the writing of Noel Ignatiev, whose work on the racialised history of Irish immigrants to America can easily be read as a major development in a theory of subjectivation, but we see it that way only if we take that theory as always rooted within concrete historical contexts and particular political formations (Ignatiev 1995). Indeed, one way to understand Norton's contribution to thinking the relation between culture and politics, to conceptualising what I have called, following Norton, "cultural politics," is to see it as a specific kind of argument concerning political subjectivation. Subjectivation only ever occurs within culture (Norton thesis 7), which also means that it only ever occurs within practice (Norton thesis 17; Norton 2004). From this perspective, there can be no theory of subjectivation that is not also a theory of social formations; ultimately, then, Butler's philosophical "theory of subjection" proves to be neither.[26]

"THE SOCIAL" WITHOUT A SOCIAL FORMATION: BUTLER'S LIBERAL POLITICAL PHILOSOPHY

I am not the first to challenge Butler on her conceptualisation of "the social." Indeed, the widely read and much-discussed conversation among Butler, Laclau, and Žižek placed the question of "the social" at the center of debate. In his first response essay, Laclau straight away calls attention to Butler's frequent use of the social (her rejection of the presocial) as a form of critique:

> Throughout her text, Butler establishes a set of oppositions between what she calls the field of structural limitation, on the one hand, and what she refers to as the "social," the "cultural" or the context-dependent. It is difficult to comment on these distinctions properly because Butler never defines what she understands by the "social" or the "cultural"—taking them, rather, as

26. In chapter 5 of *PLP* Butler stages a more focused and concrete engagement with social and cultural practices, reading them for their materiality, and one might catch a glimpse here of something like a richer account of the social formation. Yet, even in this context Butler's articulation of "the social" still sounds very similar to the usage in *Gender Trouble* and *Bodies That Matter*, where the word mainly fits into a chain of terms—each of which functions as a contrast with, or opposite to, the natural, the transcendental, or the prediscursive. Butler's discussion of both ritual and the work of repetition remains isolated to an abstract social field and never connected to a concrete social whole. Hence my conclusion that the later chapters of *PLP* move no closer toward a concept of the social formation, although given her discussion of concrete practices, the absence of such a theory proves less conspicuous than in the sections of *PLP* on which I have focused my analysis. *Excitable Speech* uses "the social" as a weapon of critique against Derrida: Butler suggests that Derrida's account of citationality remains structurally universal and thereby incapable of accounting for "social iterability" (Butler 1997a: 150). But here again the social has very little meaning or sense other than in operating as the opposite of the "presocial," or in this case, the "structural."

> self-evident realities to which she points in a purely referential way. I think, however, that one can safely say that the distinction is, roughly, for her, that between an aprioristic quasi-transcendental limit, on the one hand, and a field of purely context-dependent rules and forms of life, on the other, which are historically contingent and escape the determination by that limit. (Laclau, in Butler et al. 2000: 183)

Here Laclau identifies the very function of "the social" in Butler's early books; as I suggested in my brief account of those works, above, in them the social—like the historical, the cultural, the political, or the anthropological—has little or no positive content of its own, but functions as the opposite of that which is transcendental or universal, natural or "presocial." Butler herself responds to this critique in her final essay for the volume, but she mistakes Laclau's deeper challenge for a mere protestation against a lack of contextual specificity. Thus, Butler "answers" Laclau's charge, first, with something of a non sequitur: she says that sometimes we have to take concepts for granted and resist the temptation to put every word inside scare quotes (Butler, in Butler et al. 2000: 269). Second, Butler goes on to elaborate her concept of the social. She explains that "the 'social' *as a sphere* has its history," that it has been debated, and that her use of it does not entail the assumption of its status as a causal ground (Butler, in Butler et al. 2000: 270, emphasis added). She then offers her most direct, positive account of her usage: "The category of the 'social' reintroduces a conception of language as a practice, a conception of language in relation to power and, hence, a theory of discourse" (Butler, in Butler et al. 2000: 270). In other words, Butler uses "the social" as a synonym for "discourse" in Foucault.

While this response may well offer more specificity concerning Butler's deployment of the term, it does not really differ at all from Laclau's own account of how "the social" operates in Butler's logic.[27] More to the point, Butler responds not at all to the crux of Laclau's critique. He challenged Butler not merely to specify her usage of the term, but to explain and defend that very usage in the face of his critique. Thus, in the essay to which Butler purportedly responds here, Laclau goes on to explain *what is wrong* with Butler's implementation of the term. He writes: "My difficulty with Butler's position lies in the fact that by identifying the 'abstract' with 'structural aprioristic limitation' she subscribes to a notion of the 'concrete' which . . . *lacks any principle of structuration* . . . is more or less equivalent to indeterminate contingent variation, and closes itself to the possibility

27. Something similar could be said for Butler's chapter in *Undoing Gender*, which, while titled "The Question of Social Transformation," remains confined to the frame discussed in the text here (Butler 2004b).

that abstraction itself is concretely produced" (Laclau, in Butler et al. 2000: 187, emphasis added). In specifying the principle of "structuration," Laclau is gesturing toward the social formation. For Laclau, a Gramscian, the concrete must not be conflated with empiricism's conception of the empirical. Butler points to "the social" as merely the contingent or variable, that which stands as the opposite of the transcendental. Laclau rejects this notion on two fronts. On one hand, we can understand the concrete as itself a part of a particular social whole; it can never therefore be purely arbitrary or free-floatingly contingent. On the other, abstractions are themselves real; they reside "at the core of the actual concrete workings" of societies (Laclau, in Butler et al. 2000: 86). And in this latter sense, nothing is more "concrete" than the social formation itself. Both in these debates with Laclau and Žižek and throughout her early writings, Butler's continued references to "the social" as the opposite of the abstractly universal leave her with no way to account for the processes of structuration that make up any social formation.

The exchanges in *Contingency, Hegemony, Universality* can clearly be read as marking out a problem in Butler's account of the social. Moreover, after these debates, and in her writings post-2001, Butler has introduced a markedly different understanding of "the social"—a move that might be read as an effort to overcome this problem. Thus, while others have noted Butler's turn toward international political concerns, and many have focused on Butler's tendency toward posing questions of ethics and calling on the framework of moral philosophy, in this section I read these later texts in the context I have now established. That is, I explore her later usage of "the social" to again ask the question of the social formation. Butler's argument in *Giving an Account of Oneself* (2005)—one of her first major works after *PLP* and the first that appears after 2001[28]—certainly operates within, even itself emphasises, this frame. The book repeatedly recurs to

28. As noted in the text above, *Excitable Speech* (1997) is published in the same year, and at around the same time, as *PLP* and therefore does not come "after" it. *Antigone's Claim* (2000), which I would indeed describe as a major text in Butler's oeuvre, appears prior to what I am marking as the 2001 turn, and while I have discussed it in the past I do not address it here. *Precarious Life* (2004a) proves to be a very different kind of text, since it contains a collection of essays and occasional pieces originally produced for specific political and non-academic contexts. Hence the book comprises a much more fragmentary and focused set of essays and does not add up to the sort of systematic philosophical project that we see in either *PLP* or *Giving an Account*. Similarly, but distinctly, *Undoing Gender* (2004b) also collects together a variety of disparate, focused engagements on sex, gender and sexuality. In this section I focus mainly on *Giving an Account* and *Frames of War* (2009), the two most important systematic books that Butler has published since 2001.

the idea of "the social" and of the relevance of "social theory" (perhaps explaining West's description of Butler as a social theorist). In this text the social emerges persistently (and much more richly than in the past), appearing as an element that no moral theory can eliminate: it proves impossible to account for the "I," and the responsibility of that "I," without recourse to something beyond the "I." Butler gives a few different names to this "something more," this element that always exceeds the "I": sometimes she calls it "ethical norms" and "moral frameworks," while at other moments she describes it in the language of "the social." "Ethics," she states early on in the text, "finds itself embroiled in the task of social theory" (Butler 2005: 7). Hence it might appear that Butler's so-called turn to ethics goes hand in hand with a turn to a thinking of the social.

But what does Butler mean here by *the social*? She uses the term pervasively throughout the first chapter of *Giving an Account*, but the usage proves somewhat curious. Perhaps the clearest way to bring this odd usage to light is to show how Butler mobilises her idea of "the social" to link Foucault with Arendt. In simple terms, she does so by faulting Foucault and praising Arendt. Butler starts with Foucault's concept of regimes of truth so as to deepen her point that no moral account (no moral philosophy) can proceed without reference to norms, to context. Butler reads Foucault as establishing the fact that the critique of a discursive regime, "a regime of truth," must always also be an auto-critique, since any given regime of truth provides conditions of possibility for the "I" who would launch the critique. Here, however, Butler opens her own line of criticism of Foucault, and she does so by way of a series of "as if" postulates that echo her mode of criticism in *PLP*. Butler's critique takes shape in one paragraph, wherein she moves from asking a question of Foucault, to presuming that he cannot answer it, to concluding that this failure marks a significant limit for his project. She writes, and I comment in brackets:

> What are these norms . . . [and] where and who is this other . . . ? It seems right to fault Foucault for not making more room explicitly for the other in his consideration of ethics. [Is seeming right to find fault with Foucault somehow equivalent to mounting a critique of him?] Perhaps this is because the dyadic scene of self and other cannot describe adequately the social workings of normativity that condition both subject production and intersubjective exchange. [Yet Foucault does not work with a dyadic scene of self and other; Hegel does. Foucault works with a rich understanding of historical epistemes, with a concrete and material understanding of social and political orders through which power relations flow.] If we conclude that Foucault's failure to think the other is decisive [Wait, now we are not only coming to a decision that there is a failure here, but we are concluding that such a failure proves *decisive* in our

> reading of Foucault, even though the entire logical move is premised on the first "if"] we have perhaps overlooked the fact [who is the "we" here, given that the failure was attributed to Foucault?] that the very being of the self is dependent, not just on the existence of the other in its singularity [Butler cites Levinas for this claim about singularity, but I note that the logic and grammar of the passage actually attributes this failure to Foucault, since it is he that Butler is undertaking a critique of here], but also on the social dimensions of normativity that governs the scene of recognition. This social dimension of normativity precedes and conditions any dyadic exchange. [This might well be a valid claim, but who is it refuting? Surely not Foucault. In any case, this last move again begs the question of the status of "the social" in Butler's discussion.] (Butler 2005: 23)

Butler goes on to explain that norms are never the possession of an individual; they have a certain sociality. Again, the function of "social" in this discussion seems rather vague, since Butler says nothing about concrete social orders, invokes no theories of society or the social. The consistent function of "the social" in this text is to point to something that is more than one, more than merely the "I." Something is social because it is not merely me. This sense of the social comes into clearer focus when Butler refers to the social not just as what is missing from a dyadic account (Butler 2005: 28), but as something positive in itself.

She does the latter with her reading of Arendt (or at least her reading of Cavarero's reading of Arendt). The first reference to the social as something that one might theorise (and not just an idea that points to the more-than-one) comes at the opening of this section, when Butler mentions "an Arendtian conception of the social" (Butler 2005: 31). It seems essential to emphasise here that Butler is not referring to the (in)famous Arendtian argument about the "rise of the social" and its encroachment on the sphere of action (and politics). Instead, Butler seems to be gesturing toward the Arendtian account of plurality, but using the language of "the social" to describe it. Hence, immediately following the above-quoted reference, Butler cites Cavarero citing Arendt on the necessity of action and speech as a response to the question, "Who are you?" (Butler 2005: 30; citing Cavarero 2000: 20; citing Arendt 1958: 183). But to my knowledge no Arendtian scholars use this idea in Arendt to develop a counter-concept of "the social"—that is, one that would cut against the grain of Arendt's well-known understanding of the social realm. Instead, Butler's point here, as in earlier sections in the text, seems mainly to be about moving past solipsistic accounts and toward a relation to, and dependency on, the other (Butler 2005: 32). And therefore, once again Butler displaces any answer to a question of what she means by the social.

I contend that the first positive answer to this question—as opposed to Butler's repeated negative uses of the social to contrast with the pre-social—emerges gradually throughout this text and takes sharper shape toward the end of this first chapter, when Butler rehearses the argument of the book as a whole. The thesis of *Giving an Account of Oneself* might best be captured in this line from Butler: "The account of myself that I give in discourse never fully expresses or carries this living self" (Butler 2005: 35). There can be no exhaustive account given of the self, and the self can never be a sovereign subject that would self-authorise the account. An account of oneself is always an account given in discourse, which means that the "I" who gives an account is always already given over to the other, and the account given can never exhaust, determine, or even fully authorise the self (that gives it). I am not objecting to anything in this broad set of claims. Rather, my focus lies with the way in which Butler inserts an incipient idea of "the social" into this account. Immediately following the quote above, Butler writes: "There is the operation of a norm, *invariably social*, that conditions what will and will not be a recognizable account" (Butler 2005: 35, emphasis added). What does the italicised phrase add to Butler's argument? Butler insists that the norm is "social," but as opposed to what? Non-social?

Based on a broader reading of the text as a whole, and consistent with Butler's otherwise strange references to an "Arendtian conception of the social," I submit that for Butler the exhortation of/to "the social" is an insistence on plurality. Norms cannot be possessed, controlled, or contained by the individual who gives an account. Norms "belong" to no one, and they arise in the context of everyone. In this sense they are "social" in that they are not private, and they are "social" in that they are not individual. Butler has therefore implicitly defined "the social" as two subjects relating to one another; "sociality" describes the space or scene in which the dyadic philosophical relation occurs (Butler 2005: 23). This seems fair enough, so far as it goes, though clearly from the perspective I have been articulating throughout this chapter, such a notion of "the social" as this cannot stand in for a fuller concept of the social formation. And in a peculiar way, Butler actually has a sense of the limitations of her own theory, since, later in *Giving an Account*, Butler suggests that even in Hegel "recognition" exceeds a dyadic structure because what "eventually follows from th[e] scene" of recognition is a "social account of norms" (Butler 2005: 28). However, this claim indicates the full extent to which Butler builds her theory of the social on top of, or out of, her Hegelian theory of dyadic recognition. She thereby first evacuates the social-historical context so that she may construct a philosophical account of recognition, and then she turns recognition itself into the context for the emergence of her new, thin account of "the social." Therefore, it is not so much that Butler has it upside down as that she has it inside out: starting from a de-historicised theory of recognition she builds an abstract account of "sociality" that turns out to be nothing more than plurality.[29]

Ultimately what we are left with in Butler's own theorisation of "the social" is little more than a liberal conception of the social. Let me unpack this claim. For Butler, the social simply means more than one individual; thus, it functions very much as an *aggregative* term. Just as we see the formation of political society, within a liberal social contract theory, depend upon the shift from the individuals within a state of nature to "the social" formed through consent, so we see Butler pivot from the "I" who gives an account to the social norms in which such accounts must invariably be given. The move to Arendt thereby makes a sort of sense, not because Butler really means to invoke Arendt's understanding of the social but because she (Butler) needs to draw from her (Arendt's) notion of plurality. Of course, Arendt's account of human plurality is decisively not a liberal one, but Butler is not taking up Arendt's larger political philosophy. Instead, she rests with the idea of "the social" as more than one, and it is exactly this notion that I am claiming resonates with liberalism. Liberalism's commitment to individualism means that "the social" can never be much more than a "more than one," an aggregation of individuals. And a critique of this notion is exactly Marx's point of departure in his own articulation of the social formation, as I will develop it in the next chapter.

In the case of Butler, it is not that she explicitly adopts a liberal theory, but that despite her own occasional resistance to liberalism, she winds up with a liberal account of the social. One might protest—as I myself have done with Butler, above—that I make this final move, toward a liberal concept of the social, too quickly. After all, Butler never invokes social contract theory—never cites Locke or Rawls, or anyone else of that ilk. Indeed, I have previously argued that the strategies of denaturalisation practiced in Butler's earlier work can effectively be read *against* the social contract tradition (Chambers and Carver 2008: 21, 27, 41). Nonetheless, here I wish to defend this very different claim, and to back it up by showing that, over the years, Butler's work has grown closer and closer in proximity to that of standard liberal political philosophy.[30] Her logic looks more like that of a

29. Deep thanks to Alan Finlayson for invaluable help in formulating this point.

30. I am not the first to describe Butler's work as liberal while meaning it as an accusation: as part of his critique of "reproductive futurism," Lee Edelman challenges the politics of Butler's reading of *Antigone*, saying it "seems all too familiarly liberal" (Edelman 2004: 103–4). Elsewhere I have resisted Edelman's account, showing that

liberal mode of theorising, her overriding focus on vulnerability implicitly links her project to state-of-nature stories (see Walker 2013), and more conspicuously, the language she adopts sounds more and more like that of liberal theory. To make this case, I turn to an even more recent text, *Frames of War*, where I am most interested in the framing structures for, and language used in, Butler's arguments. Butler has doubtless built a wide and interdisciplinary audience over the years, one far broader and more diverse than the presumed reader of a text in liberal theory. Despite this truth, Butler's approach and her language now look and sound a lot like egalitarian political philosophy, and we can see this starkly in *Frames of War*'s introduction (for what it is worth, this book too has no preface), where Butler makes the case for the overall philosophical and political contribution of her essays.

Butler's fundamental project in this text is to *generalise* a set of arguments about recognisability and intelligibility that have percolated throughout her previous writings.[31] Butler shows that the act by which one subject *recognises* another depends upon prior conditions. This ontic act rests upon epistemological conditions of "recognisability"—the possibility of apprehending a subject in the first place—while those very conditions themselves presuppose prior conditions of intelligibility, which Butler describes as historical "schemas that establish the domain of the knowable" (Butler 2009: 6). Butler, of course, has written about "norms of recognisability" and "schemas of intelligibility" before, and at great length (Butler 2009: 7). The problem of intelligibility lies at the center of Butler's understanding of the heterosexual matrix in *Gender Trouble*; it captures the logic of materialisation that she delineates in *Bodies That Matter*; it underlies the articulation of hate speech in *Excitable Speech*; and most powerfully, it forms the philosophical and political crux of Butler's now well-known rereading of *Antigone* in *Antigone's Claim* (Butler 1999; Butler 1993; Butler 1997a; Butler 2000). In this text, however, Butler lays out her philosophy of recognisability and intelligibility at the beginning of the text, and she does so specifically in order to show that this philosophical structure serves as "an historical *a priori*" (Butler 2009: 6).[32] That is, the philosophical

Antigone's Claim refuses a liberal model of inclusion for a more radical sense of (un)intelligibility (Chambers 2009a). Nevertheless, when it comes to Butler's philosophical account of the social in these later works, Edelman's assessment seems spot-on.

31. Elsewhere I have tried to provide a non-generalising reading of Butler's earlier texts through the concept of (un)intelligibility (Chambers and Carver 2008; Chambers 2009b).

32. On the idea of a historical *a priori*, Butler cites Foucault's *Archaeology of Knowledge* (1972). However, on my reading of *Frames*, Butler uses the idea of the *a priori* in a much more Kantian than Foucauldian sense (Butler 2009: 18).

account is both grounding and generalising; it is tethered not to immanent critique (in the tradition of critical theory) but to philosophising in a more universal voice.

Let me offer an example of the subtle but distinct difference in Butler's recent approach. In the middle of Butler's introduction to *Frames*, she turns the argument away from her broad account of how recognisability and intelligibility function toward the political dimension of the work. In a line that restates the argument from the preceding dozen pages, Butler writes, "To say that a life is precarious requires not only that a life be apprehended as a life, but also that precariousness be an aspect of what is apprehended in what is living" (Butler 2009: 13). Again we witness Butler's emphasis that the problematic of precarity goes beyond that of recognisability since *precarity* turns on bringing into view not just subjects, but the problem itself of recognising subjects. Butler then twists this argument markedly, even calling attention to the turn she makes by explicitly indicating that she seeks to reinterpret her own claims. She writes: "*Normatively construed*, I am arguing that there ought to be a more inclusive and egalitarian way of recognizing precariousness, and that this should take form as concrete social policy" (Butler 2009: 13, emphasis added). The claim is succinct and non-opaque, but I think there is a great deal at stake here—perhaps much more than there might at first appear to be.

First, Butler takes her account of intelligibility and says she will construe it "normatively." This constitutes an explicit gesture toward the language of liberal political philosophy and a significant move away from Butler's earlier arguments. Butler's earlier work showed decisively that the question of intelligibility could never be considered "non-normative," since intelligibility remains indelibly tied to the problem of "normative violence." There would be no such thing as a "non-normative construal" of unintelligibility (or precariousness), for the reason that Butler explicitly conceptualises intelligibility as tied up with norms. Here, however, Butler uses "normative" in a way very much distinct from those earlier writings on normative violence (see Rushing 2009). With the reference to "normative," this passage invokes the language of liberal political theory—that is, "normative theory," the same approach to political theory that I challenged in my Introduction. Here I would note that the very idea of "normative theory" can be traced back to the behavioralist attempt to redefine political theory as unscientific, and thereby to create a distinction between, on the one hand, "positive theory" that addresses the world and discovers facts and laws about it, and on the other, "normative theory" that tells us what we "ought" to do or what an "ideal" world might look like. It is clear that Butler borrows that language here, not only because her use of the word *normative* marks such a departure from her previous writings, but also because she signals the link to so-called normative theory directly by going on to tell her readers what "ought" to happen. And finally, she answers the very question that empiricists have always asked from their "normative" counterparts: How does your "theory" translate into concrete policy recommendations? Butler emphasises that if she can give a general normative theory of precariousness, then it will, in fact, lead to "concrete social policy."

This is liberal political philosophy.[33] It follows the playbook that says to start with *a priori* or generalised philosophical claims and then bend them toward policy claims. And I must add that Butler's move in this section is not isolated; quite to the contrary, she repeats it (or moves like it) throughout *Frames*. Butler seems either to have embraced liberal theory or at least tacitly to have accepted its terms. She reiterates those terms throughout the introduction, consistently gesturing toward the idea of "generalising" her account, of giving it a universal status (Butler 2009: 18, 20). In the process, Butler also ends up adopting much of the language and the limitations of the liberal mode of writing and thinking. Worse than this, Butler winds up speaking in flat and obvious tautologies. For example, she describes the condition of the world with which her work engages, in this language: "Precarity also characterizes that politically induced condition of maximized precariousness." Similarly, she articulates part of the goal of her philosophical project in these words: "to sustain life as sustainable" (Butler 2009: 26, 23). Quoting these passages might seem like picking nits, but I point to these examples not as a critique of Butler's writing style and not even to question her logic. My point is that the circularity of this logic resonates decisively with that of much liberal theory today.

---

33. In this chapter I focus on the internal development of Butler's work; I therefore do not speculate on the potential external forces that might help to "explain" Butler's shift into the register of liberal political philosophy, nor do I trace external influences upon her. In this context, however, I would make two comments. First, Butler has clearly become much more of a public intellectual over the past decade, and there can be no doubt that in the United States the language of public intellectualism is liberalism. Second, the architecture of Butler's argument in *PLP* indicates one plausible, structural explanation for her recent turn toward work in moral theory and in the direction of producing writings that look more like that of a liberal public intellectual than a social and political theorist. In the absence of an account of the social formation, exactly that which Butler purges from the thinkers she interprets in *PLP*, Butler shifts in the direction of normative political philosophy.

FROM "THE SOCIAL" TO THE SOCIAL FORMATION: "BACK TO THE ROUGH GROUND"

Wittgenstein's famous, endlessly cited call to return from abstract logic to the "rough ground" can serve as a guide to the turn I want to make here (Wittgenstein 1953: §107). Wittgenstein describes the journey of philosophy as one driven by prior "requirements" for a "pure" logic; this demand for purity, for abstraction, for logical rules pushes us out onto very slippery ice. And Wittgenstein wryly notes that on the ice "there is no friction and so in a certain sense the conditions are ideal"; the only problem being that due precisely to these conditions, "we are unable to walk" (Wittgenstein 1953: 107). In closely describing a few of the scenes from *Giving an Account* and *Frames*, I picture Butler rather far out on the ice: without any way to get traction, she finds herself making tautological (philosophical) claims about "the precarity of precariousness." Unlike the empty concept of "the social" that Butler frequently invokes, I contend that an account of the social formation always provides the sort of "friction" that Wittgenstein says is needed. I therefore want to leverage my critique of Butler (for her missing account of the social formation) as a call to turn back to this rough ground—as a call to develop theories of the social formation in the chapters that follow.

Before beginning that project, I should clarify the following: in showing how Butler has implicitly eschewed a concept of the social formation, I am not accusing Butler of not being Althusserian enough (my assertion is not that she fails to do just what I plan to do). Nor am I trying to play the "structure" card as counter to Butler's emphasis on agency (or on post-structuralism). To the contrary, and perhaps surprisingly, in demonstrating that Butler has made a series of mistakes in grasping the social formation, I am suggesting that she fails to account for the dynamics of the force of normativity. I would argue that this force operates across the entirety of the social formation. But Butler leaves herself with an overly narrow concept of normativity, because she circumscribes normativity within a dyadic field of "recognition." It is as if Butler comes to see normativity as itself a "structure," and while she grasps the structure of normativity as incapable of accounting for everything—because, as she so often shows, every structure always and necessarily fails in its efforts at structuration—Butler misses out on the failure of any structure to account for its own historicity.

Althusser proves important, therefore, not only to the extent that Butler reads his concept of the social formation out of his own texts but also because, unlike Butler, Althusser was a philosopher not of the subject but of structures themselves. Therefore, following Marx, Althusser insists on the historicity of a structure as itself that which makes determinist closure always impossible (and thereby opens up spaces for agency). This is why my engagement with Butler in this chapter cannot be reduced to or confused with a standard sort of so-called Marxist critique that tries to use "history" or "structure" to trump philosophy. Rather, I am trying to trace an internal and essential logic in Butler's work that plays itself out with particular consequences for how she construes certain political concerns.

There can be no doubt, as West indicates, that Butler's voice as a public intellectual proves robust and important. That voice is heard widely and has a real force; witness Butler's recent winning of the Adorno prize and the important debate that emerged around this public event (Butler 2012). I have no intention whatsoever to deprecate this crucial work. These achievements notwithstanding, something significant has been lost in Butler's recent writing—particularly when read in the context of social and political theory. Butler's early books had a dramatic and transformative impact on a number of fields, and much of this strength was tied to the theoretical radicality of those texts—their ability to think something new—which was itself linked to their concrete critical political engagement. Butler forced a dramatic reconsideration of how we understand sex, gender, and the materiality of the body; she permanently reshaped our sense of the relation between sex and gender; and her work served as a sustaining resource for two decades of feminist and queer politics. The power of Butler's political theory was linked, I suggest, to her commitment to "troubling" established norms, ways of thought, and patterns of action (Chambers and Carver 2008). In contrast to this earlier work, what Honig calls Butler's "mortalist humanism" serves as a general philosophical position—an insistence on fundamental human finitude—with which few would disagree and which many can admire (Honig 2013). While the general "truth" of this ontology can surely be linked to a set of "normative claims," what goes missing in these works is Butler's previously remarkable ability to inspire and particularly to *incite*.

Having specified what is lost from Butler's account on her own terms, I now want to shift the focus, the tenor, and the structure of my argument in the book. "Back to the rough ground" means, for me, back to the social formation, and in this particular case it means to go all the way back to Marx, whose project for many years was to problematise the figure of "society" so as to better understand political, economic, and historical development. For Marx, "society" was always so much more than "the social" in Butler's recent work; "society" always exceeded any liberal or bourgeois notion of aggregated individuals. And because he was always "bearing society in mind" in just this sense, Marx's writings offer crucial insights into how it is possible to develop theories of the social formation, of how one can give an account of the social formation.

2

Society, Social Formations: Reading the *1857 Introduction*

> Hence with the theoretical method the subject [*Subjekt*], society, must always be borne in mind as the presupposition of [any] conception. (Marx 1996a: 147)

> social formation: a concept denoting so-called "society." (Althusser 1969 [1965]: 251)

This chapter provides an indirect epistemological account of the concept of the social formation. I consider this account *epistemological* because it centers on questions of knowledge—on what it means for knowledge to be produced historically, and on the way that knowledge relations mediate thought and materiality. I characterise the account as *indirect*, however, because it is not a properly epistemological project in the Kantian philosophical sense of trying to lay out the conditions of possibility for knowing. Social formations are not the sort of objects to be known in this sense, and therefore the investigation must proceed historically. Perhaps this means dialectically as well, depending on the meaning of that term, but it surely means indirectly in the sense that there is no linear logic to the account of social formations. And finally, in focusing on the *concept*, I uphold here (and defend in the next chapter) an Althusserian distinction between the object of knowledge, on the one hand, and the real object, on the other—a distinction that I will show proves central to grasping Marx's account of society, the social formation.

I carry out this work by way of a particular engagement with Marx as a social and political theorist, an engagement that takes the form of an interpretation of his arguments in one short manuscript, unpublished in Marx's lifetime. Below, I give a number of more detailed explanations for my choice to place such heavy emphasis on this text, but first I can say in more general terms why the *1857 Introduction* proves to be an outstanding resource for thinking through the question of social formations. The *1857 Introduction* is one of eight notebooks that Marx drafted in late 1857 and early 1858 and later described as a work of self-clarification (Carver 1975: 2–6; Nicolaus 1973: 7). And we can fairly say that whatever else he was doing, Marx was trying to clarify for himself the best way to approach and to understand the social formation. That is, while Marx never published a theory of the social formation, nor did he publish any obvious methodological texts, he was required (in order to begin to formulate his magnum opus[1]) to think through exactly the question of the social formation—that is, to think "society" as a complex, uneven, and open whole, one that cannot be segmented off from "economy," "politics," or "culture."

MARX AND CONTEMPORARY POLITICAL THEORY

The relationship between the actual, written words of Karl Marx and the academic field of political theory proves vexed; to enumerate the reasons why is only to proliferate them. For example, Marx obviously does not fit easily within the canon of modern political theory because he did not write the same sorts of texts as other modern thinkers. Hobbes, Locke, and Rousseau lie at the core of almost any survey of modern political theory, and any graduate student in political theory would be expected to know them well. They proffered distinct, sometimes radically different, theories of politics, yet they can easily be read together since all three try to set out an abstract set of theoretical principles that tell us something about what "the political" might be. They offer philosophical accounts of the origins, sources, and limits of political power and authority. They consider the meaning and role of law and of rights. In short, they philosophise about politics. Marx never does any of this.

Moreover, many thinkers fit within the canon of political theory because they write about other political theorists. Even if those other thinkers are left off the syllabus—because they do not quite make the cut in terms of impact,

1. Carver helpfully reminds his readers that Marx's critique of political economy was intended to be only a part of his magnum opus, and "*Capital* was only the beginning" of that part (Carver 1975: 4).

fame, importance—one can still recognise them *as* political thinkers. Locke argues with and against Grotius, Filmer, and Hooker, none of whom are read alongside Locke, but all of whom can be recognisably made out as political theorists. While Marx, in contrast, cites far more sources than most modern thinkers, scant numbers of them are political theorists. Instead, Marx's chief interlocutors are philosophers like Hegel and Feuerbach, utopian socialists like Proudhon and Lasalle, or classical political economists like Ricardo and Smith. And while Marx surely cites his share of political theorists, he does so far less frequently than he cites Shakespeare.

I could go on to talk about the indirect relationship between Marx and political theory by way of Marxism as a political movement in the world. I could cite Hobsbawm's much-repeated claim, now almost thirty years old, that "the shadow of Karl Marx presides over a third of the human race" (Hobsbawm 1987: 336; cited in Thomas 1991: 23). This would lead one down the path of distinction between a *Marxian* position or argument (attributable to Marx himself) and a *Marxist* position (part of the political legacy of Marxism as a worldwide movement/ideology) (see Thomas 1991: 25). But it strikes me that writing today, already in the middle of the second decade of the twenty-first century, the Marxian/Marxist distinction no longer carries much weight. And the reason is simple: *my students haven't read Marx*.[2] When I say this, I do not mean to be glib; on the contrary, I think it necessary to emphasise both the banality and the seriousness of this point. Not only do US university undergraduates have absolutely no sense of what sort of arguments Marx might have written, but even political theory PhD students are unlikely to have ever really engaged with Marx's texts. Thus, for my students, "Marxist" is a weak political label that refers either to some form of far-left political radicalism or to countries with socialist or communist economic systems. The one text written by Marx (and Engels) that they may have encountered, *The Communist Manifesto*, only confirms this position for them: it all sounds like weird radical chanting.

This problem leads directly to the following question: besides the *Manifesto*, what other choices does one have available in teaching Marx? There are many options to choose from since Marx's output is greater than many modern political theorists. Yet, in contrast to others in the canon, Marx's

2. My discussion here and below about students and teaching should not be taken as tangential to my broader argument. One of the ways that political theory is related to, and indeed, mediates the world, is through teaching, and the question of how a student (at various levels) might approach or encounter a text or author tells us something significant about how any reader might approach same. The phrase *the teaching of a text* is obviously a double genitive: to consider how one might teach a text *to a student* should also be (but often is not) to consider what a text *teaches its reader*.

texts prove terribly difficult to excerpt or boil down. A few key passages from Locke's second *Treatise*, the right chapters from Hobbes's *Leviathan*, Machiavelli's short, famous work *The Prince*—all work quite well to convey the core of those thinkers' political theories. Even a less-canonical thinker (as a political theorist, that is) like Freud provides us with an appropriate, and also short, text, *Civilization and Its Discontents*: a perfect package for teaching political theory. What we have in Marx, in comparison to all this, is the infamous so-called guiding thread, which is literally one long paragraph from a short and hastily produced preface to the 1859 *A Contribution to the Critique of Political Economy*. This is not the place to engage with the deep and vast piles of commentary that have been devoted to the 1859 Preface. To cut to the chase: "The 1859 'Preface' represents the traditional and by far the most influential and familiar way of approaching Marx," an approach that commits Marx to a faith in universal laws and determinist structures (Carver 1996a: xv). Thus, the 1859 Preface further entrenches the dismissive view of Marx: not only was he a crazy radical, but his radicalism was also based upon a naive faith in historical progress and scientific truth. Carver trenchantly resists the enormous weight placed on these few lines. He does so, first, by showing that Marx himself never emphasised them much, and by stressing that Marx had already incorporated what mattered of them (to him) into a footnote in the first volume of *Capital*; it was Engels—and at least at the beginning, Engels alone—who decided that this paragraph could provide the scientific key to all of Marx. Moreover, the emphasis on these "guiding insights," as Marx calls them, turns attention away from Marx's historically specific analysis of politics, and distracts from his more conceptually refined study of political economy and history. Carver's comments are incisive:

> "Guiding" these insights may have been, but *what Marx actually wrote and published contradicts them in detail* often enough to put paid to any notion that they were supposed to be true in some necessary or invariable sense. Indeed, the propositions themselves display an ambiguity that reflects haste and inattention—Marx was late to the press as usual. . . . the mixed metaphors Marx employs . . . are now world famous, *but are arguably confused even in the original*. Marx did not seem to see these propositions as the foundation for a doctrine, but even if he did, he would surely have expected readers to move well beyond them in seeking to understand what he had to say. (Carver 1996a: xv, emphasis added)

Of course, Carver's rejection of the idea that we can start and stop our reading of Marx with a base/superstructure model of scientific historical progress only returns us to square one when it comes to approaching

Marx's body of writings. One can start with *Capital*, of course, and that is probably the logical thing to do in terms of the development of Marx's thought, but for this strategy to work one needs to teach *an entire course* on Marx, not just a week or two. And it hardly needs saying: no one who has never read Marx is going to sign up for an entire course on *Capital* (well, perhaps some of the aforementioned graduate students might, but they are a captive audience and therefore, in this case, hardly count). I myself, like many others, have often chosen a different route: to teach Marx as philosopher.[3] The process here is mostly straightforward: one assigns early writings of Marx (what Althusser famously labelled the Young Marx), which are a bit more excerptable. These writings center on Marx's engagement with Hegel and Feuerbach, and they emphasise his theory of man as a creature that *produces*, a labouring animal deeply and essentially connected to a supersensuous nature. This is a nature from which man has been sundered by the capitalist mode of production that alienates the worker from: 1) his labour, 2) the object of his labour, 3) other labourers, and 4) his species-being. To be estranged from one's own "species-being" means to be rendered something less than who one is, less than human. The return to full humanity, therefore, requires an overcoming of the capitalist mode of production, an overcoming of alienation through "true communism." It all adds up to a very interesting and provocative argument, and it provides a great deal of philosophical support for a communist political position, thereby nicely complementing a reading of *The Communist Manifesto*.

But reading Marx as a theorist of human nature only leads to unflattering comparisons with the social contract theorists, who seem to do this kind of work much better than Marx. Moreover, the exploration of Marx's humanist philosophy does nothing to counter the prejudice to dismiss Marx as a political theorist, since it sounds to most students like Marx is complaining unnecessarily about a condition (alienation) that must simply be accepted as a fact of life today. Indeed, these early texts do not position Marx much on the terrain of political theory anyway; all predispositions aside, the arguments about alienation only link up with politics tendentiously.[4] In other

3. I get the sense that Carver would offer students *The Communist Manifesto*, but with a *very different take* on it.

4. For a broader reading of alienation—broader both in the sense that I am using it here and, I think, in the sense typically conveyed when Marx is taught in political theory—see Carver's discussion of the continuities between Marx's early and later works (Carver 1975: 38–45, especially 39). And for a recent reading that rejects alienation even more strongly than Althusser did, see Carver (2008). For an important effort to hold on to a rethought concept of alienation, see Connolly (2012, footnote 4; cf. Connolly 2013). For a reconsideration of the broader problem of alienation (in and out of Marx), as something not be overcome but rather "ameliorated," see Walker (2013).

words, a committed communist might well find these early works compelling, but Marx's early philosophy of nature, man, and alienation is not in itself a theory of society, of history, or of the political.

EINLEITUNG (1857)

My argument in this chapter centers on the claim that we find just such a theory in Marx's *Introduction* (*Einleitung*). The *Introduction* is a draft manuscript, which originally existed only as one of dozens of notebooks (notebook M) that Marx generated during the 1850s while both reading the texts of classical political economy and thinking through his own critique of their concepts and categories. The *Introduction*—that is, the material later found in, and extracted from, notebook M—was drafted in late August and early September of 1857 (Carver 1975: 3). From October 1857 through March of 1858, Marx filled seven more numbered notebooks (I–VII) with what he described on two occasions, in letters to Engels from December 1857, as "outlines" (*Grundrisse*) of either his "economic studies" (8 December) or "political economy" (18 December) (Marx and Engels 1983: 214, 224; see Mann and Wainwright 2008: 849). Marx published none of the material from these notebooks during his lifetime.

Given the title Marx gave the draft manuscript, it seems pertinent to ask what the *Introduction* was an introduction to. Marx himself provided a clear and direct answer, when, in 1859, he published *Zur Kritik der Politischen Ökonomie*: in the Preface to this text Marx points out that he is "omitting a general introduction which I had dashed off, because on further reflection any anticipation of results yet to be proved seems disruptive"—a criticism, I would add, that might apply to *any* introduction (Marx 1897; Marx 1996b: 158). Notwithstanding his decision not to include the *Introduction*, Marx suggests here that it was definitely an introduction to *Zur Kritik*, and indeed, in keeping with this claim, the original English translation of *Zur Kritik*, *A Contribution to the Critique of Political Economy*, includes the *Introduction* as an appendix, marking the first appearance of the *Introduction* in English (Marx 1904).[5]

However, Marx's answer to the question "what is this an introduction to?" is not the only one that has been given in the history of publishing/

5. The first publication of the *Einleitung* in German predates the English version by only one year (Marx 1903). This is not a coincidence, since Stone's translation was based on Kautsky's 1903 publication of the *Einleitung*.

reception of Marx's work, and, more importantly, the alternative answer has become the dominant one. This second answer's origins lie in the decision of the Marx-Engels-Lenin Institute in Moscow to collect all eight of Marx's notebooks from the 1857 to 1858 period and publish edited extracts from them in two volumes (originally in 1939 and 1941, respectively) under the title, inspired by Marx's letters to Engels, *Grundrisse der Kritik der Politischen Ökonomie* (Marx 1953).[6] Out of this editorial decision a new "book" by Karl Marx was born. It was translated (partially) into English by McLellan (1971a; cf. 1971b) and then again (fully) by Nicolaus (Marx 1973), and even in English translation it was called the *Grundrisse* (quite probably because "Outlines" would have provided far too little weight for the title of a major text by Marx, which is how both McLellan and Nicolaus present the publication of the notebooks[7]). All three of these editions of the *Grundrisse* include the material from notebook M, the *Introduction*, as the *Grundrisse*'s own introduction. Indeed, the weight of these editorial decisions, combined now with many decades' worth of readers having approached this new book by Marx, the *Grundrisse*, with the *1857 Introduction* as its starting point, has led to a received opinion that the *Introduction* is the introduction to the *Grundrisse*.

It is beyond the scope of my project here either to deconstruct or even challenge this now common wisdom about the *Introduction*'s relation to the *Grundrisse*. However, I do refuse to follow this assumption and, taking my cues from Marx's own description of the *Introduction* as a *discarded*

---

6. Given the common equivalence drawn in the secondary literature between "the notebooks" and the *Grundrisse*, it is significant to note that the latter is not a transcription of the former but rather a selection of materials, editorially arranged.

7. The *Grundrisse* is itself something of a hypostatised entity. As I noted above, English-language commentary refers to the single German word for the title, but even the full German title is a gift of editors and was not assigned to the text by Marx. Thus, when referring to the *Grundrisse* we are really pointing to an artifact of editorial and critical work, and not to any sort of object that Marx produced directly. In making these claims I follow Carver's general approach to Marx and Marx-reception in his refusal to accept as a natural object (i.e., a book by Marx, or by Marx and Engels) what actually proves to be an editorial *production* that went on well after Marx's death (see Carver 2010; Carver 2014). Carver's own treatment and analysis of the *Introduction* is consistent with my approach here: it looks at the text as its own work, and not a part of the larger "whole" that would be the *Grundrisse* (Carver 1975). Nonetheless, I depart from Carver's specific presentations of the *Introduction*, which appears in both of his translations (on the title page and also in the running heads) as "*Introduction* to the *Grundrisse*" in a way that could serve to reify the very object the existence of which Carver might otherwise contest (Carver 1975; Carver 1996b).

introduction to *Zur Kritik*, I will simply refer to the text on its own, as a work of Marx, under the name of *1857 Introduction*.[8]

In many senses the *1857 Introduction* is a little-known and little-read text. Carver has placed the *Introduction* quite literally at the center[9] of his edition of the Cambridge volume *Marx: Later Political Writings*, but Tucker's more frequently assigned *Marx-Engels Reader* only includes parts of the *1857 Introduction* within the seventy-three pages of excerpts from the *Grundrisse* (Tucker 1978; Carver 1996b). Thus, the *Reader* surely makes the *1857 Introduction* available to the devoted scholar of Marx (who will own more than the "Reader" anyway), but almost everyone teaching the course will assign excerpts from *Capital* before excerpting the *Grundrisse*. The *Reader*'s presentation of the *1857 Introduction* gives its own reader no reason to think that there is anything to be found in it other than an early draft of *Capital*. And, I might point out that they have good reasons for thinking so. Marx himself obviously never finished the text: the manuscript we have is clearly *less* than a complete draft. While some of Marx's arguments seem well conceived and perhaps almost complete (if not fully fleshed out), many of the claims he makes are in what we would call today

8. I focus my analysis here on the *1857 Introduction*, treating it as a critical text of Marx's in its own right, separable from the other seven notebooks, and certainly separable from the afterlife of the *Grundrisse*. This choice marks a departure from the reception of, and work on, the *Grundrisse*. Nicolaus, for example, claims that "the Introduction and the main text [of the *Grundrisse*] form an organic whole from the bibliographic, or textual viewpoints" (Nicolaus 1973: 13). Nicolaus's logical mistake here is that in calling the *Introduction* a part of a larger whole, he has to presuppose the very existence of that "whole," and regardless of whatever else we might say about Marx's 1857 to 1858 notebooks, it seems safe to assert that they are not a "whole" (much less "organic") anything; they are an editorial compendium of material extracted from Marx's notes. Moreover, Nicolaus himself provides no real response to what (to be fair) he identifies as a real problem: the fact that Marx "omitted" the *Introduction* upon publication of *Zur Kritik*. At the same time, my decision to treat the *1857 Introduction* as a text of its own links up with other treatments of the *1857 Introduction* (as I discuss in the text below), and it also makes a certain intuitive sense. Nicolaus's claims to organic holism to the contrary, the Introduction that Marx wrote in 1857 is arguably a distinct text, since it appears in its own notebook, catalogued differently from all the rest that now comprise the *Grundrisse*. As itself also an editorial artifact, the *1857 Introduction* has led a separate life, with many commentators arguing for its central place in understanding Marx's methodology. For this reason, I find it very important to refer to the *1857 Introduction* in a way that allows it to stand on its own feet, rather than folding it into the other notebooks that make up the *Grundrisse*.

9. I simply *note* that the text runs to 257 pages and the *Introduction* starts on page 128; my own hermeneutics has nothing to say by way of numerology, but as we know, others are better armed on this front.

"bullet point" form. Why not, then, let the text return to relative obscurity, a curiosity for the Marx scholars?

I argue here that despite (perhaps because of[10]) this text's relative obscurity and incomplete structure, the *1857 Introduction* offers a unique understanding of Marx's conception of the historical and political development of social formations, and that it can serve as a key to a renewed conception of a critical political theory of society.[11] I am by no means the first one to suggest that there is something distinctly significant about the *1857 Introduction*. Althusser has both implicitly and explicitly placed the *1857 Introduction* at the core of his entire rereading of Marx, as offered up in his two widely read, frequently translated, and enormously influential books on Marx, *For Marx* and *Reading Capital.*[12] I say "implicitly" because, especially in *For Marx*, Althusser makes no direct arguments for the specific importance of the *1857 Introduction*[13]; nevertheless, he consistently and repeatedly returns to interpretations and lengthy quotations from that text at the most important moments in his own argument. A careful reading of Althusser's early engagement with Marx already shows quite clearly that

---

10. That is, and as I show in my reading of the text, the elision of the *1857 Introduction* from Marx's oeuvre makes it much easier to reduce Marx's political thought to a sort of orthodox economism, on the one hand, and/or to a philosophical humanism, on the other.

11. With this move, and as I show in the text below, I follow authors as far apart as Carver (1975) and Althusser (1969 and 2009) in taking the *1857 Introduction* as a text of critical importance based on the methodological arguments Marx makes here (and rarely makes anywhere else). By corollary, I depart from McLellan in his insistence that the *Grundrisse* in its entirety proves to be the central work in Marx's oeuvre (see McLellan 1971a; 1971b; see also Carver 1975).

12. Both texts appeared for the first time in English at around the same time (*For Marx* in 1969 and *Reading Capital* in 1970), and they share the same original publication date (1965) in French. (The 2009 Verso version of *Reading Capital* gives, wrongly, the original French publication date as 1968.) So while these texts are often taken to be coeval, it would be a mistake to elide the timeline of production of these texts. *For Marx* collects a series of essays published between 1960 and 1964 (only the introduction of the book dates from the year of its publication). *Reading Capital* collects a series of papers given in Althusser's seminar in 1965. When published in French in 1965, it contained essays by Althusser and a number of his students; the English translation of 1970 omits the essays by Rancière, Macherey, and Establet. See my Chapter 4 for more on the curious construction and reception of this "book."

13. In *For Marx*, Althusser actually mis-cites the *1857 Introduction* as the "*Introduction to the Critique of Political Economy, 1859*" (Althusser 1969: 182, 183). The repeated quotations make it clear that Althusser is drawing from the *1857 Introduction* and not the distinct 1859 Preface; later in the very same text he switches to calling it the *1857 Introduction*, and the earlier error is not repeated in *Reading Capital* (Althusser 1969: 193, 195 and ff.; Althusser 2009).

the *1857 Introduction* shapes his interpretation of Marx in significant ways. But I also say "explicitly" because in his later reflections on that early work, Althusser reflects on the text's centrality: "In the whole of this affair I based myself as closely as possible on Marx's *1857 Introduction*, and if I used it to produce some necessary effects of theoretical provocation, I think that I did nevertheless remain faithful to it" (Althusser 1976: 189).

But putting aside the importance of the text to Althusser's own wider project (a topic I will return to later), Althusser himself makes clear, even early on, that the *1857 Introduction* is a unique and uniquely important work. In *Reading Capital*, for example, Althusser offers a particularly strongly worded set of claims that go to the core of what makes this text significant. He writes:

> The third chapter of the *1857 Introduction* can rightly be regarded as the *Discourse on Method* of the new philosophy founded by Marx. In fact, it is the only systematic text by Marx which contains, in the form of an analysis of the categories and method of political economy, the means with which to establish a theory . . . of the conditions of the process of knowledge. (Althusser 2009: 95)

I would not be surprised to hear some readers cry foul at this point, since Althusser is surely neither neutral nor representative in his approach to Marx. Althusser *starts* from his position as a communist (and active member of the French Communist Party, PCF). This position dictates his Marxism. His Marxism leads him to a reading of Marx—and a very particular, probably unique, one at that. But I cite Althusser not as representative but precisely as radical. He helps to demonstrate the crucial importance of the *1857 Introduction* not on his own, but when read in comparison with a very different interpreter of Marx.

Carver's conjuncture is not Althusser's, and Carver's initial approach to Marx comes not in terms of personal communism or French radical politics, but in the context of the discipline of the history of political thought at Oxford. Carver focuses first and foremost on the reconstruction of historical context in a project centered primarily on translating Marx. Here, then, we have a rigorous, scholarly, and non-polemical approach to Marx. Nonetheless, in a book whose very title, *Texts on Method*, echoes Althusser, Carver calls the text "unique with respect to the type of material it provides for the study of Marx's methods and his views on what they should be. In his manuscript he recorded certain methodological innovations" that would prove central to all of Marx's later writings, especially *Capital* (Carver

1975: 4). The tone and rhetoric put the reader a long way from Althusser, but the latter author would, I think, wholly embrace the argument.[14]

ZŌON POLITIKON

The above work both indicates the reasons for turning to the *1857 Introduction* to give it a careful and nuanced reading and suggests that doing so might provide us with that sense of Marx as a theorist of the social formation. The payoff, however, does not come easily. Notwithstanding the claims from Carver and Althusser, this is not a "text on method" in any sort of straightforward or traditional sense. Marx does not start with a description of his methodology or an account of his approach. He does not lay out epistemological (or ontological or metaphysical) propositions from which he plans to proceed. Instead, Marx begins with the specific terms and concepts of classical political economy. He therefore gives part 1 the wholly unimaginative title "production, consumption, distribution, exchange (circulation)." And this section does what it says on the tin, as Marx analyses each of these concepts in turn, as they have been developed and understood by classical political economists. Thus we see that Marx's method does not *precede* critical engagement, but emerges from that engagement.[15] There

14. I referred above to the *1857 Introduction* as a text that is not widely discussed, particularly in terms of thinking about Marx as a political theorist. But, of course, there is a separate sense in which the *1857 Introduction* is quite "famous." Given the unpublished draft nature of a text devoted directly to "methodological" concerns and containing Marx's own process of "self-clarification," it is no wonder that for many committed Marxists the text wields a powerful force. Still, despite the fact that following McLellan's work in the early 1970s there appeared a brief flurry of attention to both the *1857 Introduction* and the *Grundrisse* as a whole, there has been no abiding, mainstream interest in this text (McLellan 1971a; McLellan 1971b). By turning to the recent literature from scholars most devoted to the minutiae of Marx's body of work, one could, of course, easily enough multiply recent quotations that continue to emphasise the unique importance of the *1857 Introduction*. I will limit myself to just one example, a recent reference to "the famous Notebook M (also known as the '1857 Introduction') [which is] arguably Marx's most comprehensive comment on method" (Mann and Wainwright 2008: 849). When referring to scholars devoted to "minutiae," I mean those who not only know the labels of Marx's unpublished notebooks but also understand some of them to be "famous."

15. I have no interest in engaging in meta-theoretical squabbles over the status of "Marxism"—nor with identifying who counts or does not count as a "Marxist"—but it should already be more than apparent that my approach to Marx's writings shares nothing in common with so-called Analytical Marxism. As the leading advocate of that school puts it, "The fateful operation that created analytical Marxism was the rejection of the claim that Marxism possesses valuable intellectual methods of its own" (Cohen

is no method apart from Marx's reading of political economy (see also Marx 1959).[16] As Marx put it in a letter to Lasalle, referring to a never-written "work" for which the 1857 text was likely meant to serve as the introduction,[17] "[it is] the system of bourgeois political economy critically presented. It is the presentation [*Darstellung*] of the system and, at the same time, through the presentation, its critique" (Marx and Engels 1963 [1858]; quoted in Carver 1975, Carver's translation). The *Darstellung* is the *Kritik*.

The presentation of political economy is simultaneously a re-presentation of it in a critical light.[18] The idea that *Darstellung* is *Kritik* tells us something obvious (but perhaps also important) about Marx's project, in the sense that Marx's work emerges out of classical political economy. In a line that perhaps underplays the significance of Hegel's thought for Marx, Stuart Hall puts it this way: "Political Economy remains Marx's *only* theoretical point-of-departure" (Hall 2003 [1974]: 145, emphasis added). Whatever Marx may be doing politically or theoretically he is doing it either in or out of the context of the classical political economists. But the idea of presentation as critical re-presentation also tells us something about

---

2000: xvii). My return to Marx's *1857 Introduction*, and to his understanding of the social formation, represents an effort to rediscover not just the intellectual value but also the politico-theoretical value of Marx's work.

16. As close readers of Marx have already noted, his familiarity with the political economy literature of his day proved wide and deep, and in his own writing Marx sometimes presupposes a similar familiarity on his readers' part. This makes it difficult for contemporary readers to sort out Marx's arguments from his simple recapitulation of what would have been taken as "standard arguments" of the time, since, indeed, some of Marx's strongest critiques of the socialist utopians are simply sharp exegeses of Ricardo (Marx 1955). Clarifying Marx's problematic can shed a great deal of light on confusions over Marx's so-called labour theory of value (i.e., and in short, it was never "Marx's" theory).

17. The letter is written just a few months after the *1857 Introduction* had been drafted. In it, Marx refers to his "*Critique of the Economic Categories*," but in letters throughout the 1850s Marx frequently referred to his "book on political economy," a "work" whose title, scope, outline, and structure changed from letter to letter (Marx and Engels 1983). The notebooks that were published a century later as *Grundrisse* are one version of that project; the 1859 *Contribution to the Critique of Political Economy* is another; *Capital* is the final version, at least from Marx.

18. In this context it is worth emphasising that "political economy" was not just a random theory that Marx fixated upon as some sort of intellectual puzzle. Rather, Marx was obsessed with the theory of political economy because it was the conceptual (or ideological) distillation of the most significant everyday concepts (e.g., value, money, capital) through which our lives are lived. That is, classical "political economy" was a non-reflective theory of the capitalist social formation of Marx's time (and to a great extent, of ours as well). Here we see one important way in which Marx was never a "normative theorist" in the sense I criticised in my Introduction.

Marx's general approach, what for lack of a better word we might call his "method." That method looks a lot like our generic understanding, today, of so-called deconstruction, since rather than starting with a series of negative criticisms that would clear the ground to set out a distinct series of positive declarations, Marx allows his argument to emerge within his critique, while he offers the latter only in terms of a "reading" of others' texts.

Part 1 of the *1857 Introduction* thus appears to be a summary of the four key categories of political economy, presented in order. Marx proceeds by showing that each category of classical political economy is understood by the political economists in one way, yet can be demonstrated, by Marx, to be something else entirely. For classical political economy, each of these four concepts remains clearly distinct from the others, and the relation between them is linear: we start with the production of a commodity; then we follow its distribution; after that, it is exchanged; and finally we witness its consumption. Each step in the process operates according to its own logic, and each follows sequentially from the one that precedes it. Consumption completes the process and returns us back again to production.

Marx's *Darstellung* operates by putting into motion the static concepts of the political economists; Marx reveals their interdependence and their inter-relational aspects in such a way as to call into question their very identities. Here are a few of the (deconstructive) claims that Marx makes during the course of this argument, all of which serve to undermine the static, formal, and linear nature of the political economists' traditional arguments:

1. production is consumption
2. consumption is production
3. distribution determines production
4. exchange is internal to, and constitutive of, production

I could continue to add to this list until it grew quite long, but even stopping here we can see that Marx has undermined and/or rethought all four categories of classical political economy. Note, however, that the list above cannot be considered as Marx's *alternatives*. While he defends these theses, he simultaneously notes his positive *agreement* with classical political economy over the claims that production determines distribution, or that production and consumption are separate activities. He holds both their theses and his new ones simultaneously. And he can do so precisely because Marx's account has a dynamism and motion wholly lacking in the account of classical political economy.[19]

19. It is this dynamism that David Harvey so frequently emphasises in his important reading of Marx (Harvey 2010a).

It would be easy to call this a dialectical approach and, as Carver shows, there is strong evidence to indicate that Marx was reworking the economists' categories through the terms of Hegel's *Logic* (Carver 1975: 43, 130–33). But if by dialectical we simply mean "applying Hegel to political economy," then it would be far *too easy* (and in a number of important senses, simply wrong). Instead, the relationality that emerges in Marx's account, and the dynamic element that he injects into the four categories, is *historical* in a very specific sense. In fact, here my goal is to prove that the key both to making sense out of the sparse (and sometimes cryptic) lines from the *1857 Introduction* and to glimpsing some of the profound theoretical insights of this short text depends on reading it for this sense of history. Nietzsche famously declared that "lack of historical sense is the family failing of all philosophers," and while I have no interest in proclaiming Marx to be or not be a philosopher, I think we can show that he has a great deal of what Nietzsche calls "historical sense" (Nietzsche 1996: 13).

We can see an example early on in the text, in a striking passage that has received relatively scant attention in the secondary literature. Marx opens this introductory text with the subheading on "production" and a sub-subheading titled "Autonomous individuals. Eighteenth-century ideas." Here Marx argues that Smith and Ricardo begin with a conception of man that occupies a position within literature, not within prehistory. "The individual—and individuated—hunter and fisher . . . *belongs to the unimaginative conceits of eighteenth-century Robinsonades*" (Marx 1996a: 128, emphasis added). "Robinsonades" were a popular eighteenth-century genre of stories that mimicked, repeated, or reworked in some way the story of Robinson Crusoe as told by Daniel Defoe in his novel of 1719. With his reference to Robinsonades, Marx argued that the idea of a prehistorical natural man comes not from past historical realities, but from present literary narratives. Smith, Ricardo, and the other classical political economists are not referring to any actual historical *origins* with their conception of hunters and gatherers, or men in states of nature; rather, they are calling on an archetype that belongs to a particular literary genre, itself a product of a particular time and place—eighteenth-century Europe. This idea of man as an autonomous individual is an "ideal form" that emerges in the eighteenth century; it is only *as an ideal* that Smith and Ricardo (not to mention Locke and Rousseau) can *project that ideal back into the (artificial) past.* Marx refers to this "fallacy" as the idea of the individual as "posited by nature" (1996a: 129). This individual has no historical existence; he is not a historical product in their accounts, even though their accounts would not be possible were it not for a particular history—that is, the one in which Robinson Crusoe stories predominate.

And those very stories do not come from nowhere. They are a part of a larger social formation, one in which the bonds of feudal society have been broken, in which bourgeois revolutions have created the conditions of equalisation and individuation—conditions that themselves make it possible to conceive in the first place of the *individuated individual*. Moreover, Marx continues, if we actually *look* (rather than project) backward into history, we find individuals "dependent, belonging to a larger whole" (1996a: 129). Only in the current epoch, that of what Marx calls "the most developed form of social relations," do we first encounter the idea of the autonomous and individuated individual. Only a particular, developed social formation could give us the notion of an individual that can exist on its own, apart from society. Only a developed social order could provide us with the argument that at the origin of society lies individuals coming together to freely form that society. Marx concludes this line of critical presentation with a striking reference to Aristotle: "Man is in the most literal sense a *zōon politikon*, not only a sociable animal, but *an animal that can individuate itself only in society*" (1996a: 129, emphasis added).

The reference to Aristotle proves significant to the extent that it forcefully situates this argument in the context of the history of political thought, but Marx does not merely *cite* Aristotle here—in the sense of backing up his position with the weight of authority. Instead, in this formulation, Marx radically reconceives the concepts of both "the political" and "man." Of course, Aristotle's original thesis that "man is a *zōon politikon*," a political animal, serves to resist or refute Plato's argument that human beings could live in a "city of pigs," in a minimalist society that fulfilled only their base needs.[20] For Aristotle, man is a creature called or built to live in a polis, where the polis is a shared community (*koinōnia*), and thus an explicitly political formation, not a simple social order. Living in a polis allows the human animal to transcend mere life (*zēn*) in pursuit of the good life (*eu zēn*). Aristotle supports this argument with his conception of *anthrōpos* as a properly political creature precisely because he, unlike the rest of the animals, possesses *logos*. *Logos* is the capacity for reasoned speech, but it is also the capacity to *deliberate* and the ability to *judge*, and these are, for Aristotle, the political actions *par excellence*.

Marx takes up Aristotle's term, calling the human being a *zōon politikon*, but what he means by this could hardly be further from Aristotle. Marx suggests that man is a political animal because the very idea of man belongs to

---

20. Platonists will of course point out that Plato's *Republic* abandons the city of pigs in order to build a higher form of political community. I am not challenging that reading, but simply narrating the position as Aristotle himself saw things.

a particular form of historically and politically developed social formation. Only having built a society could the idea of man, of the autonomous animal, emerge. We are political creatures not because we are wired that way (which, in a sense, is Aristotle's argument, despite the fact that the language of being "wired" is surely anachronistic when applied to the ancient Greeks), but because we are a product of history, a history that is also political. For Marx, we are political animals because we are social creatures that recreate our own conditions of existence. This last part is, for Marx, the political part: we need a set of institutions, systems, and structures through which we reproduce our conditions of existence, and while these may arise out of nature, they are not simply given—they are not simply natural. This means that only within the particular context of bourgeois society would we, or could we, even come up with the (mythical) notion that we are autonomous individuals in "nature." Only the separation and distance between human animals, a separation directly produced by the capitalist mode of production and the broader social formation of which it forms a part, could make us into the creatures who would think we are separated this way by nature itself.

LABOUR *SANS PHRASE*

This *Darstellung* of classical political economy raises the thorny but important question of the nature of critique. Clearly Marx refutes the political economists' *projection* of the autonomous individual back into a prehistory. But does this make the entire idea of the individuated individual a myth? Is it simply false to refer to the autonomous individual? Would we instead refer to the "truth" of the individual as a creature dependent upon a broader social order, linked to others in relations of responsibility that undermine any "conceit" of autonomy? In other words, wherein lies this very conceit? For now I wish to defer the larger question of critique and stay close to the main lines of argument that Marx lays out here, since—regardless of how we understand what it means to be critical—*Marx does not argue in this text that the autonomous individual does not exist*. His challenge to classical political economy absolutely cannot be reduced to the idea that for the economists the individual is autonomous whereas for Marx the individual is dependent.[21] To turn the argument into this sort of account would be to

---

21. One *might* derive this sort of argument from the *1844 Manuscripts*, but I would cite this fact as evidence to avoid what Althusser calls an anthropological reading of Marx—since such a reading pushes the reader toward a misunderstanding of some of Marx's most crucial political insights. Instead, I might suggest, both with and against Althusser, that we return to those passages in the *1844 Manuscripts*—such as the discussions of

rob it of its dynamic element; it would be to turn Marx's critique of formalism into another formal account. This reading would render Marx as a "philosopher" of the very sort that Nietzsche always criticised, and it would thereby smother his historical sense.

To show *why* such a reading proves so flawed, I need to turn to another crucial passage in the *1857 Introduction*, one that also has received less than its fair share of critical and interpretive commentary. It comes in section 3 of the text, the section that most readers of Marx *do* focus on—the one that Althusser calls Marx's *Discourse on Method.* Most readers cannot seem to get past the opening paragraphs—perhaps for good reason. In those passages Marx lays out two different ways of "proceeding" within the project of the study of society (i.e., the social formation)—two ways to approach Marx's *Subject* (i.e., subject of investigation). After a rather obscure formulation of these two "ways" (the editor must provide "[of proceeding]"), Marx then asserts with apparent force: "The latter is obviously the scientifically correct method" (1996a: 146). No wonder that interpretive debates over this text endlessly circle around the dozen or so lines that precede and follow this statement, since (so these interpreters often presume) if we can figure out exactly what Marx means by "the latter" and distinguish it from "the first way," then we will not only have grasped "Marx's method" but also be able to claim for it the status of "science."[22] Marx's two "ways of proceeding" both concern the manner in which we grasp "the whole"—that is, they concern the ways of thinking a complex social totality. The first approach starts with the whole and breaks it down; this is an *analytic method.* The second approach starts with smaller parts and builds them up into a whole; this is a *synthetic method* (see Carver 1975: 129–33). But we cannot reduce this account to the idea of Marx (or Marxists) simply

---

history and nature, of evolution—armed with the idea that Marx means to say more to the political economists than that they have the wrong idea of Man and that Marx (and perhaps the communists) have the right idea. This step goes *with* Althusser to the extent that it resists the humanist/anthropological reading of Marx, but it departs from him to the extent that it opens up a space for productively rereading (and not just dismissing) the *1844 Manuscripts.*

22. With the slightly sceptical tone I take up here I mean to dismiss neither these passages (in their importance) nor their readers (in bringing out that importance). However, I do believe that it is a mistake to reduce the *1857 Introduction* to a half page of text on either side of the phrase *scientifically correct method*—as if Marx's own label of "scientific method" could somehow provide a golden key to Marxist science. As should become consistently clear throughout my engagements with both Marx and Althusser, I place little weight on the status of "science," whether it be that of Marx, of Engels, or of Althusser.

choosing, formally, between analytic or synthetic approaches, for two reasons, which I will summarise here and defend below:

1. Marx's text places little or no emphasis on the method as such (and surely he puts no effort into naming it as a method or to developing it as a singular approach). Instead, Marx's words here focus heavily upon *the conception of the whole* that we work with. *Starting* with the whole gives us a "chaotic" conception of it, whereas *building toward* the whole gives us "a rich totality" (1996a: 145, 146). The difference of which Marx speaks ("first way"/"latter way") lies in the difference between two types of social wholes.[23] The key for Marx is to understand social formations as complex, uneven, and *rich* totalities, rather than taking them as simple, monolithic entities.
2. To start with the smaller parts and build up to the complex whole *is not to start with the empirically given.* Thus, while Marx's movement is synthetic, it does not go from the particular and observable to the abstract. Marx's "synthetic method" cannot be translated into the empiricist method of induction (from observable particulars to a general law).

Marx asserts that the starting point for the synthetic process is not a simple given and the ending point is not the general abstract. Thus, Marx rejects both a straightforward empiricism (or a crude so-called materialism) and a Hegelian speculative idealism. The starting point is *the abstract conception* as already given to us to think, and the ending point is the *concrete in thought.*[24] In other words, the process of synthesis allows us to think a

23. On this difference between social wholes also hangs the weight of countless debates over "structure." Warren Montag (1998) shows eloquently that Althusser worked with two different concepts of structure, and his elucidation of the differences can clearly be traced back to the differences between "wholes" that Marx points out in the *1857 Introduction*. This tracing is not a mere academic exercise, since Althusser's concept of structure depends much more on his reading of Marx than on the (so-called) influence of (so-called) structuralists.

24. It is exactly in an effort to make sense out of this complicated and non-intuitive notion of starting with an "abstract" that is not simply the universal, and then moving to a "concrete" that is precisely *not* empirical, but rather a concrete *in thought*, that Althusser invents the language of Generalities I, II, and III. Nothing sounds more obtuse than Althusser's language of "generalities," and it comes as no surprise that critics point to this language when dismissing Althusser as the prime example of French theoretical jargon. Yet here, as elsewhere, Althusser's language is designed not to create a new system of Philosophy (with a capital P) but, quite simply, *to make sense out of Marx.* And when understood as a particular *reading of Marx*, as I discuss in the following chapter, Althusser's terms actually help quite a bit.

structured, complex whole, in concrete terms, but we are still *thinking* it and it is still a *whole*. The synthetic method that Marx outlines here helps us to move from more abstract concepts to less abstract concepts. Nonetheless, we neither start nor end outside the realm of concepts, and yet, contra Hegel, it is not concepts that carry out the synthesis. Carver explains by showing that the whole with which we start, in this case population, remains an abstraction until we build into it "other contextual elements" and do so "in the proper synthetic way" (1975: 130).

In order to get a better sense of this "proper synthetic way" and so as to avoid entirely unproductive debates about science, we have to grasp what Marx means by the abstract as a starting point and the concrete as an end point. And it is here that we can turn the page beyond the famous lines (upon which I too have now heaped more commentary) to the passages I wish to emphasise. In these paragraphs that follow, Marx provides a specific example, that of labour, wherein he makes a number of crucial clarifications—both for the above argument and for this text as a whole. Most importantly, Marx tackles the category of the "abstract," also referred to as the "simple," and he gives his readers an utterly radical reinterpretation of this category. As always, Marx works up his argument from within the terms of the classical political economists. They, he shows, deal with simple, abstract concepts such as money, labour, and value. For them, these categories are universal and ahistorical, applicable to all times and all places, and this is so precisely because the categories are abstract, simple.

Marx's critical insight is itself singular, and it again depends upon what I am calling his historical sense. In the particular case of the concept of "money," Marx argues "that wholly simple category does not appear historically in its intensiveness as it appears in the most developed states of society. By no means [is that simple category] wading through all economic relations" (1996a: 148). The second sentence seems to be an obvious historicist criticism that would run as follows: contrary to the claims of political economists who call the concept of money universal and predict its appearance in the same form throughout history, we proclaim that it cannot be found everywhere in history, and it surely does not take the same form in those places where it does appear. But such an interpretation sits unevenly with the more difficult first sentence. What does it mean to say the category appears "*in its intensiveness*" in developed states of society?

Marx explains by turning from the short example of money to a much fuller example, labour. Here Marx begins by intentionally stating two contradictory theses:

A) labour is an old and universal category
B) labour is a specifically modern category, a product of modern history

Marx explains by showing that the physiocrats had no concept of labour in general. For them, there existed a special, particular form of labour (agriculture) that was the source of wealth. Marx praises Adam Smith for "throwing away" this old notion and for helping to develop the concept of *abstract labour*. The concept "abstract labour" contains the essential (and essentialist) idea of individuals as producing (labouring) creatures; this category of labour (abstract labour) applies therefore to all societies (across time). Again, Marx comments elliptically: "This is correct in one way, [but] not in another" (1996a: 150). Abstract labour is a valid concept, in some sense, but in another sense it is incorrect to say that there is a thing called labour that applies to all time and space. How is this possible? How can general labour as a concept be true and false? How can labour be universal and also modern? To see the answer requires a sense of history, and that answer can only come out of a particular understanding of history and historical development. Marx writes:

> The indifference towards a specific form of labour presupposes a very developed totality of actual types of labour, of which one is no longer dominating [over] the others. Thus the most general abstractions generally develop only with the richest concrete development, where one [abstraction] appears common to many, common to all. Then one ceases to be able to think only [in terms] of a particular form. On the other hand, this abstraction of labour generally is not merely the mental result of [abstracting from] a concrete totality of labours. The indifference towards the specific type of labour corresponds to a form of society in which individuals transfer with ease from one type of labour into another and the specific type of labour is contingent to them, hence indifferent. (1996a: 150)

In order to emphasise how novel a line of argument Marx takes here, and in an effort to draw out how radically he reconceives of the relation between thought and history, it is worth starting with more common understandings of the abstract. A dictionary entry for the noun "abstract" gives: "existing in thought or as an idea but not having a physical or concrete existence; dealing with ideas rather than events; not based on a particular instance; denoting an idea" (Oxford University Press 2010). The abstract is therefore specifically opposed to the concrete historical particular. To be abstract, as the *OED* emphasises, is precisely to be *withdrawn* from history, to be separated, extracted, or removed from the historical instance (Oxford University Press 2011). The abstract is the ahistorical. On a typical account, then, we would oppose the abstract to the historical. To be abstract would be to be without history. We might, on the other hand, reject the validity of the abstract on just these grounds: there is no facticity to the abstract because it has been withdrawn from historical reality.

Marx, however, refuses any simple opposition between the abstract and the historical. Instead, he holds that the abstract abstracts *from* history while also only emerging *within history*. Only the rich, concrete development of a particular social formation can make it possible for us to think the abstract. Only under the particular forms of capitalist labour can we conceive the idea of labour in general, of labour *sans phrase*. In specific terms, Marx suggests that the most advanced social relations with respect to labour emerge in the United States, and that the concept of abstract labour, labour in general, "only here becomes truly practical" (Marx 1996a: 150). As the extended quotation above makes clear, this is not arbitrary. It is the particular social relations of production under capitalism that lead workers to *think* of labour "in general" precisely because they *experience* labour "in general." It no longer matters, under capitalism, quite so much *what* job one is doing, as long as one earns a wage for one's labour-power. Thus, contrary to commonsense notions about the dichotomous relation between the historical and the abstract, we see here that *it is only a particular kind of historical development that could give rise to an abstract concept*. The abstract withdraws *from* history, but it is made possible *by* history.

This logic tempts us, again, to the historicist position; it tempts us to argue that there is, in truth, no labour in general, but only particular forms of labour. Such a line of logic would tell us that it is a mistake to abstract *from* particular instances of labour (especially those under capitalism) to create the false impression that labour in general is real. But most significantly, Marx refuses this path as well. From the fact that abstraction depends upon historical development, Marx does not derive the thesis that the abstract is untrue. In the case of "the most abstract categories," Marx refers to "their validity for all epochs" (1996a: 150). *There is nothing false about labour in general*. "Labour in general," Marx insists, must be grasped by us as a remarkable *insight* of Smith; in discovering this concept he reveals a significant and very much *valid* category—"a relationship valid for all forms of society." It is—and Marx also implies that it *should be*—"the starting point of modern [political] economy" (1996a: 150).

This means, as Marx more famously explains in the passages that follow, that the starting point is actually the end point. That is, the starting point of analysis in political economy is the end point of historical development, with "end point" understood not as a projection into some teleological future, but as the current conjuncture—our current location in history.[25]

25. This is one reason why—as Marx famously remarks elsewhere, and as I briefly discussed in my Introduction—the logic of explanation proves distinct from the logic of historical development (Marx 1990: 102).

Political economy (and therefore also Marx's dramatic reworking of it) starts with abstract categories: labour, commodity, value, capital. And, in a certain sense, Marx wants to emphasise that political economy is correct to proceed in this manner. He suggests as much because he shows that we can productively study earlier periods in history from the perspective of concepts developed only in later periods. Marx argued that bourgeois society, as a highly developed social formation, actually provides us with a powerful perspective from which to understand earlier social formations: "The categories which express its relations [the relations of bourgeois society] . . . *allow* at the same time *an insight into the arrangement* of production and the relations of production *of all extinct forms of society* with whose fragments and elements bourgeois society is constructed" (1996a: 151, emphasis added). Marx would appear to imply here that only from the perspective of capitalism can we even understand feudalism.[26] Can he really mean this? Absolutely:

> In the anatomy of man is a key to the anatomy of the ape. The indications of the higher types in the subordinate types of animal life can only be understood, on the other hand, if the higher type is itself already well known. Thus bourgeois economy offers the key to [the economy of] antiquity. (1996a: 151)

Therefore, the political economists are, without doubt, right to begin with their abstract conceptions, to start with categories made possible only by the bourgeois society in which they live. But the difference between the Marxist account and that of classical political economy hinges on distinct understandings of the starting point. Political economy *projects* those abstract concepts back into history and hypostatises their empirical emergence therein. This is why they tell state-of-nature stories: to pretend as if the bourgeois concept of man actually existed in the past. The emergence of the "individuated individual" may, according to Marx, tell us something very important about the dependent, non-individuated individual, *but this does not mean that the individuated individual has always existed.*

---

26. This would suggest, in turn, that we absolutely cannot understand communism from the perspective of capitalism. And Marx himself says that certain relations appear within bourgeois society only in "stunted form. [. . .] For example, communal property" (1996a: 151). In other words, it is not simply that Marx "refused to give blueprints" for communist society, but rather that it is impossible to grasp the social order of a future society prior to its emergence. We can never know communism, or any other social formation that would follow capitalism, until *and unless* capitalism falls apart (and in a sense we will only gain our clearest perspective on capitalism, after capitalism has been replaced with some other social formation).

For his part, Marx accepts that abstract concepts are precisely *abstractions*, and that the process of abstraction depends upon the contemporary form of society. But this does not mean we can simply apply those abstractions equally to all of history, that we can reduce all particular historical forms to our contemporary form. Marx is emphatic about this point when he clarifies the argument by showing that our ability to understand past forms from later forms is not practiced by political economy, who "obliterate all historical differences and see in all forms of society the bourgeois forms" (1996a: 151). In contrast, Marx's understanding of using later concepts to understand earlier forms lies exactly in revealing and highlighting the differences that the political economists would "obliterate." The key, for Marx's historical method, is to understand earlier forms from the perspective of later forms, but not to equate forms that do and must remain distinct. We may better understand apes because we understand human beings (indeed, our understanding of apes may reach a level otherwise unattainable without our knowledge of human beings), but *apes are not human beings*. Barter within agrarian societies may be made better sense of from the perspective of a fully developed capitalist money system, but that doesn't mean that agrarian barter can be equated with money exchange under advanced capitalism.[27]

THOUGHT/REAL

Marx stakes out a position much more subtle than either universalism (in which contemporary categories would be not contemporary, but rather timeless, valid across history) or historicism (in which all "validity" would be confined by historical context, with each concept valid only within its own time). The abstract is valid in all epochs, yet only made possible within later, more developed epochs. It is true for all time, while also a product of this time. How can it be both? To see how Marx can, or at least attempts to, pull this off requires resituating Marx's thought. In offering a simultaneous critique of both the idealism of German philosophy and a certain empiricism of classical political economy, Marx articulates a novel and complex relation between philosophy/concepts/thought, on the one hand, and "the real," on the other. Both of Marx's opponents here have more concise, less complex understandings of this relation: for Hegel, *thought is the Real*; for empiricism, the real is given, and thought must find a way to correspond to

27. On the "myth of barter," which involves just this false equation, see the important work of Graeber (2011).

it, to model it, to map it, perhaps even to grasp it, but certainly to *approach* it. Any answer to the question, "What is the relation between thought and the real?" will be pulled toward one or the other (sometimes both) of these poles. Marx offers a novel answer because he plods a path between these two poles, which, importantly, does not mean charting a course "down the middle," since to avoid both poles is to actively resist each of their pulls—to tack back and forth. For this reason, Marx's answer is neither simple nor concise—as Althusser says, it is never simple to be a Marxist in philosophy (Althusser 1976).

In contrast to Hegelian idealism or a crude empiricist materialism, Marx always maintains two theses. First, thought is not the real. "Hegel falls into the illusion of understanding the real as the result of self-summarising, self-engrossing, self-motivating thinking" (1996a: 146). Thinking and thought are never their own processes for Marx; they are always the product of thinking beings, themselves situated in the material world.

> The production of ideas, of conceptions, of consciousness, is at first directly interwoven with the material activity and the material intercourse of men, the language of real life. Conceiving, thinking, the mental intercourse of men, appear at this stage as the direct efflux of their material behaviour. The same applies to mental production as expressed in the language of politics, laws, morality, religion, metaphysics, etc., of a people. Men are the producers of their conceptions, ideas, etc.—real, active men, as they are conditioned by a definite development of their productive forces and of the intercourse corresponding to these, up to its furthest forms. Consciousness can never be anything else than conscious existence, and the existence of men is their actual life-process. (Marx and Engels 2000: sec. 4; cf. Carver 2010)

Thought does not think; human beings think. And human beings can only think from within the context of the social formation in which they find themselves. *There is thus no such thing as epistemology, a theory of knowledge, that is not also and at the same time a theory of the social formation.* As a corollary to Marx's first thesis, we would also say that "the real" is a condition of thinking; thought only emerges from out of the real.

This corollary would seem, for some, to slide toward the conclusion that thought is thought *of* the real; that the duty of thought is to correspond with or model the real—to grasp it. Yet Marx refuses this line of logic and rejects this conclusion. Hence, his second thesis: thought does not grasp the real directly. Thinking is not a mirror of reality, and the task of thought is not to model the real. To try to grasp the real directly is always to reduce what is possible to what is given. Bourgeois society, in Marx's time and in our own, is the real; that is, the material conditions under which we live are the conditions of (neo)liberal capitalism. This social formation does indeed condition all that is possible in thought; it is the reason why for the first time political economy could think, as I showed in detail above, "the individuated individual." But to operate as if the job of thinking is to grasp the real directly is to make precisely the mistake of classical political economy: it is to universalise and dehistoricise that individuated individual, to project it back into history as some sort of universal truth.[28]

In stark contrast, the task that Marx assigns to thinking is to see how thought itself arises from the real. We might, then, derive a third thesis from Marx's first two: *thought thinks the relationship between the real and thought.*[29] And, for thought *to think the relation to the real means to think the social formation.* This is how we can come to see, for example, that the real conditions of bourgeois society make the concept of a state of nature possible. The thought of the state of nature depends upon the real, but it does not correspond to it. And our own conceptual thinking, in grasping the real conditions under which the theory of the state of nature emerges, does not seek to grasp reality directly. Reality is not out there to be approached by our thinking, for the real will always be the condition of and for our thought. To say, then, that the task of thinking is to grasp *not* the real, but the *relation* between the real and thought, means that there can never be an unmediated relation to the real. "Thought attends to the relation between thought and the real." This claim has numerous implications:

1. The real can never be reduced to thought.
2. Thought can never be reduced to (a correspondence with) the real.
3. Therefore there will always be a gap, a border, or a limit between thought and the real.

This third point proves deeply contentious, and understanding it fully has significant implications for the status of Marx's thought; moreover, its ramifications prove crucial for any effort to give an account of the social

---

28. This concluding logic of Marx's sketch in the *1857 Introduction* can serve as a response to Butler; it can operate as a follow-up to the critique of Butler that I offered in the previous chapter for exactly the reason that Butler, especially in her later writings, is tempted by the "method" of the political economists. She wants to take the status of "vulnerability" and "precarity" in our current conjuncture and project them backward and forward in time as universal features of human existence.

29. Althusser attempts to specify the terms of a claim like this with his distinction between Generality I (the first thought, the one that we start from) and Generality III (the final thought, the one we arrive at). For further elaboration of this idea, including the mediating role of Generality II, see my Chapter 3, especially footnote 15.

formation. In the next chapter I take up one particular debate over this claim, exploring in detail Stuart Hall's rejection of point number 3, both in his reading of Marx and in his own suggestions for how to think and how to study (which also means how to intervene in) the social formation. I make this turn deeper into these debates not in order to score intellectual points against Hall, in an old and mostly abandoned dispute. I shift to Hall's critique of the Althusserian reading of Marx because it helps focus attention on the political stakes of "bearing society in mind"—the political stakes of giving an account of the social formation. The interweaving of epistemology with a theory of the social formation demonstrates that an account of the social formation cannot be purely epistemological in a Kantian sense, and this is because political practice itself always forms a major constituent part of any social formation. Marx's concern with the status of "thought" in relation to "the real" is always a concern with definite (i.e., specific, concrete, historical, political) *practices*. The social formation is made up of practices, and it is made up of thoughts of practices. Above all, the conceptualisation of practices itself organises, structures, and potentially directs those practices. It is for this reason that Marx's effort to always bear society in mind, his attempt to grasp the social formation—such a project is also always simultaneously a theory of politics. The hermeneutic dispute between Hall and Althusser over how to interpret Marx on the social formation is thereby, both in terms of the concrete history of the event and in terms of the theoretical stakes, a political conflict through and through. My reconstruction of, and intervention in, the debate will serve to specify my own account of the social formation and its importance for contemporary theory and politics.

3

❖ ❖

Thought and the Real: Conceptualising the Social Formation

I concluded the previous chapter with the claim that Marx's account of the social formation depended upon maintaining a certain type of gap between "thought," on the one hand, and "the real," on the other, and I suggested that this epistemological claim also amounted to a broader politico-theoretical argument, since, for Marx, thought arises from a social formation, and a social formation is constituted by both thought and social practices (and thought *of* those social practices). In my interpretation of Marx's *1857 Introduction*, I have attempted to demonstrate that Marx himself holds an important commitment to the idea that thought does not directly grasp the real, and that the purpose of thinking (of concepts, of ideas) is not to model or approximate the real. In a certain sense, this chapter's primary concern lies with developing a richer sense of what concepts are for—if not to approach the real, then what? This chapter shows that the concepts (the "thought") that help make up the social formation are not the same as analytical concepts, for example, of "table" and "chair," and that, ultimately, concepts play a crucial role in both the constitution of a social order and any effort to maintain or transform that order—exactly the task of politics.

The previous chapter made the case for understanding the idea of a gap between thought and the real as inherent to Marx's understanding of the very constitution of society, and particularly of his grasp of the historical transformations of social orders. In drawing attention to this gap, I have already pulled my reading of Marx toward Althusser, who carefully articulates and vigorously defends a distinction—one he takes to be absolutely fundamental—between "the real object" and "the object of knowledge." In an infamous phrase, Althusser refers to this border between thought and the real as "the absolutely impassable frontier" (Althusser 2009 [1965]: 210). I call the phrase "infamous" because if Althusser's chosen words prove to be well known, this is not due to their celebrated nature, but because they have frequently been the target of critique, even ridicule. To clarify this situation and get at the stakes of this argument, I now turn to perhaps the most famous and consequential reader of the *1857 Introduction*, Stuart Hall.

CROSSING THE BORDER

Hall's "Marx's Notes on Method: A 'Reading' of the '1857 Introduction'," was a long-standing and extremely significant working paper in the Centre for Contemporary Cultural Studies (CCCS) at Birmingham University.[1] The first version appeared within CCCS in 1973 as a "Stencilled Occasional Paper"; a shorter version appeared the following year in CCCS's so-called house journal, *Working Papers in Cultural Studies*, but it was not included in the book publication of those papers in 1980. Therefore, the paper itself, while clearly very important to the work of Hall and the CCCS over the decade, has not been widely available outside of Birmingham (for this history, see Wise 2003). The essay was first published in widely accessible form in 2003, the year after the closing of CCCS (Hall 2003). As such, we might say that the essay has led a rather mystified life, as it animated the work of the Centre and was taken by many as central to Hall's understanding of the relation between theory and practice (while providing a crucial stage for his engagement with both Marx and Althusser). Yet the essay itself was never addressed directly by thinkers and writers outside of CCCS since it had little or no status as a publication. Its eventual publication was surely untimely, appearing well after the peak of the debates to which it spoke.

Nevertheless, even with its delayed publication, the essay proves highly significant in that it offers one of the most sustained and direct engagements with the *1857 Introduction*, and perhaps more importantly for my purposes here, Hall reads Marx with Althusser's interpretation in mind.

1. CCCS is often shorthanded as "The Birmingham School" (of cultural studies) and just as often referred to synecdochically as "British cultural studies."

Any reader of Althusser will notice how frequently, and with such relish, he cites Marx's 1859 description of the unpublished 1845 manuscripts (appearing much later as *The German Ideology*) as his and Engels's resolution "to settle accounts with our erstwhile philosophical conscience" (Althusser 1969 [1965]: 32; citing Marx 1996b: 161).[2] Althusser's entire reading of Marx hinges on the idea of 1845 marking a dramatic epistemological break, as Marx leaps laterally from the problematic of Feuerbach and Hegel to a new problematic of his own, one that he constructs out of the concepts of political economy.[3] I raise this argument here because it nicely parallels Hall's reading of the *Einleitung*. That is, we can read Hall's previously unpublished manuscript as his own settling of accounts with Althusser. Hall, as is well known, borrows and refines a number of concepts from Althusser, but in a distinction that would make all the difference to Althusser, I would stress that Hall does not take over Althusser's own problematic (Althusser 1969: 46). Hall uses (certain) Althusserian concepts to construct his own problematic—one appropriate to the field of cultural studies as it is articulated by the CCCS within the particular conjuncture of 1970s Britain—and he breaks with Althusser precisely on the question of how to read Marx's *1857 Introduction*.

First, it must not be forgotten that Althusser and Hall are Marxists, and both are very similar sorts of Marxists. They both reject any type of technological determinism in Marx, while also denying a fully humanist reading of his writings; they both resist Hegelian interpretations of Marx; each insists, in his own way, on the importance of history and dynamic historical movement to a full understanding of Marx's work. And thus it should come as no surprise that much of what Althusser says about the *1857 Introduction*—in the countless locations where Althusser cites that text (and always at the most crucial moments of his arguments) across both *For Marx* and *Reading Capital*—goes unquestioned by Hall. Similarly, a great deal of Hall's own close textual reading of the *1857 Introduction* resonates powerfully with the approach to the text taken by Althusser. Keeping this background of immense agreement in mind, let me come straight to their crucial differences. Starting at the most general level allows me to stake out their opposition in the starkest terms, by announcing the critique that each

2. Only the English translation of Althusser's French translation of Marx's German comes up with "erstwhile"; direct English translations of the German merely give "former philosophical conscience."

3. I discussed the Althusserian idea of *problematique* in my Introduction; see Althusser (2009: 50, 171).

author would make of the other. Hall would accuse Althusser of "theoreticism." Althusser would accuse Hall of "empiricism."[4]

This critique (by Hall) and the moment of potential counter-critique (which I will reconstruct from Althusser's works) emerge at the same location in Hall's text. The first half of Hall's somewhat lengthy reading of the *1857 Introduction* (Wise calls the reprinted article a shortened version of the original stenciled paper, but at thirty-seven single-spaced pages it is by no means short) follows a fairly standard Althusserian line. Hall starts by echoing, without citing, Althusser's repeated claim (itself an echo of Marx) that while Marx gives his readers examples of historical materialism, Marx himself never transcribes his dialectic—never outlines the method by which one conducts such analyses. And as I noted earlier, Hall agrees completely with Althusser that this particular text of Marx's proves crucial to understanding Marx's method. Hall proceeds to show, as I've done in detail above, that Marx's critical approach takes shape through his presentation of political economy; Hall calls this "a critique of the ideological presupposition of political economy" (Hall 2003: 115). Hall demonstrates the way in which Marx's reading of the key concepts of political economy sets those concepts into motion and reveals them to be a part of a larger, complex whole. From here, however, Hall goes on to insist on a point that Althusser will reject: for Hall, the critique that Marx offers depends upon "*unmasking*." Indeed, according to Hall, the fact that Marx unmasks the truth that lies beneath false surface appearances is just "what is *scientific* in his dialectic." Hall describes such a process as follows: it is "a method which reveals the 'essential relations' behind the necessary but mystifying inversions assumed by their 'surface forms'" (Hall 2003: 116).

Of course, no contemporary theorist will be all that surprised by this argument. The notion that the Marxist "science" is one of finding a deeper truth within capitalist structures, the idea that Marxism counters the "false representations" of ideology with the materialist realities that underlie them, indeed, the very notion that "ideology critique" (Hall's phrase) amounts to showing ideology to be false—*all of this* resonates with received conceptions of Marx and Marxism. They echo the claims of Frankfurt School Critical Theory and other neo-Marxisms of the twentieth century. I mark out these arguments here because, following Althusser, I will reject them

4. On Althusser's reading, even Gramsci was a particular type of empiricist, and obviously Hall is a self-professed Gramscian. I explore Althusser's unique understanding and critique of empiricism both later in this chapter and in Chapter 4.

in my own reading of Marx.[5] For now, I simply want to show that Hall's emphasis on "unmasking" and so-called ideology critique in his reading of Marx highlights and amplifies his break with Althusser. I am thus drawing out what is at issue between them in that break, which comes after a long and crucial passage from Hall in which he articulates a very much Althusserian understanding of structure in Marx's text.

> We must "think" the relations between the different processes of material production as "members of a totality, distinctions within a unity." That is, as a complexly structured differentiated totality, in which distinctions are not obliterated but preserved—the unity of its "necessary complexity" precisely requiring this differentiation. (Hall 2003: 127)

As Hall will explain in a later lecture focused directly on Althusser, this idea (which Hall here traces out of Marx's text) derives from Althusser—from Althusser's interpretation of Marx. Hall opens that later essay in biographical mode: "Althusser persuaded me, and I remain persuaded, that Marx conceptualizes the ensemble of social relations which make up a whole society . . . as essentially a complex structure, not a simple one" (Hall 1985: 91). For this very reason, Hall goes on to show that contradictions and differences within the Marxist totality—what Hall often follows Althusser in calling the "social formation"—cannot be removed, obliterated, or "sublated" (in Hegelian fashion). A social formation is what Marx calls "a rich totality," one capable of holding within it contradictions, tensions, and a certain "unevenness" between its levels. In other words, the "correspondence" between levels, which Marx so famously refers to in the 1859 Preface, cannot be read as a functional causality (Marx 1996b); there is never a one-to-one relation between levels. As Hall says Althusser taught him: "The notion of simply reading off the different kinds of social contradiction at different levels of social practice in terms of one governing principle of social and economic organization . . . [is] neither useful nor [is it the way] in which Marx, in the end, conceptualized the social totality" (Hall 1985: 91). Given all this agreement between them, and given that Hall's reading of Marx *follows* Althusser so closely in many places, the critique of Althusser may at first seem subtle or easy to miss. It comes right in the middle of the article, and it hinges on Hall's reading of the well-known passages concerning the "scientifically correct" method.

---

5. For another strong rejection of "demystification," and an extremely powerful and historical reading of Marx, see Postone (1993). I have previously addressed some of these broader issues around critical theory in chapter 4 of Chambers (2013).

These theoretically important passages matter for a reason that I failed to remark upon in my above interpretation. The reader who can find a way to pick up the *1857 Introduction* with fresh eyes—one who works through its elliptical, outline format and thinks hard about its philosophical and historical claims—cannot help but be struck by the fact that here, in these particular sections, Marx makes the most radical epistemological reversal of empiricism. Marx rejects directly, what is, for many of us, the most intuitive and commonsensical idea in empiricism: the claim that *knowledge begins with the empirical.* Empiricism tells us to start with the concrete, to begin with what lies right before our eyes or in our hands. But in the *1857 Introduction* Marx says just the opposite: *knowledge begins with the abstract*. When I first taught this text I was somewhat dumbstruck by it—at a loss as to how I could convey such an idea to students.[6] And this is the very idea that fascinates *both* Hall and Althusser concerning this text. Each author comments in later texts, reflecting back on their reading of this one. I quote Althusser first, and then Hall:

> Marx argued that knowledge does not proceed from the concrete to the abstract but from the abstract to the concrete . . . what fascinated me in all this argument was that one had to begin with the abstract. (Althusser 1976: 190)
>
> Marx's insight that critical thought moves away from abstraction to the concrete-in-thought . . . is one of his most profound, most neglected epistemological propositions. (Hall 1985: 92)

Hall and Althusser agree completely on the importance of this argument in Marx's work; they both insist on its significance for social and political theory. Yet for just this reason (the depth of their shared starting point), Hall's subtle criticism of Althusser amounts, in fact, to an important and ultimately decisive departure from him. In the later text from which I quote above, Hall concludes his thought as follows: "which even Althusser himself *somewhat misinterprets*" (Hall 1985: 92, emphasis added). "Somewhat misinterprets" seems like the mildest form of criticism, the sort a teacher would write in the margins of a paper written by a good student with a fragile ego. Yet at the end of this quote, and in order to explain this criticism, Hall cites his own paper on the *1857 Introduction* (still largely unavailable at that time).

---

6. Dwelling on this problem has led me here: the project of this chapter develops in detail the concerns that come from trying to explain and unravel Marx's idea that to understand and to know (especially to understand and to know the arrangement of a social order) one must start with the abstract.

Turning back to Hall's central text on Marx, we see that he takes issue with the conclusions that Althusser draws from his reading of the passages in the *1857 Introduction* on the abstract/concrete relation. First, Hall offers an exegesis of Marx, explaining the idea that the resultant of knowledge and thinking is the concrete. Althusser calls this the "concrete-in-thought" in order to distinguish what Marx means by the concrete we arrive at through thinking, on the one hand, from the idea of starting with an empirical given, on the other. One can clearly see that, on this issue, and as his own starting point, Hall follows Althusser:

> The concrete is concrete, in history, in social production, and thus in conception, not because it is simple and empirical, but because it exhibits a certain kind of necessary complexity. Marx makes a decisive distinction between the "empirically-given," and the concrete. In order to "think" this real, concrete historical complexity, we must reconstruct in the mind the determinations which constitute it. Thus, what is multiply determined, diversely unified, in history, already "a result," appears, in thought, in theory, not as "where we take off from" but as that which must be produced. (Hall 2003: 129)

All of this raises the crucial question of how to understand the nature of thought, of thinking itself, in relation to the world (i.e., vis-à-vis any historically given social order). It becomes a thorny question for Marx and those who are following him here, for reasons I suggested in the previous chapter. That is, empiricism has an easy answer (thought *models* the real) and Hegel has an easy answer (thought *is* the real), but Marx has rejected both of those alternatives. For his part, Althusser has a specific and fully worked-up response that depends upon insisting on a distinction between "the real object" (a "concrete" entity in the world) and "the object of knowledge" (a concrete-in-thought). Hall and Althusser each follow Marx closely when he rejects the Hegelian answer to this question; their detailed readings here track each other tightly.

However, Hall implicitly argues that Marx's rejection of Hegel also undermines the Althusserian position. Thought, says Marx, surely occurs in the head of an individual who thinks, an individual located somewhere in the real. Hegel's mistake, here as always, lies in giving over to a "conceptual process," one that supposedly works in and of itself, that which can only be done by thinking humans located in the material world. Marx's formulation is somewhat obscure, but still forceful: "The concrete totality is in no way a product of the self-delivering concept, of the concept thinking outside or above perception and conception" (1996a: 147). Thought and the real are therefore not the same, not only because thinking cannot be *reduced* to empirical reality but also because thinking cannot *produce* reality.

Hall then carries Marx's criticisms of Hegel one step further; he transfers them into a criticism of Althusser.

> Any theory of "theoretical practice," such as Althusser's, which seeks to establish an "impassable threshold" between thought and its object, has to come to terms with the concrete reference (it is not, in our view, an empiricist reduction) embodied in **Marx's clear and unambiguous notion**, here, that thought proceeds from the "*working-up* of *observation and conception*." (Hall 2003: 130; italics Hall's, bold mine)

Building from Marx's "clear and unambiguous notion" that thought advances by working up observation, Hall goes on to reject the idea of a fundamental distinction between the real object and the object of knowledge. Rather than an "impassable threshold" (my text [Althusser 2009: 210] actually reads "unsurpassable frontier," but the meaning seems similar enough[7]) between thought and being, Hall implies that there is a gap between the two. Most importantly, *it is a gap that can be bridged*, by practice (Hall 2003: 130). If this were not enough to make his distancing from Althusser clear, Hall then favorably cites a much stronger set of criticisms of Althusser. In an essay published in 1971 (two years before Hall's essay first appeared inside the CCCS), Pierre Vilar harshly criticised Althusser for his distinction between the real object and the object of knowledge. Hall says to his readers, in a tone that to my ears sounds simultaneously droll and biting: "We must prefer Vilar's brief but succinct gloss over Althusser's complex but less satisfying ones" (Hall 2003: 130). Hall then proceeds to cite Vilar's appeal to the commonsense notions that thought, while taking place in the head, surely *approaches* the real (Vilar 1973: 74).[8] In sum,

7. "Impassable threshold" might, of course, be Hall's own translation of Althusser's French. However, it is not at all clear from Hall's published essay which texts of Althusser's he was drawing from. Indeed, while the lengthy essay has sixty-four footnotes, and while Hall mentions Althusser by name on numerous occasions (and frequently calls on him implicitly), the text has but *one single citation* of Althusser, a reference to the English translation of *For Marx*. Neither Hall nor Vilar cite the "unsurpassable frontier" passage directly, but I can think of no other passage that Hall *could* be referring to in Althusser's work other than this one, when Hall makes reference to, in inverted commas, the "impassable threshold." In his later essay on Althusser, Hall again cites the standard English translations of *For Marx* and *Reading Capital*, and there can be no doubt that Hall was very much familiar with the latter text when he wrote his earlier essay.

8. Vilar's piece provides a great deal of evidence for my claim here that Hall criticises Althusser both subtly and in a way that marks a serious break. Pointing to Vilar allows Hall to *displace and yet affirm* a very strident critique of Althusser, all while avoiding one major problem—namely, in places, Vilar badly misreads Althusser. I briefly

Hall contends that because Marx's critique of Hegel depends upon showing that thought is always rooted in the real, it also demonstrates that *there is no limit* between thought and the real. Thought must not be confused with the real (à la Hegel), but it can, indeed *does*, *try to reach* the real. Moreover, Hall here clearly implies (without ever saying it in so many words) that to insist, as Althusser does with such force and conviction, upon the gap between the real object and the object of knowledge is to trap oneself inside of theory; it is to ignore, or worse, to eschew real practice in favour of "theoretical practice."[9]

MINDING THE GAP

Hall's critical argument raises two primary questions, one textual, one conceptual. First, what are the actual claims made within the passage in Marx where Hall locates the phrase that he will repeatedly rely upon in his critique of Althusser—"working up of observation and perception"? Second, can we maintain (i.e., is it a tenable philosophical position) a non-Hegelian, non-empiricist epistemology that allows for a *bridgeable* gap between thought and the real? (And how would this position differ from Althusser's?) Let me briefly address the narrowly interpretive question first. Hall, I contend, overemphasises the empiricist resonance, in English, of "the working up of observation"; indeed, he places too much of the weight of his critique of Althusser on this phrase—far more than it can be

mention only two examples here. First, as a historian, Vilar transposes Althusser's extremely broad understanding of empiricism into the very narrow terms in which that concept emerged in debates over historical methodology. The historian falls into empiricism by taking history as a given set of brute facts. But the social theorist falls into empiricism by thinking that his or her concepts will map reality. Hall quotes Vilar's response to Althusser's critique of Engels, where Engels argues that thought approaches the real asymptotically. Vilar's critique amounts to little more than taking up a tone of indignation. But Althusser's explication of Engels's letter shows clearly that Engels unwittingly "falls into empiricism" in the manner of the social theorist. The concerns of empiricism in the discipline of history are not really ones that Althusser shares or perhaps even sees. Second, Vilar (like many later readers) does not see the stakes of "science" in Althusser, and specifically does not see how *different* those stakes are from late twentieth-century debates over making the social sciences into "real sciences." Vilar seems to think that defenders of contemporary economic models defend those models' inadequacies on the same grounds as Althusser defends Marx, a claim that requires turning Marx himself into an empiricist (Vilar 1973: 76).

9. If the critique holds, Althusser himself would name it the problem of theoreticism (see Althusser 1976: 105–6).

made to bear. It is easy to see why this phrase would prove so appealing to Hall in making this argument, and why he would be tempted to cite it, as he does, over and over again. To a 1970s English-speaking audience or reader, this phrase cannot help but sound a bit empiricist. Empiricism is the epistemology that defines knowledge as that which is based upon, derived from, or "worked up" from *observation* and experience. Of course, as the long Hall quote from further above makes clear, Hall does not want to read the phrase as fully empiricist; he refuses, in advance as it were, the idea that this is an "empiricist reduction." This begs the question of how one can A) base thought on the working up of observation, and B) insist on bridging the gap between thought and the real, without also C) ultimately resting such an argument on empiricist epistemology.

I address this thorny issue below, but first I need to demonstrate that Marx himself is surely not making a turn to, or even *toward*, empiricism. Indeed, the phrase that Hall relies so heavily upon has much less "empirical" content to it in the original German. To return to Hall's quote, he stresses the idea that for Marx, "thought proceeds from the '*working-up* of observation and *conception*'," and he calls this notion "clear and unambiguous." However, Hall cites the phrase out of context, so let me start by quoting it more fully. It appears at the conclusion to Marx's critique of Hegel. This is Marx's clarification that the concrete in thought is not generated by an autochthonous conceptual process; rather, thought occurs in the head of thinking human individuals, themselves rooted in society. In that passage, Marx uses Hall's favored phrase twice. He says: "The concrete totality is . . . not in any way a product of the concept *which thinks and generates itself* outside or above observation and conception; [it is] a product, rather, of the working-up of observation and conception into concepts" (Marx 1973: 101, emphasis added, Nicolaus translation). It is human individuals within a particular social formation that work up their thoughts; their conceptual processes are based upon their own "perception and their conception" of and in their socio-material context.

"Perception and conception" is not my paraphrase, but rather Marx's own words from a different translation (Marx 1996a: 147, Carver translation).[10]

10. This is not the first time that an interpretive debate over these passages has been bound up with the difference between the translations by Nicolaus and Carver, respectively, of the *1857 Introduction*, nor is it the first time that the debate has centered on the status of thought in relation to both the subject and the object of knowledge. In a very short (less than four pages) but completely dismissive piece in *Society*, Hartsock and Smith accuse Althusser of utterly misunderstanding Marx, of reading "Marx as saying the exact opposite of what he is really saying" (Hartsock and Smith 1979: 487). They base this charge on Althusser's interpretation of this very same paragraph in

Marx is not saying that the individual subject's thinking process (and the creation of knowledge that would follow from it) is based in any narrow way upon "observation"—*that* is the empiricist claim. Marx is arguing instead that thinking goes on within a human mind, and that mind resides within an individual who is a part of society. "Perception does not begin, in [Marx's] view, with 'mind' or 'consciousness' on its own" (Carver 1975: 136), but this does not make the empirical object (giving off sense-data) primary. In other words, thinking always remains in a relation to the real because the thinker is always rooted in a social formation, yet Marx has no interest in the individual subject as knower who would "observe" the world. Carver's translation of *Anschauung* as "perception" is clearly a better choice than Nicolaus's "observation," but even perception has more resonances with empiricism than *Anschauung*. As Rohrhuber has recently argued, the best translation for *Anschauung*—especially within the context of nineteenth-century German philosophy—is "intuition" (Rohrhuber 2007: 1). *Anschauung* surely implies the notions of both observation and perception, but it does so within the context of Kantian philosophy that formalised *Anschauung* as *reine Anschauung*—that is, *pure intuition* (Rohrhuber 2007: 1). In Kant, *empirische Anschauungen* are empirical/sense perceptions, and *reinische Anschauungen* are "pure" perceptions, derived a priori from concepts/conceptualisation (*Begriffe, begreifen*). Thus, for Kant, perception without conceptual content is empty. For Marx, "the real concrete" (what Althusser calls the "concrete in thought") is human activity. Human activity proves to be, for Marx, both conceptual and material at the same time. Here Marx actually follows Kant's point (no perception without conceptualisation) but twists it around the other way: if humans cannot have knowledge of material things without prior concepts (Kant), then material things have no reality for humans apart from conceptualisations. But this

---

the *Einleitung* that I am discussing in the text above. Hartsock and Smith argue that when Marx says "the real subject retains its autonomous existence outside the head" he is only continuing his critique of Hegel, for whom "the head's conduct is merely speculative, merely theoretical," whereas Althusser leverages this claim to mistakenly "build a philosophy in which the head's conduct is indeed merely speculative" (Hartsock and Smith 1979: 488). In one of the few rigorous treatments of Althusser's thought in the literature of North American political theory, William Corlett (1996) pushes back against this reading, partially by contrasting the Nicolaus translation (used by Hartsock and Smith) with the Carver translation (which Corlett uses). However, even Corlett fails to note the obvious: in quoting Marx, Hartsock and Smith have *left out the last line of the paragraph*, the line that makes it clear that for Marx "the real subject" is *never* either a Hegelian subject or an isolated bourgeois individual. That last line is, of course, one I have quoted before and the one from which I draw the title of this book: "the [real] subject, *society*, must always be borne in mind" (Marx 1996a: 147, emphasis added).

latter argument cannot be understood through Hegel: "material things have reality" *not* through the philosophical activities of pure thought, but through the practical activities of ordinary life.

Therefore, Marx rejects both the matter/consciousness dichotomy and the subject/object dichotomy. This means that subjects can never be said to "observe" objects and derive meaning from them via the senses. Clearly then, we have here a notion of perception and observation as far removed from "empirical observation" as one might imagine. For his part, Rohrhuber suggests words like *presentation* or *representation* to capture the contemporary flavour of the word *Anschauung*. In any case, it would be an obvious mistake to take from Marx's repeated reference to *Anschauung* the idea that Marx starts with the empirical. The key point is different for Marx: "He is always bearing 'society' in mind—i.e., contemporary society, with class conflict, not some abstract fantasy—as the presupposition to his conceptualising work on a 'concrete' (i.e., complex) concept" (T. Carver, personal communication).[11] I insist, in turn, that while we as readers of Marx must never lose sight of his consistent efforts to "bear society in mind"—reading him this way proves essential to grasping Marx's consistent critique of a certain kind of Hegelianism—we must also resist any urge to translate, on the one hand, Marx's emphasis on society as the always-given *background context* for all thought into, on the other, the empiricist idea of "observation" of the world as the starting point for thought. As Hall himself emphasises (but perhaps forgets within his critique of Althusser), thought, for Marx, *emerges from* society, but *starts with* the abstract.

Nevertheless, and as I have already noted, Hall himself does not wish to make Marx into an empiricist, so my textualist critique of Hall's reading of Marx still leaves unanswered the question of the relation between thought and the real (in Marx, in Hall, in Althusser). On this front I want to advance an even stronger argument: despite Hall's claims to the contrary, when he commits himself to understanding the relation between thought and the real as one of a "bridgeable gap," he commits himself to an ineluctable empiricism. One of the tasks of Althusser's work is to prove this point, to show that the idea of thought "approaching the real" *always leads to empiricism.*

---

11. In a general commentary on Althusser's work, Étienne Balibar makes the following comment that fits tightly with Althusser's specific reading of the *1857 Introduction*. He states: "There is of course no philosophy without presuppositions, but the 'real' presupposition is neither Man nor Consciousness (nor the Subject); it can only be the material or structural conditions of the production and transformation of these abstractions" (Balibar 1994: 164). For clarification about the arguments, the concepts, and the German here and in the preceding paragraph, I am deeply indebted to Terrell Carver.

Indeed, Althusser insists so resolutely upon the fundamental distinction between the object of knowledge and the real object because he finds no other way to avoid the pitfalls of both empiricism and Hegelian idealism. Ultimately, Althusser even conceives of Hegelian idealism as but a *variant* of empiricism. Arguments like these hinge upon Althusser's very particular (and perhaps peculiar) understanding of empiricism as a broad ideological notion. In the preface to the English translation of *For Marx*,[12] Althusser explains that he understands the essays in that volume to contain a double intervention into a specific political conjuncture.

> The object of *the first intervention* is to "draw a line of demarcation" between Marxist theory and the forms of philosophical (and political subjectivism) which have compromised or threatened it: above all, *empiricism*, and its variants, classical and modern—pragmatism, voluntarism, historicism, etc. (Althusser 1969: 12)

This passage indicates clearly, first, that Althusser makes empiricism *much more important* as a theoretical enemy than most other Marxists and most other political theorists writing at this time, and, second, that Althusser conceives of empiricism *much more broadly* than most other thinkers would do. A late twentieth-century text on social science methodology would undoubtedly *distinguish* between the various forms of thought that Althusser collapses together here under the heading of empiricism. And, no doubt, most social theorists would argue that historicism and pragmatism are very much distinct epistemologies, perhaps even best understood as *critiques* of empiricism. In this post hoc account of *For Marx*, Althusser is quite obviously working with a unique account of empiricism.

Yet he cannot be accused of smuggling this account in, as ammunition for his critique, or of defining the term in his own way without explaining why. In *Reading Capital*, Althusser devotes a large section of his substantive introductory essay to his broad conception and fundamental critique of empiricism. This argument has received relatively little attention by readers of Althusser, possibly because the introduction also contains Althusser's dense defence of a "symptomatic reading" of Marx, and the hermeneutic

---

12. This preface appears under the heading "To My English Readers," a title probably meant only to convey that the text would be read in the English language. Yet the title also conveys traces of either French parochialism on Althusser's part (where the only non-French speakers that matter are the English across the channel) or a general English parochialism on Brewster's (where those who read English are English). In any case, the title does say something about the nature of the debates over Marxism at the time, in which it probably was true to some extent that Althusser would be read in English translation mainly by English Marxists.

argument that Althusser makes there (while certainly defensible on its own terms) also proves enormously easy to cite out of context in such a way as to make Althusser appear naive. That is, a few choice quotes can turn "symptomatic reading" into sheer stupidity. Tony Judt offers the following, which he seems to intend as a genuine summary of the project in *Reading Capital*: "Althusser was engaged in what he and his acolytes called a 'symptomatic reading' of Marx, which is to say that they took from him what they needed and ignored the rest," and then "interpreted the 'silences'" to make up anything they felt was missing (Judt 2008: 107). I mention these critiques not to address them directly here but because Althusser's more significant engagement with empiricism seems to have been buried underneath them.

That engagement commences in section 10 of the introduction, and Althusser marks it clearly as a "detour" for which he requests "the reader's indulgence" (Althusser 2009: 37). In section 9 Althusser has just reached a key stage in his logic when he articulates an interpretive paradox, a new wrinkle on the hermeneutic circle. He concludes that section with the claim that a rigorous reading of *Capital* depends upon working with the very conception of knowledge that is only really produced by *Capital* itself—produced by the entirety of the Marxist revolution in thinking. This specific set of claims about interpreting Marx mirrors Althusser's broader argument about Marxist philosophy and science. Using the Kuhnian language that may be more familiar to readers of this text (but was not used by Althusser), I would put it like this: *Marx's work produces a paradigm shift that it never announces as such.* Readers of Marx (i.e., Althusser, his students, and their readers) must themselves describe the shift, must sketch out the new paradigm, so as to reread Marx's texts within the paradigm that those texts themselves produce (rather than confining the texts to the old paradigm). Therefore, for Althusser, accounting for what I am calling a new paradigm requires articulating what he describes and emphasises as "*a new conception of knowledge*" (2009: 37).

It follows that this new conception of knowledge must first and foremost be distinct from "*the empiricist conception of knowledge*" (again, Althusser's italics), a term that Althusser uses—he tells his readers this immediately—"in its widest sense" (2009: 37). This broad understanding of empiricism, for Althusser, depends upon a few key elements. In empiricism, one always begins with a given subject that remains distinct from a given object. Between them lies the key *process* of empiricist epistemology: "to know is to abstract from the real object its essence, the possession of which by the subject is then called knowledge" (Althusser 2009: 38). According to Althusser, for empiricism knowledge always depends upon a process of *extraction*, of separating out the essential from the inessential. Empiricism "scours" the real object, seeking to purge the inessential, to capture the essential among the "dross" (a word Althusser uses repeatedly to capture the sense of this process, to make digging for gold resonate with empiricist knowledge production).

Here we see emerge a concept of "the real"—a phrase that Althusser repeats throughout his writings, and which, as I have shown above, proves so pivotal to the criticisms of his work. By sketching out this account, however, it becomes quite clear that for Althusser "the real" is never a given thing, and for this reason Althusser's references to "the real" should never be taken as evidence of some sort of brute "realism" on his part.[13] In his accounts, in contrast, the real always takes on a precise specification depending upon the conception of knowledge at work. *For empiricism*, then, we can say that "the real . . . is structured as a dross of earth containing inside it a grain of pure gold" (Althusser 2009: 38). The real, for empiricism, is that field of the object from which the knowing subject will extract (through the process of abstraction) *real knowledge*. This means that the real is a field containing two absolute distinct elements: the essential and inessential. The function of knowledge lies in removing or eliminating the "inessential real" so that the knowing subject winds up with only the essential real. Althusser says this occurs through "a whole series of sortings, sievings, scrapings, and rubbings" (2009: 39).

He then adds a crucial final dimension to his interpretation of empiricism: this entire series of "extraction processes" *is itself excluded* from the empiricist conception of knowledge. The "scouring procedures" produce the essential real, the pure form of the object of knowledge, yet they "leave no trace in the extracted part" (Althusser 2009: 39). In the place of scrapings and sievings and all the rest, empiricism leaves us only with the knowing subject and the real object (the shining, pure gold); between them lies only abstraction. The work of extraction that abstraction must do is always rendered mute and invisible; we neither hear it nor see it. However, Althusser contends that we can locate a trace of the trace of this process. We can find this mark not in the real object that empiricism produces, but in the very structure of the field of the real. Empiricism structures the field of the real such that the inessential part appears on the *outside* and the essential part lies on the *inside*. "If the essence is not immediately *visible*, it is because it is concealed, in the strong sense, i.e., entirely covered and enveloped by the dross of the *inessential*" (Althusser 2009: 39). This structure

13. Here I disagree entirely with Hall's comment that the early Althusser takes up "a 'realist' philosophical position" (Hall 1985: 105).

provides Althusser with a space, a "critical distance," to think a conception of knowledge truly distinct from empiricism.

The key insight lies here: for empiricism, knowledge is ultimately always already *contained within* the real; that is, knowledge is "*inscribed in the structure of the real object*" (Althusser 2009: 40). Knowledge is always a knowledge *of* the real, a process invested *in* the real. Knowledge only arises, can only be produced, as a relation *inside* the real object (through the process of separating the inessential from the essential). For Althusser, the empiricist conception of knowledge itself contains the key element of, or suggestion for, an alternative conception of knowledge. It does so because empiricism at once *sees the difference* between the real object and the object of knowledge—it conveys the all-important sense that the process of knowledge produces a different object than that which already lies before us in the real—and at the same time it *obliterates that difference.*

> When empiricism designates the essence as the object of knowledge, it admits something important and denegates it in the same instant: it admits that *the object of knowledge is not identical to the real object*, since it declares that it is only a part of the real object. But it denegates what it has admitted, precisely by reducing this difference between two objects, the object of knowledge and the real object, to a mere distinction between the parts of a single object: the real object. (Althusser 2009: 42–43, emphasis added)

By obliterating that difference, empiricism ultimately reduces knowledge to the real; "in the denegation there is no longer more than one object: the real object" (Althusser 2009: 43). Empiricism insists that the gap between the real object and the object of knowledge—the very gap that the empiricist epistemology itself has opened—must ultimately be closed. Empiricism demands that the gap is only temporary, that the process of knowledge is itself a process that closes the gap; the knowing process can *reconcile* the object of knowledge with the real object. Ultimately, there is *nothing but* the real object.

Despite this conclusion—this final reduction to the real that remains central to empiricism in its self-understanding—Althusser nonetheless glimpses in empiricism a possibility for a new conception, one that would maintain the difference between the object of knowledge and the real object. That new conception can be culled from Marx, and it will come as no surprise at all that for that new conception Althusser turns to the *1857 Introduction*—section 3, of course. Thus, it is exactly here, in the context of describing empiricism and in articulating a critical alternative to it, that Althusser offers his own reading of the famous passages in Marx's *1857 Introduction* that I have explicated above. In this context, Althusser shows how Hegelian idealism is really a special variety of empiricism. Marx's criticism of Hegel for reducing the real to thought parallels Althusser's criticism of empiricism for negating the difference between the real object and the object of knowledge. Althusser argues that

> Marx defends the *distinction* between the *real object* (the real-concrete[,] the real totality, which "*survives in its independence, after as before, outside the head*") and the *object of knowledge*, a product of the thought which produces it in itself as a thought-concrete (*Gedankenkonkretum*), as a thought-totality (*Gedankentotalität*), i.e. as a *thought-object* absolutely distinct from the real-object, the real-concrete, the real totality. (Althusser 2009: 43–44)

Althusser thereby insists on a distinction between an order that produces the real object in history, and an order of knowledge that goes on in thought.

He follows this argument with a strong clarification: to maintain rigorously the distinction between the real object and the object of thought does not mean that Marx "fall[s] into an idealism of consciousness." Thought, the thought-concrete (*Gedankenkonkretum*) that we must distinguish from the real object, is not somehow merely or purely mental. It is part of the social formation: "This thought is the historically constituted system of an *apparatus of thought*, **founded on and articulated to natural and social reality**" (Althusser 2009: 44; italics Althusser's, bold mine). I have emphasised this last phrase to stress that thought is not abstract consciousness, either for Marx or for Althusser. Thought emerges from and speaks to the social formation. Althusser's later comments about history, offered in a different context, can highlight the argument here. He writes: "History is an immense *natural-human* system in movement" (Althusser 1976: 51). Althusser argues that as long as we understand thought as the *Gedankenkonkretum* as a part of this natural-human movement of history, then we can at the same time maintain the distinction between the object of thought, on the one hand, and the real object, on the other. Having described thought's relation to the social formation in this way, Althusser can defend Marx's lines in the *1857 Introduction* where Marx asserts that the process of knowledge itself *takes place entirely in the domain of thought*.

Crucially, at just this point Althusser gives his own rendering of Hall's favored phrase.[14] Brewster's translation of Althusser's French gives us the following in English: "It is perfectly legitimate to imagine . . . thought's

---

14. Hall's critique of Althusser, as I have shown, relies heavily on this phrase, but the critique remains at a very general level with respect to Althusser's writings. Hall hardly cites Althusser's texts, and he certainly does not mention Althusser's specific readings of the passages in question in Marx.

labour on its raw material (the object it works on) as the '*labour of transformation* (Verarbeitung) of *intuition* (Anschauung) *and representation* (Vorstellung) *into concepts* (in Begriffe)'" (Althusser, 2009: 45; citing Marx 1996a, 147). This is obviously a non-parallel comparison of translations, but by coming to Brewster's English by way of Althusser's French, we end up with something very much distinct from the Nicolaus translation that Hall works with. For Hall's (i.e., Nicolaus's) "working up" we have the "labour of transformation"; for his "observation" we have "intuition"; and for "conception" we have "representation." Contrary to Hall's attempt to read this as a place where Marx concedes to a bridgeable gap between thought and the real, Althusser interprets these passages as further insistence on, and clarification of, the limit that separates the two.

Moreover, in *For Marx* Althusser relies on just these passages to propose his *infamous* typology of "Generalities," so commonly taken as damning evidence of Althusser's obfuscation. However, when read in context, one need not stretch to see Althusser's language of "generalities" as a genuine attempt to interpret and clarify Marx's admittedly "most difficult, compressed and 'illegible'" (Hall 2003: 113) text. Thus, Althusser coins the notion of "Generality I" in an attempt to make sense of Marx's radical claim that thought starts not with the concrete (or the empirically given object) but with the abstract. The starting point for thought, in the abstract, is Generality I; it is what Althusser calls the "raw material" for a theoretical or scientific practice, in the simple sense that *given generalities are what we go to work on in thinking* (1969: 183). The importance of this point lies not in the idea that intellectual work is labour in the same sense as physical work would be. Many of Althusser's critics have taken him to task for this idea, for both privileging the role of the intellectual and denying the uniqueness of the proletariat's labour. It is by no means clear on my reading of the texts that Althusser intends to do either of these things, but, in any event, "Generality I" proves significant for a different reason entirely. It shows us two things: 1) thought does not begin with the empirical object (an old, repeated claim); 2) thought does not simply seek to dispel the myths of the given abstract generalities it starts with (a new claim). In other words, the job of thinking cannot be to reveal that abstract universals are false, or naive (Althusser 1969: 183). The task of thinking is to move from the abstract, the given generality (Generality I) to what Marx calls the concrete in thought (*Gedankenkonkretum*) and Althusser names Generality III.[15]

15. Generality II plays a minor and, as he himself admits, underdeveloped role in Althusser's arguments. It is comprised of the given body of terms and concepts of the theory or science of the day—"the corpus of concepts . . . at the (historical) moment of

The language of generalities does nothing more than translate Marx's argument from the *1857 Introduction*. It does so, however, with an important twist, since it allows Althusser to leverage Marx's arguments in order to make a forceful critique of empiricism in the broad sense that Althusser has already outlined. Althusser asserts: "when Marx declares" that thought or science starts with and works on a given generality (the "raw material" of Generality I), "he is putting before us *a new model which no longer bears any relation to the empiricist model* of the production of a concept by good abstraction" (1969: 190, emphasis added). And this is not just a *critique* of empiricism, but an *alternative* to it. Althusser explains by way of a simple yet robust example: the concept of "fruit." The concept does not derive from the abstraction of a knowing subject who would look at many examples of fruit and then derive their concept from those individual empirical instances of it. It is simply naive to think that this is where concepts come from. "[T]he concept of fruit is itself the product of distinct practices, dietary, agricultural, or even magical, religious, and ideological" (Althusser 1969: 191). Concepts, abstractions, are themselves products of a social formation and its historical development. This simple point has numerous implications, yet one of them stands out: the process of thinking will work on concepts that are "ideological," but the goal of this process will *not* be to dispel the myth of ideology, or to pierce the veil and find what lies behind them. We work with concepts that are "ideological," simply because ideology "is one of the basic practices essential to the existence of the social whole" (Althusser 1969: 191).

Therefore, "the real object" is never the goal that Marxist epistemology seeks. At the very end of the section on empiricism in *Reading Capital*, Althusser clarifies how and why we must distinguish between the "real object" and the "object of knowledge":

> Knowledge working on its "object," then, does not work on the *real* object but on the peculiar raw material, which constitutes, in the strict sense of term, *its* "*object*" *(of knowledge)*, and which, even in the most rudimentary forms of knowledge is distinct from the *real object*. (Althusser 2009: 46)

The object of knowledge always emerges within Generality I. It is an abstract and general concept produced by history. The real object is always society itself, but only where "society" must be thought as an uneven and complex social whole—the social formation. For the empiricist notion of a

---

consideration" (Althusser 1969: 184; cf. Althusser 1969: 251). To translate, once again, Althusser's understanding of science into Kuhnian language, we might call Generality II "normal science."

real object whose essence would be abstracted from the inessential dross of the broader field of the real, Marx substitutes the social formation—what Althusser calls "a pre-given, complex structured whole" (1969: 193). In the *1857 Introduction* Marx repeatedly demonstrates that production, distribution, exchange, and consumption are all, simultaneously, both valid abstract categories *and processes that go on in society*. And when Marx stresses that the category of "production" can and must always be connected back to "production at a determinate stage in social development of the production of individuals living in *society*" (1996a: 130), Althusser continues by saying, "that is, *in a structured social whole*" (1969: 195, emphasis added).

Ultimately, by insisting that the real is not the real object of knowledge, by showing that "the real" is a real society, a social formation, Althusser makes his case for his commitment to the idea of an "impassable frontier" between thought and the real. We see that the understanding, explanation, and transformation of the social formation can never be carried out by an empiricist project that would seek an origin or try to grasp the real directly.

> Instead of the ideological myth of a philosophy of origins and its organic concepts, Marxism establishes in principle the recognition of the givenness of the complex structure of any concrete "object," a structure which governs both the development of the object and the development of the theoretical practice which produces knowledge of it. *There is no longer any original essence, only an ever pre-givenness*. (Althusser 1969: 198–99, emphasis added)

In asserting that there is no longer any original essence, Althusser succinctly conveys here, at the end of *For Marx*, what he will explain in such detail in the introduction of *Reading Capital*: Marx's project and our understanding of it must be distinguished *in toto* from the empiricist conception of knowledge. This effort to maintain the difference between a new Marxist paradigm (with a new conception of knowledge) and all variants of empiricism, drives Althusser to insist continually, and sometimes seemingly dogmatically, on the difference between the object of knowledge and the real object. And it is precisely from those more strident formulations of this distinction, which come toward the end of Althusser's contribution to *Reading Capital*, that both Hall and Vilar want to take their distance.

BEYOND EMPIRICISM

However, if we look at those passages closely, and if we read them in the context of Althusser's very consistent project to formulate Marx's conception of knowledge in opposition to empiricism, then we are drawn, I argue, to two conclusions. First, the grounds on which Hall and Vilar criticise Althusser are nothing less than the grounds of empiricist common sense.[16] And second, to pose the relation between thought and the real (between concepts and their real objects) as asymptotic, ultimately reduces—and despite explicit protestations to the contrary—to an empiricist conception of knowledge. I will defend these two claims in the process of setting out one more reading of Althusser, this time covering not only his most pointed arguments about the thought/real distinction but also those passages in which he is called to task by Vilar and Hall.

In chapter 3 of part II of *Reading Capital*, Althusser turns *yet again* to section 3 of the *1857 Introduction*. It is at just this moment that he makes the comparison, which I quoted at the beginning of Chapter 2, between this section of Marx's unpublished manuscript and Descartes's famous *Discourse on Method*. With this framing in mind, Althusser argues that this text allows Marx to distinguish his method from both speculative philosophy and empiricism (and we have already seen that Althusser sees the former as a peculiar species of the latter). "The decisive point of Marx's thesis concerns the principle distinguishing between the *real* and *thought*" (Althusser 2009: 95). From this fundamental principle we can derive, in turn, two theses: Althusser names them "the primacy of the real" and "the specificity of thought." Although it sometimes seems forgotten in criticisms of Althusser, he maintains the first thesis for obvious reasons: the real is primary because all thought is rooted in the real—in a particular social formation. Althusser identifies the latter thesis in the lines I have already quoted concerning the "concrete in thought": the *Gedankenkonkretum* is neither the real itself (Hegel) nor reducible to it (empiricism).

At this point Althusser clarifies the meaning and stakes of the real/thought distinction, and does so in a way that shows the subtlety and nuance of what he will nonetheless later refer to as a limit. For this reason, I quote at length:

> No doubt there is a relation between *thought*-about-the-real and this *real*, but it is a relation of *knowledge*, a relation of adequacy or inadequacy of knowledge, not a real relation, meaning by this a relation inscribed in *that real* of

16. And the grounds of common sense are brought in for devastating critique by Hall himself, following Althusser, in his later essay. In response to appeals to common sense, Hall says: "Here, we are most under the sway of the highly ideological structures of all [*sic*]—common sense, the regime of the 'taken for granted'. The point at which we lose sight of the fact that sense is a production of our systems of representation is the point at which we fall, not into Nature, but into the naturalist illusion" (Hall 1985: 105).

> which the thought is the (adequate or inadequate) knowledge. This knowledge relation between knowledge of the real and the real is not a relation *of the real* that is known in this relationship. **The distinction between a relation of knowledge and a relation of the real is a fundamental one**: if we did not respect it we should fall irreversibly into either speculative or empiricist idealism. Into speculative idealism if, with Hegel, we confused thought and the real by reducing the real to thought . . . ; into empiricist idealism if we confused thought with the real by reducing thought about the real to the real itself. In either case, this double reduction consists of a projection and realization of one element in the other: of thinking the difference between the real and thought about it as either a difference within thought itself (speculative idealism) or as a difference with the real itself (empiricist idealism). (Althusser 2009: 96; italics Althusser's, bold mine)

Althusser's first line here emphasises a crucial point that I would argue is missed by Hall and Vilar's critique: Althusser does not circumscribe thought from the real so radically as to make them mutually exclusive. There are clearly important *relations* between thought and the real. In this passage, and as I have emphasised to bring out this point, what is *fundamental* is not a thought/real dichotomy. What is fundamental is the difference between two different relations: on the one hand, a relation *between* thought and the real, and on the other, a relation *within the real.* For empiricism, the difference between the essential and inessential is a difference written within the real itself. For Marx, thought has a specificity; thought about the real is not contained within the real itself. And therefore the relation of thought to the real is a knowledge relation and not a "real relation." Moreover, to deny that it is a "real relation" is not to suggest that it would somehow be "false" but rather to indicate that it is not a relation to be located within the real itself.[17]

All of this means that when Althusser criticises Engels for promoting an understanding of thought and the real as "asymptotic" (2009: 89), or when he insists on an "impassable frontier," he is not suggesting that there is no relation between thought and the real. Quite to the contrary, he underscores the importance of that very relation in a way that is diametrically opposed to the empiricist conception of it. We can now see how problematic Hall's rendering of Althusser's argument truly proves to be: Hall criticises Althusser's supposed effort to "establish an 'impassable threshold' between

---

17. When read in this context, we can see Althusser as providing something of his own example in *For Marx*, where he writes: "In reality, the bourgeoisie has to believe in its own myth before it can convince others, and not only so as to convince others, since what it lives in its ideology *is the very relation* between it and its real conditions of existence which allows it simultaneously to act on itself . . . and on others" (Althusser 1969: 234).

thought and its object" (Hall 2003: 130), whereas Althusser himself affirms a relation between thought and the real. Moreover, Althusser's "impassable frontier" is not simply a line that cannot be crossed, as Hall tends to suggest. Instead, Althusser's "impassable frontier" reads much more like a Derridean conception of *limit*, as Althusser explains in the remainder of the passage. Althusser italicises the passage himself, but this does not seem to have called Hall's attention to it. Althusser says we do not

> set foot beyond the impassable frontier which separates the "development" or specification of the concept from the development and particularity of things—and for very good reason: *this frontier is impassable in principle* **because it cannot be a frontier**, *because there is no common homogeneous space (spirit or real) between the abstract of the concept of a thing and the empirical concrete of this thing which could justify the use of the concept of a frontier.* (Althusser 2009: 210; italics Althusser's, bold mine)

In other words, *the very idea of a frontier is an empiricist one.* It is empiricism that sees a frontier between the knowing subject and the real object to be known. It is empiricism that conveys the idea of that frontier being crossed by the extractive process of knowing. Empiricism passes through the frontier in order to pierce the veil of inessential appearances and find the essence within, deep inside the real. Althusser's reference to an "impassable frontier" is therefore not meant to fix or instantiate a barrier between thought and the real but to challenge the entire empiricist understanding of the relation between the two.

Something quite similar goes for Engels's asymptotic relation between concepts and things. Let me quickly recall Vilar's response to this short chapter in *Reading Capital*: "I fail to see what 'astounding' mistake Engels was committing when he wrote (in a letter, incidentally, as a casual image) that conceptual thought progressed 'asymptotically' towards the real" (Vilar 1973: 75). Vilar's tone, both in this passage and in the longer excerpt from which I draw it, proves very significant: his disdain suggests that Althusser is protesting too much, that Althusser cannot see what lies right before him in common sense. How can he complain at such length about a few lines in a letter? What on earth could be wrong with saying that thought approaches reality? I contend that Vilar's implied rhetorical questions (they are implied by the attitude of his critique) are quite possibly excessive and surely misplaced, since Althusser gives a specific (and, he thinks, important) answer. Althusser's comments on Engels's letter come only a dozen or so pages after his initial outline of empiricism (and it is just this context that is consistently elided in the critiques). The engagement with Engels is intended to show that even within a Marxist tradition there are numerous layers of reception and interpretation (see Carver 2010). Moreover, these layers run across different political conjunctures, making it very difficult to see Marx's work as a paradigm shift. That is, it is easy to read Marx through the lens of the very paradigm that he is, in fact, supplanting (even Marx often uses a classical language of opposition between appearance and essence, Althusser 2009: 211). To grasp Marx's "breakthrough" requires a consistent effort to resist reading his arguments within the frame of the empiricist conception of knowledge.

Althusser argues here that Engels falls into this trap (falls back into the empiricist paradigm) in the letter to Schmidt. Schmidt had criticised Marx for proposing "metaphysical," "philosophical," and perhaps above all, "non-economic" concepts that do not bear directly on economic reality. One can almost hear Althusser's suppressed answer to Schmidt's objection: it is not the job of concepts to capture or describe a relation within the real. Instead of responding, however, Althusser points to Engels's own reply as an example of the phenomenon under discussion in this chapter. Engels tells Schmidt that his criticisms do not apply to Marx insomuch as they "apply to all concepts, regarded from the standpoint of reality," and such concepts correspond to reality "only with asymptotic approximation" (Engels 2000 [1895]; quoted in Althusser 2009: 90). Contra Vilar, in his commentary on this letter Althusser never says that the final phrase is an "astounding error"; rather, he calls the entire response "astounding." And Althusser never refers to an "error" on Engels's part; Althusser asserts instead that Engels's "answer is beside the point" (2009: 90). What, then, is the point? Althusser wants to make clear, and he uses Engels's reply for just this purpose, that the object of knowledge does not coincide with the real object. Thus, "Marx's object" in *Capital* is not an object in the real, and the conception of knowledge advanced by *Capital* cannot be based on extracting the essential from the inessential within the field of the real. Instead, the object of *Capital* must be an object of knowledge; as with all thought, it may therefore contain a relation to the real, but that relation (a knowledge relation) will be very much distinct from a relation *within* the real.

The question of the "adequacy" of Marx's object of knowledge in *Capital* cannot be translated into the adequacy of that object to approximate, or to approach asymptotically, a real object. Therefore, when Engels tries to defend Marx by saying that all concepts are inadequate—inadequate "by virtue of some original sin which affects all concepts" (says Althusser derisively)—he misses the point. Althusser's crucial response to Vilar's rhetorical question (what's wrong with saying concepts approach the real?) appears at this juncture: "Engels therefore transfers to an empiricist theory of knowledge, as a native weakness of the concept, precisely what constitutes the theoretical strength of Marx's adequate concept" (Althusser 2009: 90). Let me unpack this claim. First, the idea that all concepts are inadequate to their objects must be understood as part and parcel of the empiricist conception of knowledge. The dream of empiricism, we might say, would be to do away with the process of knowledge and live an unmediated relation to the real, to be *in* the real, to *be* the real. It is only from this perspective that all concepts fail to live up to standards, because no concept can be perfectly adequate to the essential real relation that it hopes to grasp. So for empiricism, concepts have a "native weakness." But for Marx, concepts are not supposed to "live up" to the real; they can only be "judged" in relation to the objects of knowledge that they produce. Their goal is to think the concrete in thought, not to grasp the real. And this means that an adequate Marxist concept will be exactly one that eschews correspondence to the real, one that embraces what Althusser calls the "native weakness" of empiricist concepts. Hence, Engels's reply astounds Althusser because it is guided by an implicit "empiricist theory of knowledge" (2009: 90), and he quotes Engels at length so as to provide an illustrative example of the temptations to reduce Marx's thought to empiricism, even by Engels himself.[18]

A THEORY OF SOCIAL FORMATIONS

My extended interpretation and defence of Althusser's insistence on maintaining a distinction between the real object and the object of knowledge serves as a direct response to what I would now be prepared to describe as Hall's misreading of Marx's *1857 Introduction.* When Hall departs from Althusser he also departs from Marx. This claim should in no way be taken to indicate the infallibility of Althusser's reading of Marx, but it does suggest the power and importance of Althusser's reading when it comes to this particular issue. Much more importantly, however, and as I promised at the outset, this final discussion of Althusser's subtle-yet-radical critique of empiricism shows the centrality of the real object/object of knowledge

---

18. At just this location in the reading of the *1857 Introduction*, one could return to the much more famous 1859 Preface and read it in the context it was written—that is, as another take on introducing the approach to political economy that Marx would carry out in *Capital*, as another way of thinking through methodological guidelines for how to study Marx's subject, society (the social formation). To reread the 1859 Preface in the context of the arguments I have just worked through here is to bring to light an entirely different sense of what Marx may have meant by "base," by "superstructure," by "correspondence," and so on. For one attempt to read the 1859 Preface in this way, see Carver (1982).

distinction to a theory of the social formation. To give an account of the social formation requires bearing society in mind, and it requires bearing in mind the gap between the real object and the object of knowledge. Thus, tracing through and defending this Althusserian argument ultimately helps to complete the indirect epistemological account of the concept of the social formation that I proposed to offer at the beginning of Chapter 2. Put succinctly, we can say that the real exists within the social formation, yet a political theory ("scientific" or not) of social formations cannot be carried out by way of an attempt to grasp the real directly. Instead, such a theory must start from a definite, particular social formation (and the "abstractions" that are its givens) in order to think the relation between the real and thought. Marx's *1857 Introduction* can thereby be seen to sketch the outlines not of a "*Marxist* political theory" but of a theory of politics spurred, provoked, and inspired by the writings of Marx. This is a political theory of the social formation.

4

The Temporality of Social Formations

The last two chapters developed a particular understanding, a more exact conceptualisation, of the social formation. That is, my layered readings of Marx's *1857 Introduction* served to build up a specific sort of "concept" of the social formation, while at the same time showing specifically why the concept "social formation" is precisely not the sort to be applied to a putative reality "out there." Rather, the work of conceptualising the social formation is itself always a part of, and made possible by, the concrete historical conjuncture. In illustrating this claim through the engagement with Althusser's epistemological arguments, I have demonstrated the point I asserted in my Introduction: the social formation cannot be abstracted from its *problematique*. Concomitantly, "the real" cannot be separated from the social formation. These conclusions can be shown to have numerous consequences, but one rather direct one is as follows: theories of the social formation impact, constrain, and help determine both the way that we approach the work of conceptualisation in political theory and how we relate that work to politics. Such linkages cannot be worked out well in generalising or abstract terms, and for that reason I turn in this chapter to reassess one particular area of contemporary political theory: that devoted to radical understandings of non-linear temporality. Put differently, I want to rethink this strand of thought through the terms of the social formation and thereby further illuminate the crucial issue of structure and change vis-à-vis social orders.

RADICAL TEMPORALITY IN CONTEMPORARY THEORY

Many recent works in contemporary political theory have focused on a topic that Heidegger long ago identified as "the concept of time." In particular, certain contemporary theorists have called for a turn toward a more radical thinking of temporality—one that would prove more appropriate to, and more robust in thinking through, contemporary politics. While this work has certainly not attained the status of a central debate in the field (others eclipse it in terms of both quantity of work and intensity of dispute), I contend that it marks an important turn in contemporary theory. The language these thinkers use to describe their own understanding of time differs, but the various approaches all converge on the idea of a distinct temporality (a "second time" as it were) that we can clearly and sharply distinguish from dominant, mainstream, or everyday concepts of time. Under the former heading—that is, a new thinking of time—we find a diverse set of names/concepts: duration, disruptive time, time as becoming, spectrality, time out of joint, untimeliness, hauntology. Under the latter heading—that is, that which these concepts resist, subvert, or offer alternatives to—we find a narrower grouping: clock time and chrono-time, progress and progressivism, teleology, and, above all, *linear time* (Chambers 2003; Brown 2005; Connolly 2002; Connolly 2005; Grosz 2004; Widder 2008; Hutchings 2008; Rahman 2009).

There can be no doubt that these works differ, sometimes dramatically, in their theoretical targets and their political goals, with investigations that range from liberalism, to pluralism, to evolution, to ontology, and back to democracy. I have no wish to minimise the diversity of these distinct articulations of radical conceptions of temporality, nor to downplay the importance of this overall turn to untimeliness in political theory. Nonetheless, in an effort to advance the very enterprise on radical temporality and politics to which these works are committed, I suggest that we view them from a perspective that reveals a certain set of commonalities, commonalities which may also mark the limits of this project as currently formulated. One such shared attribute can be found in the fact that "time" often enters into the discourse of contemporary political theory in phenomenological and existentialist flavors. What I mean by this is not that the work on temporality is dominated by phenomenological and existentialist philosophy, but that time is taken to be important *as the experience of a subject*. Contemporary theorists try to reconceptualise temporality in a manner more suitable to politics by starting with different experiences of temporality. Thus, we experience time not only as clock time but also as duration; we experience the linear flow of time, but we also experience its disruptions; our very encounter with time reveals to us that time is out of joint. These experiences therefore provide guidance for new concepts of time, and these concepts are meant to be more suitable for politics to just the extent that they reflect the experience of subjects.[1]

By reconsidering temporality in relation to the structure of larger social orders, this chapter defends a thinking of time that goes beyond experience. To unpack this claim and to articulate an argument in support of it, I start by suggesting that the recent turn in contemporary political theory toward untimeliness might itself be considered untimely in the sense of arriving on the scene *late*. The ground that a writer like Derrida appears to uncover may have already been trod by his teacher, Althusser. Althusser certainly has no reputation as a thinker of great historical sense (the "structuralist" label rescinds such a title before it could even be granted), nor as a theorist of radical temporality; none of the contemporary theorists cited above rely on or even mention his work. Yet contained within Althusser's project of rereading Marx we can find just that: a theory of untimeliness prior to the coining of the term; a thoroughgoing rejection of linear and everyday time (Althusser 1969 [1965]; Althusser 2009 [1965]).

Moreover, as should already be clear from my engagement with Althusser on epistemology in the preceding chapter, Althusser does a great deal more than simply "think untimeliness" earlier. Rather than *contribute* to a debate over "the concept of time" (in which, I think, much of the recent discussions have been trapped), Althusser—along with the approach to the social formations that I have been developing throughout the book—makes it possible to reconceive the debate entirely (perhaps even to mark or effect an epistemological break with the current terms of debate). Because he, like Marx, is always giving an account of the social order, always bearing society in mind, Althusser's work enables a reconsideration of radical understandings of temporality, one that eschews the temptation to derive a concept and apply it to "the real." Put simply, Althusser relates temporality to questions of history and of the social formation, thereby extracting "untimeliness" from existential, phenomenological, and human-centered contexts. In so doing, he introduces a number of conceptual innovations that, I argue, can help to significantly rework the terrain of temporality and politics—while simultaneously placing into relief the stakes of both theories and politics of the social formation.

---

1. One might go further to argue that the existential account of temporality tends to point toward a subject's experience of temporality (in the form of event, of rupture, of disjointedness) as an experience of *freedom*. Under this line of logic one could also explore the extent to which, from Althusser's perspective, contemporary accounts of temporality are humanist in their approach and implications. I place these considerations to the side, and herein I neither advance this argument nor distance my account from it.

As I explained in detail in the previous chapter, Althusser was opposed, perhaps most of all, to what he saw as the "ideology of empiricism," and he understood empiricism very broadly as an epistemology that took knowledge as the experience and possession of the knowing subject, who would *extract* knowledge of the "real object" from all that is inessential. In this light one might fairly describe Althusser's entire project as the effort to give a non-empiricist reading of Marx. He thus always worked diligently and consistently to produce a non-empiricist concept of temporality and history. Althusser's treatment of temporality insists on the idea that time must exceed experience, that no conceptualisation of temporality can start or rest with the experience of a subject. It is for this reason, first of all—and not simply because he thought untimeliness "first"—that I turn to Althusser on time.

Moreover, I suggest that the entire critique of linear/progressive/chrono time may be flawed to the extent that its focus on the experience of time overlooks a crucial dimension of the relationship between time and politics: a radical conception of temporality must be directly tied to a concept of the social formation.[2] Even though I have been developing a concept of the social formation over the preceding chapters, it is worth remembering here what I specified back in the Introduction: at the most basic level, social formation "denotes so-called 'society'" and it seeks to capture the interconnectedness between what we often call "the social," "the political," and "the economic" (Althusser 1969: 251). Althusser thinks time differently and more deeply because he makes the crucial move of *linking temporality to the social formation.* I call this move crucial because it allows Althusser to produce a conception of temporality that cannot be reduced to spatiality,[3]

---

2. Here I use the phrase *radical conception of temporality* descriptively (and non-polemically). It describes what I take to be one primary goal of most of the "untimeliness" literature: to develop a conception of time that is radical because it breaks with our everyday, intuitive sense of "clock time" and that is also potentially radical to the extent that it might provide the conceptual resources for a radical politics. In the extant literature "non-linear" often appears as the answer to this search for a radical concept of time. While I share the goal of producing an idea of temporality that is radical in just these senses, I want to suggest that "untimeliness" is not enough to achieve those goals.

3. Other thinkers have also attempted to resist this reduction of time to space. Henri Bergson's work on memory tries to conceive temporality beyond a spatial representation (and, in turn, to think space as duration). As should be clear, below, Althusser's resistance to the "spatial reduction" works toward very much distinct ends, and so my claim in the text is that Althusser *leverages* this non-spatial conception of time toward a particularly salient political theory (Bergson 2009). On the connections between Deleuze and Althusser, including Althusser's critical commentary on an early draft of Deleuze's important essay on structuralism (Deleuze 2004 [1972]), see Stolze (1998).

and this, in turn, makes it possible to theorise a time appropriate to politics. Rather than conceive of temporal alternatives (duration vs. clock time, e.g.) that human subjects might experience or invoke, we must grasp temporality as emanating from society,[4] and a theory of time must therefore be linked to a theory of the social formation.

READING *READING CAPITAL*

Capital is a very difficult text to read; Marx himself said so on numerous occasions (Marx 1990: 104), and to my knowledge no interpreter after Marx ever contradicted him on this point (see Harvey 2010a: 7). Given the difficulty, not to mention length, of the text, there could be great value in a guide to reading *Capital*, and many such texts have been produced (e.g., Harvey 2010a, as the latest example). Despite its title, *Reading Capital* (hereafter, *RC*) is not one of them. Instead, *RC* proves arguably more difficult to read than *Capital* itself. The text is an odd one, the joint product of a seminar that Althusser conducted with his students at the École Normale Supérieure in 1965. The book is therefore collaborative in spirit, but more than this, its collaborators initially presented the text more as a large quilt than as a singular, coherent whole. The original French edition began with a long introduction by Althusser, to which he gave the title "From *Capital* to Marx's Philosophy," and which was clearly designed to try to make some larger sense out of the collaborative project of the entire seminar—to describe the hermeneutics behind the collective reading of *Capital* and to suggest how one might develop Marx's larger philosophy from that reading. This introduction was then followed by a collection of what the book's authors themselves refer to as seminar "papers." Each of these papers, however, is four to ten *chapters* in length, and thus the book as a whole runs to well over six hundred pages. As originally presented, the seminar contributions were ordered as follows: Jacques Rancière, Pierre Macherey, Louis Althusser, Étienne Balibar, and Roger Establet. The book therefore genuinely reflected the work of the seminar, and the text was by no means a single-authored monograph by Althusser.

4. This is not to say that contemporary work on temporality somehow ignores society or history; quite to the contrary (Brown 2005; Rahman 2009). As I show in this chapter, however, the *link* between temporality and the social order and the idea of a social formation as *temporalised* do very different theoretical work and should be distinguished, perhaps sharply, from arguments that focus either on a rejection of progressivism or teleology or on a historicisation of temporal concepts.

However, publishing, editing, and translating demands changed all that. In 1970, Italian and English translations were published, and for both of these editions approximately half the text was cut, including the entire contributions of Rancière, Macherey, and Establet. Perhaps just as significantly, the order of presentation was changed, with Althusser's "paper" now preceding Balibar's. This has the effect of creating a text of roughly 320 pages (still in very small font), with the first 220 pages all written by Althusser—his introduction and his own seminar paper. No wonder the book came to be read and referred to as "Althusser's" alone, with the work of Balibar (not to mention the other three contributors) often downplayed when not ignored entirely. Aside from the consolidation of the Althusser "author function," this publishing history has another, more significant effect on how the English translation of the text is received. That is, even if one takes it as a given that *RC* has been consistently interpreted over the years as Althusser's book, the forgetting of the fact that the work was originally collaborative has had certain systematic structural effects upon *how RC* has been read during that time.

Let me unpack this point. In taking *RC* as "a book by Althusser," most readers, obviously, only consult his contributions to the book; moreover, since many readers quickly get bogged down in the density of the argument, they often never make their way out of the lengthy introduction, which runs to almost eighty pages. But finally, since the introduction—for reasons I do not know—is not even marked as an introduction, it is easy to read only the first half of Althusser's contribution to the book and take those sections as the core argument of "the book," which one takes to be "Althusser's." This approach leads many (perhaps most) readers to some very strange conclusions about the core arguments of *RC*, and it surely leads them to see the book as a very odd text. The reason is straightforward: the first part of the text was originally written as an overview and introduction to the entire work of the 1965 seminar; *it was designed to introduce readers to all five seminar papers.* Thus, to read this text outside the context of that body of papers is to see it as a strange piece of writing. Given the original context, it is not surprising that Althusser, in a text written originally as an introduction, focuses almost exclusively on interpretive questions, on how the group as a whole attempted to "read" *Capital* both during the seminar and in their papers, and it seeks to specify how their interpretive approach differs from others. Many readers, however, wind up taking away from *RC* merely an argument about "symptomatic readings," and they mistake Althusser's interpretive guidelines for the concrete theses of the book.[5]

5. The fame attained by one of Althusser's other students, Jacques Derrida, from his work on textual methodology, clearly lends encouragement to such a reading.

But even if we accept the fact that in its English translation and through its reception over the past forty-five years *RC* does in fact function as a work of Althusser's, such acceptance does not justify this sort of misreading of "the book" since to approach the text this way would require one not only to *accept* the elision of the other contributions to the volume but also to *pretend* that this elision never occurred. In other words, this reading has to take part I of *RC* as it is presented in English as the central argument that Althusser makes, when in fact the comments in part I were written to serve an entirely different function. It makes more sense, then, to look at part II of the English version of *RC* to see what specific arguments Althusser himself sought to advance in the seminar. Such a move gains legitimacy when we note that Althusser's paper, in part II, has its own title, *does* include an introductory section, and is followed by eight more numbered chapters and an appendix. In other words, if we are going to read *RC* as if it were a book by Louis Althusser, then it proves much more tenable to read part II on its own, *as that book*—thereby setting aside part I, as we would have already set aside part III, written by Balibar (not to mention the other three parts by Rancière, Macherey, and Establet).

Focusing on part II circumscribes and clarifies the argument of *RC* and it makes this "book" much easier to read. Since part II is really nothing more than Althusser's original seminar paper, it has a very specific focus, and despite the obvious ways in which the text remains difficult, Althusser could not be clearer about the task he sets himself in these chapters. In his brief introduction (to part II), Althusser explains that the division of labour of the seminar assigned him the task of articulating Marx's "relation to his work" in *Capital*, in order to make sense of Marx's concepts, his innovations, and specifically his distinct differences from classical political economy. However, Althusser claims that such a relation is itself not clarified in any obvious way, either by the text of *Capital* itself or by the methodological writings that surround it. According to Althusser, in a move that resonates with the discussion from my previous chapter, these texts lack any clear articulation of the precise *object* of Marx's investigations. For Althusser, this "lack of a clear object" (my paraphrase) applies both to the specific "*object* of *Capital*" (2009: 84) and to the precise "*object of Marxist philosophy*" (2009: 80). One cannot locate the latter without first identifying the former; thus, Althusser's one task is to specify the object of *Capital*. Althusser's seminar paper proves to be a seminar paper in a fuller sense: it is tasked with answering the question "what is the object of *Capital*?" and its thesis emerges in and through that answer.

It proves tempting to misread Althusser on this point: to think by the question "what is the object of *Capital*?" that Althusser is asking an empirical question, as if the object of *Capital* could simply be located somewhere in the economy (or the world more generally). But in the last chapter I gave the specific reasons why such a reading cannot be tenable. What Althusser refers to as the "philosopher's question" (2009: 14–15) concerning the *object* cannot be answered empirically. Indeed, as I briefly expand upon in my final section, below, the question makes sense only within the context of the history of science out of which Althusser's work emerges—"*my debt to Canguilhem is incalculable*" (2009: 352). Marx's so-called object is thus not an empirical object, but an object of knowledge—that is, a concept that Marx produces. Marx's object is not something we can find in the world; it is nothing like the empiricist's object, while it is very much like Lavoisier's object, O_2, which Lavoisier did not "discover" in the world but "produced" conceptually—and ironically, this, says Althusser, makes him the true "discoverer" (2009: 166).

Given this goal, Althusser is consistent in his focus throughout the eight chapters. Chapter 2 begins with long quotes from Marx that, as Althusser glosses them, can help us to specify the difference between his object in *Capital* and the object of classical political economy. Chapter 3 then illustrates the ease with which readers of Marx can be seduced into mistaking *his* object for that of classical political economy, particularly because Marx locates and values a great number of strengths in the authors that precede him. Thus, to locate Marx's object we must see not only how it emerges out of his reading of Smith, Ricardo, and others but also how and why it cannot be the same as their object. In order to underline and clearly maintain this difference, chapters 4 and 5 are devoted to explaining Marx's most important critique of the classical economists. These two long chapters, which take up just less than half of the entirety of part II, therefore constitute what Althusser will call at the beginning of chapter 6, a "long digression." Constant in his aim, Althusser begins chapter 6 by reminding the reader of the purpose of his essay. The sentence stands on its own: "We are looking for Marx's peculiar object" (160). However, in order to specify Marx's object in the final four chapters of part II, Althusser must specify, and elaborate in great detail, Marx's "fundamental criticism" of classical political economy, and this makes his digression in chapters 4 and 5 much more than a digression: these chapters contain Althusser's central argument concerning the relationship between Marxism and history. Althusser insists that we can only distinguish Marx's project from that of classical political economy by way of this critique. In other words, without a clear and concise understanding of Marx's concept of history, we will conflate Marx's object with that of Smith and Ricardo. And if we cannot see the difference between Marx's object and theirs, then we cannot see the revolution in thought that Marx brings about.

BEYOND HISTORICISM, AGAINST HEGEL

For these reasons, I anchor my reading here on chapter 4, as it contains the core arguments of this fundamental digression; my section heading above draws from the titles of chapters 4 and 5, as Althusser first shows the necessity of a non-linear concept of history and then demonstrates that historicism cannot meet these needs. Here I argue that these two chapters add up to much more than a digression, by suggesting that Althusser's reading of Marx on history and historicism proves as significant to contemporary debates about politics and temporality as it does for Althusser's own circumscribed project in *RC*. It does so because in these chapters Althusser develops a thinking of temporality in and through social orders. Thus, I interpret the chapters to two ends: 1) elaborating and articulating Althusser's own reading of Marx for the purpose of augmenting his, and my, understanding of the social formation, and 2) clarifying the stakes of current debates around time and temporality by reading them in relation to the concept of the social formation. My reading makes the case for Althusser as an untimely discoverer of the untimely, and it demonstrates that an account of the social formation can refigure the idea of radical temporality (untimeliness). His argument from five decades ago not only prefigures or preempts the turn to the untimely in political theory but also unravels two common equations that circulate within contemporary political theory. The first equation holds: structuralism = absence of history. The second maintains: poststructuralism = historicisation. To the extent, then, that we might still associate Althusser with structuralism, these chapters undo any easy assumption that the work of "the structuralists" lacked a sense of history.[6] And to the extent that Althusser's work, instead, informs the generation of poststructuralists (including Althusser's most famous students, Foucault and Derrida), then these chapters call into question the often unstated connection between Fredric Jameson's famous slogan "always historicise" and the central thrust of post-Marxism and poststructuralism (Jameson 2002).

6. On the massive topic of Althusser's relation to the vexed history of structuralism, English-language readers now have available the amazing resource of Warren Montag's book, *Althusser and His Contemporaries* (2013). Montag's rich work of contextual history undoes almost all the received wisdom about both "structuralism" and Althusser's relation to structuralism. To illustrate this point, I will pick, almost haphazardly, just one short quote: "Althusser rejects the very problematic that defined structuralist activity" (Montag 2013: 32). While almost all of my own work on Althusser in this book was completed prior to the appearance of Montag's text, his interpretation resonates with my own in numerous ways, and his historical work provides a deep background to some of the more narrowly textual arguments I make here.

While Althusser, of course, has none of these broader ends in mind in his 1965 "seminar paper"—his task in these chapters lies in showing the absolute centrality of a novel understanding of history to Marx's project—the connection to Jameson's later arguments proves much more than indirect. Althusser begins chapter 4, titled "The Errors of Classical Economics," by delineating Marx's fundamental criticism of the entire project of political economy up to the time of Marx's writing. Hence Althusser's summary of Marx's criticism resonates with the Jamesonian mantra:

> Classical Economics . . . had an ahistorical, eternal, fixed and abstract conception of the economic categories of capitalism. Marx says in so many words that *these categories must be historicized* to reveal and understand their nature, their relativity and transitivity. The Classical Economists, he says, have made the conditions of capitalist production the eternal conditions of all production, without seeing that these categories were historically determined, and hence historical and transitory. (Althusser 2009: 102, emphasis added)

Althusser then proceeds to give his own long, offset quotation of Marx, revealing Althusser's lines to be nothing more than a paraphrase. Both quotations will likely strike the contemporary political theory reader as filled with common sense, since the cornerstone of twentieth- and twenty-first-century political theory seems to be the commitment to understanding all objects, categories, and concepts as "historically determined, and hence historical and transitory."[7] Indeed, returning to my argument from Chapter 2, one of the many reasons why Marx is so hard to read *as a political theorist* today is that he sounds like either a very bad one (making predictions about revolution and declaring edicts about human nature) or a very common one (telling us the same thing that everyone else is saying). Doubtless, if all Marx offers conceptually concerning history is the insistence on historicising, then it proves much easier to read someone who writes about products of more recent history.

Althusser tells his readers, however, that it would be a terrible misstep interpretively, and a grave mistake politically, to take Marx's so-called fundamental criticism of classical political economy as his "last word." Marx's "*real* critique" must be understood to move well beyond this starting point, which itself should be grasped as "superficial and ambiguous" (2009: 102). Marx's critique of classical political economy cannot be reduced to the historicisation of their categories, as if all Marx did was identify the ways in which the categories that Ricardo and Smith take as eternal instead

7. But see Finlayson (2003) for a much richer and more complex account of political theory today.

prove to be historically contingent (see Young 1990: 55). This approach would not give us Marxism, says Althusser; it would produce nothing other than *a historicised version of classical economics*. Yet, widening the gap between Marx and classical political economy proves to be a complex task because—as I showed in detail in Chapter 2, with the example of Smith's notion of "labour in general"—Marx works so closely with its categories. In other words, it is both easy and tempting to elide the difference between Marx and the classical economists because Marx's theory would not be possible without their work—because Marx develops his project not from scratch but rather *through theirs*. Althusser asserts that these difficulties arise due to "*the confusion that surrounds the concept of history*" (2009: 103). The commonsense understanding of history serves to reduce Marx's project to that of a historicised political economy, and therefore the only way to grasp the radical break that Marx makes from classical political economy is to first bring to light his radical concept of history. Marxism, says Althusser, requires its own theory of history. More to the point, and as he will conclude at the end of this chapter, *Capital* offers its own theory of history, a theory absolutely necessary to the theory of the economy (2009: 131). But this means that *Capital*, and those other important works that surround it, must be read as producing a unique Marxist theory of history, one that resists both empiricism and historicism.

Althusser begins to derive such a theory by going back to Marx's critique of Hegel, since it is Hegel who provides the fullest illumination of the intuitive sense of history that must be displaced if one is to see that (and how) Marx is not merely historicising when he takes on the political economists. Put differently, the Marxist concept of history only comes to light in contrast to the Hegelian concept. Moreover, for both authors (Hegel and Marx) their conceptions of time are reflections of their understandings of society, of the social order. Marx's conception of time diverges from Hegel to exactly the extent that the Marxist social formation deviates from the Hegelian social totality. This is a key distinction that I have been working with tentatively throughout this book, and which is announced directly in my 6th hypothesis. Here I want to elaborate on this crucial difference that Althusser introduces when he articulates the distinction between the Hegelian *totality* and the Marxist *whole*:

> Marx did not have the same idea of the nature of a social formation as Hegel . . . Hegel thought of society as a *totality*, while Marx thought of it as a complex whole, structured in dominance. . . . it seems to me that we can leave to Hegel the category of *totality*, and claim for Marx the category of the *whole*. . . . within the totality a double temptation is always present: that of considering it as a pervasive essence which exhaustively embraces all of

> its manifestations, and—what comes to the same thing—that of discovering in it, as in a circle or a sphere (a metaphor which makes us think of Hegel once again), a centre which would be its essence. (Althusser 1976: 181)

As I mentioned briefly in Chapter 1, according to Althusser, the Hegelian totality is "made up of circles within circles"; that is, while there are multiple levels within this totality, each level is but the expression of an inner core, what Althusser refers to as "a spiritual unity" (Althusser 1976: 182; Althusser 2009: 104). This unity of the Hegelian totality finds expression in Hegel's concept of historical time, a concept that "merely reflects the essence" of that totality (Hegel 2009; Althusser 2009: 104). Althusser emphasises two elements in the Hegelian understanding of time: 1) the continuity and homogeneity of time, and 2) the contemporaneity of time, the centrality of the *present*. Time must be homogenous for Hegel precisely because the dialectical unfolding of the Idea must occur *in time*. From the notion that the Idea develops within homogenous time we get a conception of history as marked by *periods*, periods of different Ideas that have emerged within the uniform *space* that such a concept of time provides (Althusser 2009: 104). Here, then, we see a common move by which temporality is reduced to spatiality; time becomes a *medium* for actions, events, history—or, in Hegel's case, the teleological ascendence of the Idea.[8] Any period in history can therefore be *marked* by the singular Idea that defines it and gives it meaning, and periodisation then proceeds by the discovery of distinct Ideas for different periods (see Read 2005). Althusser suggests that, in this instance, Hegel merely offers a way to work through a common contemporary problem in the practice of historians—how to think, for example, the difference between the age of Louis the XIV and Louis the XV (2009: 104).

Moreover, according to Althusser, this continuity of time—what I am calling a particular reduction of time to space—actually depends upon a prior determination by Hegel: the historical present (Althusser 2009: 104; Althusser 1969: 115). Hegel conceptualises the totality such that all components within it "always co-exist in one and the same time, one and the same present" (2009: 105). Althusser explains this idea of the contemporaneity of time (Hegel's version of "presentism") by showing that, in Hegel, any historical formation is understood to take on a particular structure. To wit, the social formation is structured such that one can make a "vertical break" at any point in time: "a break in the present such that all the elements of

---

8. Marx's conception in the *Grundrisse* of capital's "annihilation of space by time" (Marx 1973: 524) and Harvey's theory of the "spatial fix" (Harvey 1981; Harvey 2001) are distinct, if very much related, matters.

the whole revealed [by this break] are in immediate relationship with one another" (Althusser 2009: 105). Althusser therefore contends that, with Hegel, it is always possible to point to the "essential section." This "essential section" refers to the elements of a social order that make possible a *legible presence* of all elements of the formation; within this section, "all elements of the [totality] are given in co-presence" (Althusser 2009: 105). That the Hegelian totality contains an essential section (one that always allows for this vertical break) explains the contemporaneity of time in the Hegelian understanding. Moreover, it is precisely the fact that Hegel's totality contains such an essential section that prevents it from functioning as an adequate conceptualisation of the social formation. Hegel's concept of totality is philosophically impoverished because it is temporalised by way of presence. The unity of Hegelian social totality depends upon, and simultaneously entails, that every element in the social totality is also a co-present *moment* in the totality. Time can be continuous (and homogenous) based upon the "continuity of presence" ("co-presence") of every element within the Hegelian understanding of a "social formation," which is always a "totality" and not a Marxist "whole" because of its determination by the centrality of this present (i.e., presentism) (cf. Montag 2013: 32). For this very reason what we might otherwise call the Hegelian "social formation" is, in a strict sense, no such thing, since the totality can never give an adequate account of a social formation that, as we will see in the next section, is never continuous or unified in this way but is always discontinuous, untimely, and overdetermined.[9]

A MARXIST CONCEPTION OF HISTORICAL TIME

Althusser uses this interpretation of Hegel to offer a scathing critique of one of the central planks of so-called structuralist history: the fundamental

---

9. To the extent that, as Althusser himself says, "social formation" is just another name for a society, then in a general sense there can be a variety of different and competing concepts of the social formation, including the Hegelian totality. In this way it would make perfect sense to refer to Marx's and Hegel's (and others') competing concepts *of* the social formation (and I have previously done just this, Chambers 2011). At the same time, however, Althusser is calling for a specific delimitation of "social formation" as a concept discovered/invented by Marx, and to a certain degree I follow Althusser here in trying to give a more specific, more definite account of the social formation. Above all, for clarity I therefore try to reserve "social formation" for the account that Althusser is developing out of Marx (and that I am developing out of Althusser) and to use other terms, such as totality, for understandings of the social formation that are subject to critique, revision, or rejection.

distinction between synchrony and diachrony (Althusser 2009: 119). This is just one of the many reasons why Althusser was never a "structuralist," or, perhaps better, why "structuralism" was never really what it has been taken to be.[10] Montag's recent arguments prove highly relevant here, as he opens a wide gap between Althusser's actual arguments about structure and history, on the one hand, and the standard account of "structuralism," on the other:

> In opposition to the mechanistic determinism attributed to him by Thompson and others, Althusser worked to overcome the opposition between chance and necessity by defining historical necessity as the product of chance encounters between absolutely singular entities. In place of the Stalinist establishing "the laws of historical development" or the structuralist revealing order and unity beneath the appearance of disorder and diversity, there thus emerges an entirely unexpected Althusser, heir to the aleatory thought of Epicurus and Lucretius, as well as Spinoza's absolute nominalism. *What is perhaps most surprising about this current in Althusser's thought is that, even if it was made explicit only at the end of his life, it was present, although nearly unnoticed, throughout his work*, beginning with the essays that make up *For Marx*. (Montag 2013: 9–10, emphasis added)

In addition to refuting the narrow dismissal of Althusser as a determinist, Montag also makes explicit a key point that, while implicit throughout my own treatment of Althusser's works, proves worth flagging at this juncture—namely, that there is no need to turn to the later "aleatory Althusser" in order to "save" Althusser from the dangers of structuralism. I do not mean to dismiss the rich vein of work that has now developed around Althusser's so-called aleatory materialism, but merely to insist that there is no such thing as a major "break" between Althusser's early and later work. In this context, it is worth emphasising that so much of the "aleatory" language in "the later Althusser" comes into existence through the posthumous publication of manuscripts from Althusser in which he himself took drafts of *early manuscripts* and went through in later years crossing out "historical" in the phrase "historical materialism" and writing in "aleatory" (Althusser 1999; Althusser 2006). In a move utterly consistent with Montag's work, I read Althusser as never having been the structuralist he

10. On the latter point, Montag shows powerfully how the most famous "structuralists," such as Lévi-Strauss, made explicit arguments against the very ideas that now make up the "textbook definition" (my words) of structuralism (Montag 2013: 59). On the former, and as I show below, he demonstrates in detail that Althusser was always opposed to the determinism that was attributed to him and his so-called structuralist approach by famous critics (Montag 2013: 9; Thompson 1978; cf. Connolly 1981).

was taken for. Thus, in an important sense, Althusser's conceptualisation of the social formation has always been aleatory.

Putting behind me the way in which Althusser's critique of Hegel forces us to rethink his relation to "structuralism," here I want to emphasise an aspect of Althusser's interpretation in these sections of *RC*—an aspect of central significance for my project in this book—that he himself fails to highlight. Althusser suggests that his reading of Hegel is important not because of the direct critique it produces (e.g., that Hegel's presentism is merely the sublimation of a latent empiricism), but because it puts us on the right track in developing an appropriate conception of history and temporality for Marxism, which for my purposes can be translated into a project of developing an account of the social formation (Althusser 2009: 108). What we see in Hegel is that his concept of time can be read off of his inadequate concept of the social formation (the totality). To develop a radical conception of temporality for/in Marx thus requires us to articulate Marx's concept of the social formation. We construct "*the Marxist conception of historical time* on the basis of the Marxist conception of the social totality," what Althusser later calls the Marxist whole and what I discuss throughout the book, under the heading of social formation (2009: 108). Putting the point more generally would result in the following formulation: *temporality is not a variable distinct or separate from the social order; any (theory of the) social formation contains its own temporality; any social order is temporalised through and through.*

Temporality is not an external movement of the whole, but an immanent dimension of it. Althusser glosses a passage from the *1857 Introduction* by insisting that "the *structure of the whole* must be conceived before any discussion of temporal sequence" (2009: 109). More than this: to grasp the structure of the whole is to grasp its temporality, so it is not as if we would first understand the structure of the whole and then theorise its movement in time. To try to go this route would be to presume that time somehow preceded the social formation, or existed outside of it (à la Hegel, as the medium in which the totality unfolds). Instead, we must see temporality as emanating from the structure of the social order.[11]

Moreover, to think temporality as a "product" in some sense (though surely not a derived one, not one that comes after, but one that is bound up with that which "produces" it) of the social formation, immediately means to reject the presentism of the Hegelian formulation. If temporality belongs to the social order, then we must reject the continuous and homogenous

11. David Harvey's well-known work in Marxist geography offers one of the clearest concrete examples of how such an analysis might play out (Harvey 2006; Harvey 2007).

understanding of time or history. Here we broach the possibility of a much more radical thinking of time. Althusser writes:

> It is no longer possible to think the process of the development of the different levels of the whole *in the same historical time*. Each of these different "levels" does not have the same type of historical existence. On the contrary, we have to assign to each a *peculiar time*, relatively autonomous, and hence relatively independent, even in its dependence, of the "times" of the other levels. (Althusser 2009: 110–11)

This argument gives us a conception of "differential time." Any social order has distinct, uneven levels related to one another through the articulation (*Gliederung*) of the whole, and these levels have different times. But the times are not unique and independent (though they are relatively autonomous) since they are related to one another as parts of the social formation. This is why Althusser can call each peculiar time "relatively independent, even in its dependence," because while the particular time of each level or element is independent of the other elements, all are dependent upon the particular configuration of the social order—its historical articulation. This logic gives some indication of how and why *differential time* must not be conflated with a simple notion of multiple or different times.[12] Althusser insists that a differential conception of temporality within the history of social formations cannot be confused with or reduced to the empirical observation of different times. Different times must always be "relat[ed] . . . to the concept of their difference." We can never simply proclaim in an abstract, dehistoricised sense that there are multiple times, nor can we eschew abstraction by simply "doing history" in such a way as to catalog temporal differences. "We must also think these differences in rhythm and punctuation in their foundation, in the type of articulation, displacement and torsion which harmonizes these different times with one another" (Althusser 2009: 112).

Doubtless, differential time sounds like an abstract concept, and it seems more than reasonable to ask for an example. At the same time, however, the difference between differential time and multiple times means that there can be no *simple* example. One cannot merely point to an empirical object and call it "differential time"; indeed, the idea of differential time undercuts so many recent analyses that would blandly and generically claim that time is speeding up. Instead, differential time must be analysed within the

12. Genuine *multiplicity*, as distinct from "multiple times," might prove to be another matter entirely, and might resonate more forcefully with what Althusser means by differential time.

historical specificity of a particular social formation and at a particular political conjuncture, and its differential nature must be understood in relation to the larger social order. In lieu, then, of any simple or abstract (philosophy textbook) example, I submit that in his recent work on migrant day labourers, Paul Apostolidis offers just this sort of rich, subtle, and historically situated analysis of the temporality of the social formation (Apostolidis 2015). Apostolidis shows, that is, the way in which day labourers contribute to and help sustain the particular social formation of neoliberal capitalism in the USA (with its peculiar temporalities), while these labourers themselves operate within their own unique temporality—one that is, using Althusser's words from the extended quote above, "relatively autonomous, and hence relatively independent, even in its dependence, of the 'times' of the other" dimensions and levels of the social formation. The time of the day labourer, the time of the contractor who hires them to do remodeling work, and the time of the owner of the suburban home being remodeled—these are not just "different" times that would lead us to a conclusion that time is "multiple." Rather, their differences must be related to the larger social formation in such a way as to grasp the differential time that both produces and is produced by that social formation.

The idea of differential temporalities produced by a social formation pushes Althusser toward radical conclusions about temporality, some of which, I submit, exceed and alter the recent work by contemporary political theorists. One of the central planks of current writings on time and temporality, and this despite their variety and differences, is surely an insistence on *non-linear time* (Brown 2005; Connolly 2005; Chambers 2003). Althusser's arguments predate these works by a number of decades, but he himself contends that such claims result directly from a decent reading of *Capital*. Indeed, "merely reading *Capital*," says Althusser, illustrates the centrality of non-linear time to his conception, but, more than this, it also gives rise to the crucial concept of *invisible times* (2009: 112).

Althusser's production of the concept of invisible time presages current concepts like "untimeliness" as drawn from Derrida's work, or "time as becoming" as developed out of Bergson's writings (Derrida 1992; Derrida 1994; Bergson 2009; cf. Deleuze 1988). Invisible time cannot be read off the surface of events; it cannot be observed. It goes almost without saying, but Althusser surely says it anyway, that invisible time evades empiricism. It is invisible because it is "essentially illegible, as invisible and opaque as the reality of the capitalist production process itself" (2009: 112). Althusser gives an extended reading of invisible time through the example of "the time of economic production." This time cannot be read on clock faces, counted on calendars, or discovered in biological change. Althusser insists that the time is invisible in that it has no simple empirical existence: "it must be *constructed* in its concept" (2009: 112). This means it must be pieced together and produced out of the distinct and variable rhythms and temporalities that make up the processes of production, distribution, and exchange. The time of economic production is an invisible time filled with differential time. Althusser gives numerous examples of these differences: "the difference between production time and labour time, the difference between the different cycles of production (the turnover of fixed capital, of circulating capital, of variable capital, monetary turnover, turnover of commercial capital and of finance capital, etc.)" (2009: 112). Althusser therefore concludes that the time of economic production is an invisible time due to the fact that it has "absolutely nothing to do" with the time of everyday practices—what we today might call clock time or chrono-time, and what Althusser called ideological time.

The concept of invisible time proves central to Althusser's argument concerning a thinking of a concept of history that would be adequate to Marxism and to a viable understanding of the social formation (it elaborates the difference between the Hegelian totality and the Marxist whole). At the same time, it pushes past contemporary work on temporality in its insistence that we cannot make do with two sorts of times that we might experience directly (chrono-time that we read off our watch, and time-as-becoming that we might endure in various moments of our existence). *We must instead insist on a concept of time that goes beyond experience.*[13] Invisible time "is only accessible in *its concept*, which, like every concept is never immediately 'given', never *legible* in visible realty: like every concept this concept must be *produced, constructed*" (Althusser 2009: 112–13). Here Althusser makes a set of claims that both draw on and develop the extended argument that I explicated in the last chapter, concerning the difference between the real object and the object of knowledge. Invisible time is not a real object, discoverable by experimental techniques of observation. It is in an object of knowledge, produced within the realm

13. Althusser's brief, and extremely positive, discussion of Foucault points also to a deepening and radicalisation of what today we call "untimeliness." Althusser suggests not just the occasional outbreak of untimeliness within history (not just a rupture), but the very untimeliness of history itself. He draws the following rather startling set of conclusions from Foucault's *History of Madness*: "There is nothing true in history which allows it to be read in the ideological continuum of a linear time that need only be punctuated and divided; on the contrary, it [history] has its extremely complex and peculiar temporality which is, of course, utterly paradoxical in comparison with the disarming simplicity of ideological pre-judgement" (Althusser 2009: 115; Foucault 2009 [1961]). On Foucault and Althusser, see Montag (2005).

of thought and not located within material reality. For just this reason, invisible time evades the dangers of empiricism, which I detail below, and it distinguishes the Althusserian attempt to think temporality "beyond experience" from others.[14]

His insistence on the real object/object of knowledge distinction not only underscores the importance of this point for Althusser's entire approach to Marx but also more starkly illuminates and clarifies his critique of both Hegel and empiricism on the subject of history/time. Althusser insists that to produce a concept of invisible time that makes sense of economic and historical processes also means to insist that each process within history may require its own temporality. There can be no return to an underlying "base time" that would provide the ground for the diverse and dislocated temporalities of the various elements that constitute any definite social formation within history (Althusser 2009: 116). The differential times cannot be discovered in relation to a "reference time" (2009: 118). There is no essential temporality (i.e., a source time) underlying the diverse rhythms and disjunctures, just as there is no essential section in the whole. Moreover, there is no forward and backward of one time with respect to another; since no time is linear, there can be no adjudication of various times. This means, crudely but importantly, that there is no GMT. But it also means that so-called backwardness and forwardness cannot be read off of empirical economic development. Instead, backwardness and forwardness is a metaphorical language, the meaning of which "must be sought in the structure of the whole"—an important insight for a great deal of productive work in postcolonial theory (2009: 118).

This argument has crucial implications for the concept of history that Althusser is trying to think within this lengthy "digression." Althusser continually reminds his readers that the "empiricist temptation is enormous"; he worries that no matter how much work one puts into evading the various traps of empiricism, one will ultimately lapse back into empiricist frameworks given their commonsense, intuitive nature. But Althusser insists

---

14. Deleuze describes Bergson's "method of intuition" as one in which "we go beyond experience, toward the conditions of experience," although not in the Kantian sense (Deleuze 1988: 23). Here we see an important overlap between the approaches of Althusser and Bergson (or, Deleuze's Bergsonism) not only in "going beyond experience" but also in seeking to identify that which is neither transcendental nor subject to historicisation. Nonetheless, the differences between Bergson's phenomenological approach that relies on perception and the approach of Althusser cannot be denied, since Althusser would likely attempt to categorise the phenomenological approach as still trapped within the contours of his broadly defined empiricism. I am deeply indebted to Smita Rahman for pushing me on Bergson and for calling my attention to this passage in Deleuze.

that the concept of history must refuse "any compromise with 'empirical' temporality" (2009: 117). We might say, then, that the concept of history cannot rest with the notion that there are two times (linear/non-linear, chrono/becoming, timely/untimely) but must rid itself of any reduction to linear-observable-visible-chrono-time. In this context Althusser makes perhaps his most rhetorically persuasive argument for the difference between the object of knowledge and the real object. Our concept of history, he is arguing here, must not be reducible to (or thought to be approaching asymptotically) empirical objects within history. First he paraphrases/cites (one can rarely tell when Althusser is doing the one or the other) Spinoza: "*the concept of dog cannot bark*" (2009: 117). Then, in a move that calls to mind the discussion of "the concept of fruit" from my previous chapter, Althusser develops this argument into a powerful analogy to help explain his approach to history: "The knowledge of history is no more historical than the knowledge of sugar is sweet" (2009: 117). Our concept of history, our thinking of temporality adequate to an analysis of any social order within history, cannot simply be a historical artifact or object. Here we catch a powerful glimpse of Althusser's most damning argument against the idea that Marx's critique of political economy rests with the call to historicise.

I will elaborate on that argument in the next section, but first I need to spell out some of the conclusions that Althusser himself draws from this sketch for a concept of history. First, he delivers a full-blown critique of synchrony/diachrony. While these notions are not as much en vogue today as when Althusser wrote, the distinction is often assumed to be valid and meaningful, while it is simultaneously attributed to structuralist accounts (a group into which Althusser himself is often lumped). For these reasons, it seems worth noting the thoroughgoing nature of Althusser's critique (Montag 2013). He argues, fundamentally, that the entire distinction between synchrony and diachrony is based on a Hegelian concept of history, for it depends upon "a conception of historical time as continuous and homogenous and contemporaneous with itself" (2009: 106). Synchrony is nothing other than Hegelian co-presence; diachrony is nothing more than the development of a temporal sequence within a homogenous time. Althusser can therefore safely conclude that without the Hegelian concept of history, the distinction cannot stand: there is no presence to sustain synchrony and no homogenous continuum within which diachrony could unfold (2009: 119). Yet Althusser does not merely dismiss the distinction entirely, but rather argues that after its deconstruction (my word) something may remain of each of the terms. Synchrony, then, would point not to the co-presence of actual objects in history but to the very articulation (*Gliederung*) that holds together the social formation, "that makes the whole the whole" (2009:

119). And diachrony might be sustained as a concept for thinking the transformation of modes of production (2009: 120). Althusser himself does not make sustained use of the terms after their deconstructive reworking here, but that reworking provides him with one more chance to distance himself from both Hegelianism and empiricism, and it puts one more plank into his most important argument: the concept of historical time.

Here is Althusser's "definition" of historical time:

> the specific form of existence of the social [whole] under consideration, an existence in which different structural levels of temporality interfere, because of the peculiar relations of correspondence, non-correspondence, articulation, dislocation and torsion which obtain, between the different "levels" of the whole in accordance with its general structure. (Althusser 2009: 120–21)

I put the word *definition* in quotation marks since one of the primary conclusions that Althusser draws from this abstract account of historical time is that there is no such thing as history "in general," no such thing as a singular (and therefore static) account of history. Instead of a general concept of history, the concept of historical time amounts to nothing more or less than an elaboration of the idea that there are "only specific structures of historicity." And these definite structures of historicity remain inextricably bound up with and tied to "the existence of determinate social formations" whose meaning remains indelibly linked to "their peculiar complexity" (Althusser 2009: 121).

Time is therefore nothing like the location for the unfolding of history. It is neither homogenous nor continuous, and it refuses the possibility of co-presence. This is a conception of temporality that resists most radically any reduction to space. Time is not a space in which history unfolds, or a location for presence; time is instead multiple, non-linear, and always a dimension of a particular social order, itself a historical product. History is not a general concept that unfolds within an even broader concept of time. There is no general history. *There are definite social formations produced contingently and determined historically and emanating their own peculiar, overlapping, conflicting, discontinuous temporalities.*

Many conclusions can be drawn from this account of historical time.[15] Armed with it, Althusser himself spends quite a large number of pages

---

15. Althusser's later writings, the so-called aleatory work (Althusser 1999; Althusser 2006), might be made to link up to his earlier works via this account. As I discussed in the text above, here I focus very tightly upon Althusser's earlier writings on the temporality of social orders precisely because I see more salience for a concrete thinking of politics in that project. On these later writings, see McInerney (2005); the entire 2005 special issue of *Borderlands*; and Williams (2001).

taking historians to task for their lack of attention to theory (and their substitution, in its place, of a methodology that almost always smuggles in empiricism). Most important for my purposes here, however, is the position that this concept of temporality leads one to take on the question of historicism, which bears on our most fundamental understanding of the social formation. Put simply, Marxism must never be reduced to the historicisation of classical political economy (Althusser 2009: 125). Put more strongly, as Althusser does in the title of the next chapter: "Marxism Is Not a Historicism" (2009: 132). Chapter 5 of *RC* goes to great lengths to extend, extrapolate, and elaborate the argument that its title names; it uses the concept of historical time developed in chapter 4 to show that Marxism is, in fact, non-historicist.

I will not offer an exegesis of Althusser's arguments in that chapter, which contains a number of detours—some designed to deepen Althusser's anti-humanist reading of Marx (especially against Sartre), some designed to take Gramsci to task for his forthright historicist reading of Marx without, in the process, appearing to criticise Gramsci all that harshly (ditto in many cases for Engels). The problems of historicism are many, but the central conceptual difficulty associated with historicism can be drawn out quite logically from the arguments already covered here. Historicism reduces to a variant of empiricism. Worse still, historicism transforms the Marxist whole into a Hegelian totality (Althusser 2009: 147); a historicist account can therefore never be an adequate account of the social formation. Althusser's entire reading of Marx (and by this I mean Althusser's entire politico-philosophical project) depends upon producing a non-humanist, non-historicist Marxism. We can see from the reading of chapter 4 of *RC* given here that this project requires a significant rethinking of temporality—one that, I have suggested, took Althusser along a number of paths that exceed the recent work done in contemporary political theory on time and politics. In order to draw out those arguments, I would like, in the final section below, to provide a bit more contextual framing for the work that Althusser has done here on history and time. This means repositioning Althusser more squarely in his own historical context of mid-twentieth-century French thought in order to see better how he contributes to early twenty-first-century arguments in contemporary political theory.

THE THEORY AND POLITICS OF A (TEMPORALISED) SOCIAL FORMATION

Despite my efforts to fold Althusser's older writings into the contemporary debates over temporality, I am not the first to identify, or argue for, the importance of Althusser's work on temporality. In insisting that we use a radical conception of time in order to rethink the relationship between a *concept of* "history," on the one hand, and *events in* history, on the other, Althusser was speaking straightforwardly to some of the most important political and theoretical debates within postwar France. In his 1990 book *White Mythologies*, Robert Young describes this as one of Althusser's chief contributions, succinctly summarising it as a capacity "to problematize the concept of history by addressing its presuppositions about temporality" (Young 1990: 61). And the importance of this contribution was not lost on those working immediately in Althusser's wake in France, as I will discuss in more detail below. Young's book does a brilliant job of contextualising and explicating Althusser's arguments without itself getting lost in the context—without, that is, turning the reconstruction of context into the entire point of his exercise.

Instead, Young's arguments draw out the significance of Althusser's work on the concept of history not just for the battles that Althusser was engaged in but, more to the point, for more recent debates over history and theory in the UK and North America. Young goes back to Althusser, and to the Marxist debate in France concerning the concept of history, in order to formulate a very refined response to the charge made in the 1980s and 1990s (and on through to today) that poststructuralist/postmodernist/postfoundationalist thought somehow ignores, dismisses, liquidates, or removes "history" from both politics and political analysis. Young shows astutely that the critique of poststructuralism as "denying history" merely replicates earlier charges made in the context of postwar French thought *within* debates over Marxism. Moreover, a closer reading of that context shows that "the reproach that poststructuralism has neglected history *really consists of the complaint that it has questioned History*" (Young 1990: 23, emphasis added).[16] In other words, it is not any actual neglect of historical meaning or historical events, nor is it the lack of attention to concepts of history, that is at issue in the charge against poststructuralism; rather, it is precisely the insistence, by certain thinkers within the so-called poststructuralist vein, on challenging the idea of "history" as a unifying totality that gives rise to this frequently heard complaint.

Moreover, and more to the point, the critique (both twenty-five years ago when Young published his book and today) of poststructuralism for denying history only repeats the reception of Althusser's work, "taken

16. Young occasionally capitalises the word *History* in order to indicate the extent to which certain critics hypostatise the concept as itself an entity without a history. I do not follow his usage but simply distinguish more nominally, as at the beginning of this section, between the concept of history and events in history.

by many as an attack on history as such."[17] Quite to the contrary, Young insists, and as I have demonstrated above, it was Althusser's critique of Marxists' historicism in the name of another (Marxist) concept of history that opened up "new political possibilities" (Young 1990: 47). Ironically, however, Althusser's contributions in this context have not generally been recognised by Marxists, who still often take Althusser to have broken with Marxism because he was willing to question Marx's own account of history—or at least to suggest that Marx did not have a fully developed one (Young 1990: 53). While Althusser's arguments about time and history were made within the context of the Marxist debate over the role of history (and while they can be understood as a clear, if perhaps indirect, response to Sartre's project to use the concept of history to rescue a humanist Marxism from the clutches of Stalinist economism), most Marxists refused to take up Althusser's arguments on this front.

Instead, it was just those self-proclaimed *non-Marxist* students of Althusser, students who have themselves provided so much of the inspiration for contemporary work devoted to rethinking temporality, who took Althusser's claims about history (and time) most seriously.[18] Young tacitly implies with his overall argument, and suggests directly in his setting up of a quotation, that Foucault had Althusser in mind when the former developed his most important arguments concerning genealogy and historical sense. Young writes, quoting Foucault: "Althusser constructs, as Foucault puts it, 'a counter-memory—a transformation of history into a totally different form of time'" (Young 1990: 61; quoting Foucault 1977: 160). Indeed, this effect, of turning history into a different form of time, is what both Nietzsche's historical sense (especially as read by Foucault) and Althusser's critique of historicism and arguments for invisible time carry out.[19] Derrida not only proves to be much less ambiguous about the

---

17. Young makes unequivocal the link between a critique of Althusser, within Marxism, on the one hand, and the contemporary critique of poststructuralism, on the other: "The accusation that poststructuralism neglects history *undoubtedly* harks back above all to the work of Althusser who, more than anyone else, *appears* to have attempted to eliminate history" (Young 1990: 53; the emphasis in the quotation is mine, but it proves consistent with Young's broader argument).

18. Hence Althusser is also sometimes blamed for those students' perceived ill-effects on the human subject (see Smith 1984b).

19. It is much more debatable, however, whether Foucault really meant to suggest the connection that Young has constructed here. As is well known, Foucault developed something of a reputation for failing to cite sources, much less influences. And while I have previously suggested that the reputation may not always have been fully deserved

debt that he owed to Althusser but also suggests, in the following interview response, the presumed centrality of Althusser's work in this area:

> Althusser's entire, *and necessary*, critique of the "Hegelian" concept of history and *the notion of an expressive totality, etc.*, aims at showing that there is not one single history, a general history, but rather histories **different** in their type, rhythm, mode of inscription—intervallic, differentiated histories. *I have always subscribed to this.* (Derrida 1981b: 57–58; quoted in Young 1990: 63; bold emphasis Derrida's, all italic emphasis mine)

Derrida indicates the importance of Althusser's critique of history and its attendant rethinking of temporality, but more than this, the formulation suggests a broad familiarity with both the terms of the critique and its significance. This is why I have emphasised Derrida's reference to "the notion of an expressive totality, etc.," since he speaks as if both his interviewer and the readers of this transcript will all already be familiar with Althusser's identification of an "expressive totality" in Hegel. Derrida assumes not just that readers of this piece will already have read *RC*, but more, that they too will see the "digression" on history and time to be of utmost importance. Note also that Derrida, who always sought to twist his own work in such a way that it would also resist and differentiate itself from other authors, even those he admired the most (deconstruction is an act of reading and writing that shows the utmost fidelity to—indeed, respect for—the text), appears almost uncritical or even dogmatic in his endorsement of the Althusserian position, one that Derrida says he *subscribes to* (not Derrida's typical move, nor his typical language).

Foucault and Derrida, in their more or less explicit endorsements of Althusser's work on time and history, help to point the way from Althusser's argument to the contemporary debates on time and politics. But at the risk of repeating myself, my point is not simply to indicate the influence or contribution of Althusser to contemporary work on radical temporality, nor is it to give Althusser "credit" for a "discovery" of sorts. And the last thing I would want to suggest here is that somehow the work of Althusser leads *progressively* to the contemporary authors I referred to at the beginning of this chapter. Instead, my point in developing this line of contextual reconstruction is to return us to the *differences* between Althusser's work on temporality and that of contemporary political theorists. It is here that we can locate the importance of Althusser's arguments as I have explicated them in this chapter. Such work has meaningful implications not only for

(Chambers 2003), it seems a bit of a stretch to attribute *indirect* citations to Foucault that he himself failed to make.

a history of thought but also for a rethinking, today, of the relationship between time and politics, and for a richer formulation of the theories and politics of the social formation.

Those differences might typically be ignored on the very same grounds from which Althusser's work is so often dismissed: namely, that of structuralism and so-called scientific Marxism. In response, I would suggest that it is specifically his work on time and the concept of history that reveals so forcefully that Althusser is not the theorist "we" (by which I mean English-language political theorists, especially in the USA and the Commonwealth) have taken him for. On the one hand, the charge of so-called structuralism against Althusser must be either dismissed entirely or at least modified so extensively as to lose its critical force (Montag 2013). The standard reading of structuralists, particularly on the topic of history, works by assuming that their "structuralism" leads them to focus only on a synchronic view. But this reading simply cannot account for the fact that Lévi-Strauss's critique of Sartre is actually a critique of Sartre's understanding of temporality. And in much the same vein, Althusser's critique of historicism was not a critique of history, nor its dismissal, but an intervention against the humanist misunderstanding of history (an ethnocentric misunderstanding)—and that very critique opened up new dimensions in thinking the politics of history. Furthermore, as Young shows so lucidly, Lévi-Strauss's critique (1966) of Sartre (1991 [1960]) reveals that synchrony was *Sartre's* problem, not that of the known "structuralist" Lévi-Strauss (Young 1990: 41–47). Finally, as I have elaborated in some detail above, Althusser's arguments on the concept of history demonstrate even more deftly that the very synchrony/diachrony dichotomy is a potent mistake, one that he not only does not subscribe to but also carefully and consistently rejects (Althusser 2009: 119; see also Althusser 1969, chapter 6). Boiled down, we see that when understood through and as a development of the concept of the social formation, Althusser's arguments on time and history take on a completely different hue.

On the other hand, and as I have already suggested in prior chapters, Althusser's commitment to a "scientific" reading of Marx and devotion to proving the worth and authenticity of Marx's "scientific revolution" have been woefully misunderstood, at least in the context of late twentieth-century US political science. In this setting, the emphasis was placed, not surprisingly, on the designation *scientific*, and that term's denotations were largely contained within the ambit of the behavioral revolution, as its impact continued to be felt in the US social science disciplines; hence, science is what seemed to be important, and what it meant was taken as a given (Smith 1985; see also Smith 1984a; cf. Corlett 1996). But what Althusser means by "science" has so very little to do with a search for causal laws or nomothetic knowledge as to either undermine the meaning of the term or force the word to undergo a catachresis. As Young (and others) have shown, Althusser's work must be read not only in the *political* context of French communism (and the conflicts within, and splintering of, the PCF after May 1968) but also, and perhaps more relevantly, in the *intellectual* context of Gaston Bachelard and Georges Canguilhem and their work in the history of science (Young 1990: 48; see Bachelard 1984; see Canguilhem 2000). For this reason, among others, it was the nature of the theoretical/conceptual *revolution*, and not the status of science, that mattered most to Althusser (Althusser 1969: 32). Hence it was the guiding idea of an "epistemological break" and of a discontinuous and disjointed theoretical history that structured and informed Althusser's reading of Marx and the history of Marxism; the attempt to distinguish the scientific from the non-scientific was less significant and had very different resonances in Althusser's own context. On this issue no point could be more important than the fact that in the North American context the status of science was granted to empiricist work, whereas for Althusser, as I discussed in Chapter 3, the most important enemy of Marx's science was the ideology of empiricism.

Here, then, I am doing more than just displacing the standard rejections of Althusser (as "structuralist," as "scientific Marxist"). In my readings of Althusser in this chapter, I am *both* demonstrating the way in which Althusser's work helps to articulate a theory of social formations *and* also showing something of the extent to which the misreadings of Althusser's work over the years often pivot on a certain kind of failure to approach his writings with an idea of the social formation in mind. Put differently, in reading Althusser within his own conjuncture I am also giving at least a partial account of the social formation. That is, I am relating his thought to a larger social whole (and in this way, bearing society in mind); this means refusing the move by which one would first extract Althusser's concepts from his social order and then attempt to "apply" them to "problems" in our social order. Indeed, Althusser's putative concepts prove less important on my reading than does his larger sense of the social formation. And ultimately, that is why my effort here is not to say that Althusser has a superior concept or theory of untimeliness, but rather to show how his understanding of the temporality of social orders can provide a stronger overall grasp on the social formation (and in this way make an important contribution to the broader project of this book).[20]

20. Thanks to Drew Walker for pushing me to emphasise this larger point.

At the same time, the work here challenges contemporary theorists to reassess the work on untimeliness as limited, in certain senses, by a failure to grasp temporality as *of* the social formation (and in this way I speak more narrowly to this particular debate). Thus, in closing this chapter, let me turn back to the differences that matter when it comes to distinguishing Althusser's radical theory of temporality from conceptions circulating within contemporary political theory today. Althusser, I have argued here, provides us with an earlier and also better argument about time *for politics*. This contention rests on the extent to which Althusser's conception of time, unlike today's notions of radical temporality, demonstrates the *connection* between, on the one hand, a given account of society, an account of the relationship between the economic, the social, the political, the cultural—an account of social order—and, on the other, the concepts of time and history. That is, Althusser demonstrates that any critique of the social formation requires a certain attentiveness to temporality (and untimeliness), and he does all this (as Stuart Hall might say) in a very "definite" way (Hall 1977). We must study the temporalities of the social order, but this means neither coming up with concepts of temporal experience that would derive from a subject[21] nor simply reading time/temporality directly off of empirical events. Instead, to think the temporalities of the social formation entails the production of concepts of temporality that work to grasp the articulation of the social formation, and this means understanding its constitution and considering its possible transformation. These concepts of temporality—those that emerge *from* the social order, but those that also make possible our understanding *of* the social formation—cannot themselves simply be empirical; they are neither given by events nor contained by experience.[22]

---

21. Young places great stress on this type of point in his critical reading of Sartre. This is why the Foucauldian displacement of man proves so crucial, and why Althusser's anti-humanism makes possible his radical and critical conception of time.

22. To call a concept of time "beyond experience," and to emphasise the distance of this concept from any empiricism, does not mean that such a concept of temporality is either a Kantian *a priori* or a Platonic *Idea*. The details of this argument would require a digression deep into Althusser's theory of history and metaphysics, but the conclusion is that Althusser's temporal concepts are both a part of history and that which makes it possible to grasp history. They are therefore not *simply* subject to historicisation, but they are also not transcendentally objective. As I discussed in Chapter 2, we can say about these concepts what Marx says about the concepts of classical political economy: they are *products* of history and yet at the very same time they are true *in general*. Hence Marx can describe labour in general as "a relationship valid for all forms of society" (Marx 1996a: 150). This is why Althusser's move "beyond experience" is in no way an abandonment of history.

My task in this chapter has been to read radical temporality *through* the concept of the social formation, while at the same time augmenting my earlier conceptualisation of the social formation *with* temporality. That work leads to two conclusions. First, it shows in relation to the literature in contemporary theory on radical temporality that any concept of history, of temporality, of change, of progress, depends utterly on a prior presupposition about the constitution and nature of the social formation. Second, and as I argued in my interpretation of Althusser's key parts of *RC*, it demonstrates that *the social formation is itself temporalised.* We must resist the reduction of temporality to an experience (even if diverse, even if non-linear) of a subject, and mobilise instead conceptions of temporality that explain the social formation—and this means, at the same time, to explain social, cultural, and political logics of and within the social formation. Contemporary political theory (and theorists) cannot rest, then, with "alternative" conceptions of time and history; we cannot merely offer, for example, untimeliness or "time out of joint" as an alternative to progress and clock time. Instead, the task of theory must include an understanding of the various temporalities of social formations, and it must therefore include an explanation of the work done by and through them. This requires, as I have been arguing throughout the book, giving an account of the social formation. I add the final dimension to that project in the next and final chapter, where I turn to the fundamental question of the material that constitutes the social formation.

5

Interests, Groups, and the Social Formation

An elementary particle is one that is so simple that no one has any understanding of it.

—Arthur Bentley, paraphrasing Robert Oppenheimer (Taylor 1957: 231)[1]

As previous chapters have done, this one explores a number of the hypotheses on the social formation that I laid out in my Introduction. This chapter, however, has a narrower and more direct focus; it centers on the 1st hypothesis, which, to recall, proposes that the social formation is never formed nor sustained by way of the *aggregation of individuals*. Marx put the point most concisely: "a society is not composed of individuals."[2] To say that a social formation is irreducible to, and inexplicable in terms of, individual aggregation, means to make two following claims: social order does not come about because of the choices that individuals make;

1. In his oft-cited dinner speech from his later years, Bentley presents the above words as if they are a direct quote from Oppenheimer (Taylor 1957: 231). Tracking the claim to its "source" turns out, it seems, to be almost impossible. In a review article, C. D. Anderson gives only a slightly different version of Bentley's phrasing, but Anderson presents the words as a loose paraphrase of his own, for an idea that he says he "believe[s] is due to Robert Oppenheimer" (Anderson 1961: 830). Later sources give a version of Anderson's phrasing, now placing the words in quotation marks and attributing them as a direct quote to Oppenheimer (but never with any citation of sources) (e.g., Weiss 1999).

2. I have given Althusser's favoured translation of this line, one he quotes repeatedly (Althusser 1976: 52); the standard English translation is "society does not consist of individuals" (Marx 1973: 265).

and political interest is not the sum total of individual interest (or otherwise the result of any sort of mathematics). Throughout this book I have repeatedly rejected the liberal, social contract idea of society as a creation of the free will and consent of autonomous individuals. Nonetheless, as my 1st hypothesis states, and as I would reiterate here, the social formation is still made up of human beings, of political groups, and of political interests. How, then, to understand the very "stuff" of the social formation? How to theorise the social formation, to grasp the politics of the social formation, in relation to political action? In order to respond to these central questions—questions at the heart of any work on the social formation—I turn here to an unlikely and little-known source.

THE RISE (AND FALL) OF ARTHUR BENTLEY

Aside, perhaps, from the histories of social science and the discipline of political science (Gunnell 1993), Arthur Bentley does not seem an obvious or likely choice for almost any imaginable project in politics or political theory. Over the first half of the twentieth century Bentley wrote seven books and almost three dozen journal articles, most published in respectable, recognisable academic outlets. Nonetheless, he wrote in relative obscurity, situated well outside the walls of academe; decades after the publication of his most sustained engagement with politics, Bentley remained unread, mostly unheard of within the fields of American politics and political theory. Yet it is precisely as a *source*, a specific and peculiar kind of source, that, for a very brief time in the middle of the twentieth century, Bentley became celebrated, even canonised. One could account for this unexpected yet intense surge of interest in, and praise of, Bentley's work from a number of angles (Jordan 2000; Gunnell 1993; Gunnell 1996), but for the limited purposes of my treatment here I am happy to reduce this complex historical phenomena to the work of one thinker: David Truman.

Truman's monumental work, *The Governmental Process*, not only reconfigured the terrain of American politics for decades to come, shifting decisively from an analysis of formal institutions (especially the courts and the Congress) to the activity of groups in society, but also *enacted* and *constructed* its debt to Bentley. The very title of Truman's book is a powerful homage to Bentley's most famous work, but just in case the allusion in the title proved too subtle, in the foreword to his own book Truman laid out his "debt" to Bentley in no uncertain terms, saying that of all the sources he draws from to develop his own theory of government, "one deserves special mention because it has given the subject much of what *systematization* it has so far received. That is Arthur F. Bentley's *The Process of Government*, first published in 1908. As the title of the present volume suggests, Bentley's 'attempt to fashion a tool' has been the principal bench mark for my thinking" (Truman 1951: ix, my emphasis). I call Truman's debt to Bentley "enacted" and "constructed" for a number of distinct reasons. First and last, Truman never offers even a cursory exegesis of Bentley's text, and as I will show below, ultimately Truman's approach to politics, to the individual, to social science, and especially to the social formation proves to be utterly at odds and completely irreconcilable with Bentley's. But there is more to it than this: Truman *projects* Bentley as a source for his own thinking so as to construct a prehistory of Truman's conception of interest groups, of pluralist politics, and of a nascent social-science empiricism. As Blokland helpfully describes the forward to Truman's magnum opus, Truman "pointedly refers to him [Bentley] to justify his [Truman's] conception of political scholarship as a discipline that studies the *behavior* of *groups* in an *empirically scientific way*" (Blokland 2011: 33). Blokland's original emphasis here matters in that it shows the significance of Bentley to Truman, a significance that lies not in Bentley's own arguments, nor in Bentley's almost sixty-year effort to develop a radical alternative to the very project of empiricism that Truman advances and defends. Rather, Bentley's book, and a few choice quotes gleaned from it (Jordan 2000: 793), stands in for a missing body of supporting work. Making *The Process of Government* into the key source, intellectual precursor, and fundamental "inspiration" for *The Governmental Process* allows Truman to build up the tradition that would support his project while simultaneously erasing a counter-tradition (i.e., by eliding Bentley's own powerful, prescient critique of Truman's own project).[3]

Some of the above claims might sound polemical, yet in what follows I will substantiate them in such a way as to show that there is really nothing extreme about them. Few scholars have turned to close study of Bentley's work, but those who have (despite their own disputes and differences of opinion) have all concluded that Truman probably never really read Bentley closely, and whether or not he did, his own arguments are hardly compatible with Bentley's (Kress 1970; Ward 1984; Mathiowetz 2011). My point is not to "prove" that Truman, and the empiricist pluralist tradition that developed out of his work (especially Dahl 1956), misread or failed to read Bentley (the facts prove rather clear on this front), but rather to reassess some crucial differences between Bentley and Truman as

3. Jordan describes it this way: "that Truman deferred to Bentley is, one suspects, a scholar looking for a big brother and inventing a founding father" (Jordan 2000: 796).

leverage to augment my account of the social formation. Moreover, even after the work of Kress and the fairly comprehensive account of Bentley's intellectual project in Ward's (1984) *Language, Form, and Inquiry*, there remains a great deal of confusion over the relationship between Bentley's work and Truman's. Both Kress and Ward, two of the only authors to study Bentley's work in great depth and across the range of his writings, insist on the distinctiveness of Bentley's work—a contention that rests mainly on distinguishing that work from Truman's. But recent attempts to compare Truman and Bentley on the theoretical merits of their arguments have come to strikingly distinct conclusions. Jordan's (2000) review concludes that while Bentley is often unfairly criticised for arguments he never really made, the only real value to be found for social science lies in Truman's project, which is quite different. In contrast, Mika LaVaque-Manty pushes the two thinkers much closer together: reading Bentley, like Truman, as an empiricist and reading Truman, like Bentley, as a critic of so-called methodological individualism (LaVaque-Manty 2006).[4]

This recent work on Bentley and Truman is therefore enigmatic. It leads readers to ask a simple but significant question: Do Bentley and Truman agree or disagree in their understanding of individuals, of groups, of social science—and, for my purposes, do they give similar accounts of the social formation? Here I will respond to this question with a multipart argument that shows the following: the "disagreement" between Jordan and LaVaque-Manty proves important—and in a way that goes beyond either of their purposes in reviewing the history of the study of groups in politics—because of the distinct type of "disagreement" that it unexpectedly (and unintentionally) articulates[5] between Truman and Bentley. In gesturing toward two

4. Mark Wenman (2013) has also written very recently about Truman and Bentley, but rather than compare the two, he discusses both in the context of reconstructing the American pluralist tradition vis-à-vis the work of William Connolly. Wenman offers only two paragraphs on Bentley, but overall he seems to accept the line of continuity between Bentley and Truman that Truman himself originally drew, while going on to forge a new linkage between Connolly and the mid-century pluralists. My own position would be to accept cautiously the idea of a connection between Connolly and Bentley, while strongly contesting the ties between Bentley and Truman (as I do in this chapter) and between Truman/Dahl and Connolly (something beyond the scope of this chapter).

5. I use the word *articulate* here in a somewhat unorthodox, perhaps awkward sense. I push on the meaning of the term because I am grasping for a way to describe a "becoming audible" (rather than a "becoming legible") that is not simply the work of one individual (speaking clearly). I want to indicate that there is something hard to grasp, hard to see, or hard to hear, about the relation between Truman and Bentley, and I aim to show that the continued disagreement about how to understand their relation (in Jordan and LaVaque-Manty) can help render that relation easier to see, and easier to hear. In

different types of "disagreement," I invoke Jacques Rancière's work as a way to clarify the terms of my intervention here. The first "disagreement" is the traditional sort, comfortably contained in the English-language sense of "disagreement": Jordan and LaVaque-Manty read Truman and Bentley quite differently; they do not agree on how to describe the relation between these two contributions to "group theory." To put it in a language invoked by Rancière: when Jordan and LaVaque-Manty look at this literature, they see two different things—Jordan sees X and LaVaque-Manty sees Y.[6] Here I want to show that this disagreement between LaVaque-Manty and Jordan over how to read Bentley and Truman can be understood as a product of a very different type of disagreement between these latter two authors. This second type of "disagreement," what Rancière calls *la mésentente*, is not so much a dispute wherein two parties "disagree," and it is not about two different arguments—one for X and one for Y. As Rancière puts it, *la mésentente* "is less concerned with argumentation [*l'argumentation*] than with what can be argued ['the argumentable', *l'argumentable*]" (Rancière 1999: xii). A *mésentente* is a misunderstanding wherein the very emergence of a common object (that which we might argue over, or disagree about) is at stake (Panagia 2006: 89; Chambers 2013: 154).

Here we can see the connection between Rancière's conception of *la mésentente* and my conception of the social formation as both produced by and productive of distinct objects. The conflict or dispute in *la mésentente*

---

this realm, however, the English language contains a plethora of sight metaphors and a dearth of sound metaphors. I would like to describe the relation between Truman and Bentley as "becoming audible" in the sense of the social order and the social formation that I have developed throughout the book. This is a "becoming audible" that works the same way we so easily describe a "becoming visible" with the word *illuminate*. Hence, the "articulation" of this disagreement cannot be the work of an individual subject; it happens or comes to pass in ways and for reasons that exceed the subject. Perhaps the best account of this would be a change in the mix of the sound at a concert, such that what was muffled, too loud or too soft, without presence—all becomes clear, full, powerful, and audible. Thanks to Rebecca Brown for helpful discussion on this point.

6. Jordan sees a Bentley writing for a different time and a different context, not really even working within social science "group theory," and he sees a Truman who did, in fact, develop some of the key concepts for later social science group theory. Hence Jordan can conclude that critics of group theory are ungenerous in their readings of Bentley, since he was not really even developing the type of theory they challenge, while simultaneously suggesting that only Truman's work has much relevance for twenty-first-century political science (Jordan 2000). LaVaque-Manty sees something completely different: a shared set of commitments to the group as the fundamental unit of analysis, and a shared project that the later author advances based on principles articulated by the earlier writer—"we can think of Truman as Lenin to Bentley's Marx" (LaVaque-Manty 2006: 11).

hinges not on different positions or arguments about some given thing, X; the disagreement itself is *over* this ostensibly common object. For Rancière there is an understanding, *entente*, at the core of this mis-understanding, *més-entente*, since both parties *claim* to see/hear/feel the same thing, X. Of course, precisely what they fail to share is the same understanding of the sense or meaning of X, because while they might seem to point to the same object, *it is not really the same object*. Working within Rancière's semantic field, we could say that parties to a *mésentente* lack a common sense of that apparently "same" object because they are operating within very different distributions of sensibility (*le partage du sensible*).[7] Translating these key terms into the language of the social formation that I have developed throughout this book, we would say that parties to a *mésentente* find themselves in distinct social formations: each sees the same object, X, but it is not the same object because the parties view it through different social formations, and as I have shown, distinct social formations produce distinct objects. Hence, on a general level one can draw out certain key elements of the social formation by reworking Rancière's well-known idea of *la mésentente*.[8]

On a much more specific level, I would also like to call attention to the particular misunderstanding/disagreement between Bentley and Truman: both say "group," both say "interest," and both say "observable," but this apparent *entente* is interrupted by a more fundamental *mésentente* because they do not share the same sense of any of these, or a whole host of other terms. Indeed, they work within such vastly different partitions/arrangements of sensibility that their shared use of "group" or "interest" only serves to mute what would otherwise be a radical disputation between them. The further exploration of this more fundamental "disagreement" can serve to augment my account of the social formation. To give an account of the social formation requires an understanding of the relationship between individuals and larger "groups"—what other thinkers might refer to as "constellations" or "assemblages"—that help constitute the whole (Deleuze and Guattari 1987; Connolly 2008). As I reread it here, the dissensus between Truman and Bentley revolves around the problem of how to account for the whole without reducing it to an equation that would be derived from its constituent parts. In this chapter, I develop a reading of

7. For more on this central term in Rancière's project, see Rancière (1999; 2001; 2006); Panagia (2010); and Chambers (2013), among many others.

8. This broader point helps to illuminate my specific claim, made at the end of Chapter 4, that in many ways my reading of various authors "on" the social formation itself functions performatively as an effort to articulate a social formation.

Bentley that draws out his account of groups as a radical alternative to Truman's (and the entire empiricist tradition that followed Truman); I rearticulate Bentley's project as an effort to understand individuals and groups as co-constitutive elements of the whole. That reading serves to expand my broader theoretical development of the idea of the social formation by adding specificity about the material that makes up any given social order. At the same time, my work here once again sets a theory of the social formation on ground far apart from traditional empiricist social science or traditional liberal political theory. And finally, in turning to the question of political interest, my work here on Bentley also raises the larger question (which I pose in more specific terms in the Coda that follows this chapter) of how one would develop a *critical* account of the social formation—a sense of what it would mean to contest the current configuration of society, to call for transformation, to bring about change.

TRUMAN: GROUPS AS A RELATION OF INDIVIDUAL INTERESTS

As I indicated above, Truman's book on "interest group" politics begins by telling a developmental story, one in which Truman carries on a project inaugurated by Bentley almost fifty years earlier. My reading contests this story substantively, and also structurally; hence, I start not with Bentley's work, but with Truman's own independent account of groups, individuals, and interests. I thus pursue not the chronological development of ideas from Bentley on to Truman, but instead work genealogically, pursuing a certain line of descent from Truman back to Bentley.[9] This approach helps me to interrupt and overturn Truman's story of progress, and to show that it is the earlier thinker who has the far more radical ideas, and the later thinker who accommodates his own thought to the norms and expectations of both

9. My overall project here is not to produce a full genealogy, as this is not a work in the history of ideas. Yet a genealogical *approach* does help me to represent with maximal force the disagreement between Truman and Bentley—so as to better develop my account of the social formation. I should note here that for those more interested in tracing the development of these ideas in either the history of thought or the field of politics, it would be crucial to examine the intermediary and catalytic role of the early emergence of professional political consultancy. Putting it provocatively, we might say that the transition from Bentley to Truman would not have been possible without the role of early political consultants like Edward Bernays. For a full account of professional political consultants in this period, including their influence on the development of politics and political ideas, see Sheingate (2013).

twentieth- and twenty-first-century social science. First, then, I need to lay out the framework of Truman's work on its own terms, prior to any consideration of Bentley's work.

The opening chapters of Truman's book have a curious, and I suspect unappreciated, structure. After the foreword (containing the homage to Bentley), Truman starts not with definitional, theoretical, or conceptual work. Instead, he engages in a ground-clearing effort: chapter 1 of *The Governmental Process*, as its title indicates, sets out a response to/defence of "The Alleged Mischief of Factions." Truman is clearly worried that American culture already sees "interest groups" as vile and despicable, as a problem for politics—"a modern pathology" (Truman 1951: 4). Truman wants to disprove this thesis, to show that there is both nothing new and nothing inherently troublesome about the role of groups in American politics. He does this by way of a truly bizarre reading of the American founders. To prove that "group pressures . . . are not new in America," he turns to Madison's famous definition of a faction in *Federalist 10*, quoting that celebrated, one-sentence definition as follows: "a number of citizens, whether amounting to a majority or a minority of the whole, who are united and actuated by some common impulse, or of interest" (Truman 1951: 4; quoting Madison 2012 [1787]: 24–25). Truman seeks to use this quote as powerful support for his claim that the pressures of groups, the very idea of an "interest group," goes all the way back to the founding.

Doubtless, one can see clearly that Truman's quote of Madison indicates that a faction, which Truman says is synonymous with a "party" or a "group," is nothing more than a group that shares an interest: "a number of citizens . . . united . . . by some common . . . interest." Yet before turning below to Truman's explicit conceptual development of this fundamental idea, here I must interrupt that analysis to make clear that the above is a flagrant misrepresentation of Madison's famous definition of faction. In his quoting, Truman leaves out the most important part of the definition, since after referring to a group united by a common impulse, Madison goes on to specify that a faction is a group who shares an interest "*adverse* to the rights of other citizens, or to the permanent and aggregate interests of the community" (Madison 2012: 25, emphasis added). In order to generalise Madison's account of factions so that it can serve as a broad template for any understanding of an interest group, Truman has to erase from the definition the very element that mattered most to Madison. The entire point of *Federalist 10* is to show how the proposed new US Constitution will be able to deal with precisely the sort of "group interests" that prove to be a danger to rights and freedoms. If by "interest group" we mean to denote a neutral sense in which some set of individuals share an interest, then we can never equate an interest group with a faction, since for Madison it is essential to the meaning of faction that the shared interest is a *dangerous* interest.[10] This means, ironically, that in his effort to show that group interests are not pathological, Truman turns to Madison's account of how to deal with *pathological* groups. Indeed, if the task before him (Truman) is to demonstrate, in the middle of the twentieth century, why "interest groups" are not a danger, Madison's account of factions should have been the worst choice for support. Yet Madison's definition, properly edited, tempts Truman because it gives him the chance to kill two birds with one stone: he can show that "interest groups" have always been a part of American politics, while also proving that there is nothing inherently "bad" about them. By evacuating Madison's concept of faction of its central element, Truman thus sets up the possibility that his own work on interest groups will be a further advancement of established and celebrated ideas in American thought.

But just in case going back 160 years to the American founding is not enough to prove the longevity of the "interest group" idea, Truman begins his second chapter by quickly reaching further, back to the fourth century BCE. Truman opens the chapter with the words "man is a social animal," an idea he attributes to Aristotle (Truman 1951: 14). Here again we see a deep irony in the moves Truman makes to support his notion that interest groups are an old and venerable concept: while Aristotle would surely agree that man was a social animal, that was not at all the point of Aristotle's argument in his *Politics*. Quite the opposite, really, as Aristotle believed that *all animals were social creatures*, whereas man was distinctive in being a political animal, a creature who can deliberate and judge, and thereby a creature properly fit to live, and live fully, only in a polis.[11] To remove man from the polis would be to raise him up to the level of a god, or lower him down to that of a beast. The idea that man is a "social animal" was, from Aristotle's perspective, at best a banal notion and at worst a problematic and wrongheaded idea, one that underlay the theory of his teacher, Plato,

10. Dahl (1956) does something similar with his treatment of Madison. Like Truman, he somehow manages to equate "faction" with "interest group," and like Truman, this requires misreading or misunderstanding just what mattered most to Madison about the concept of a "faction."

11. Marx mocks Aristotle on just this point. In his text, Marx gets correct just what Truman has backwards, as Marx affirms the idea of man as a social animal, distinguishing that notion from Aristotle's idea of man as a political animal. In the footnote that follows, Marx attributes Aristotle's thesis that *anthrōpos* is a being designed for life in the polis to Aristotle's own social formation. Marx writes: "This is quite as characteristic of classical antiquity as Franklin's definition of man as a tool-making animal is characteristic of Yankeedom" (Marx 1990: 444).

who imagined (much to Aristotle's horror) the possibility of humans living together in a "city of pigs," satisfying only their barest and basest animal needs.[12]

I point out these ironic misreadings (attributing to authors almost the exact opposite ideas that they themselves defended) not for the sake of critique itself and not merely to correct the record, but because the elisions are significant to our understanding of Truman—and thus, in turn, for grasping the significance of Bentley's thought. Truman's theory of groups and interests has no way to account for understandings that were crucial to Madison and Aristotle and that play a significant role in my own understanding of the social formation. First is the Madisonian idea of a faction, a group whose interests, by definition, are in extreme tension with the fabric of the social whole. This central Madisonian insight supports my 1st hypothesis on the social formation (as never simply an aggregation of individuals) and always thwarts any straightforward liberal appropriation of Madison. Next is the Aristotelian idea that the social order is never simply, neutrally, social, but always already introjected by a political dimension—an idea that reinforces my 2nd hypothesis. This is to say that both of Truman's misreadings of canonised authors remain bound up with his overall understanding of the interest group, and both help to clarify the wide chasm between a Trumanesque attempt to account for the social formation, and my own. We can say that for Truman the interest group is *relational with respect to the individual, but isolated with respect to any larger social formation.*

---

12. Given that Plato goes on to develop a much richer and fuller city (the kallipolis) than the city of pigs, it remains a point of contention whether Aristotle's criticism is a sound one, but there is no doubt that Aristotle advances this critique (Mayhew 1997). On my reading of Aristotle, the criticism matters regardless of whether it hits its target, and this is because it underscores for Aristotle the important difference between understanding *anthrōpos* as a merely social animal or a fully political animal. This is just what makes Truman's claim odd, as it entirely misses Aristotle's emphasis in the *Politics*, and that strange claim of Truman's also matters vis-à-vis his assertions about carrying on Bentley's legacy. Bentley takes Aristotle as paradigmatic of the *wrong way* of thinking about the social order. A critique of Aristotle lies at the heart of Bentley's overall project. Aristotle is, of course, no liberal, but Aristotle strongly asserts the position that the composition of the individual matches/mirrors the composition of the polis. The polis is structured by slavery, and so it simply must be the case, for Aristotle, that some individuals are naturally slaves (even if some are only slaves by convention, and therefore ought not be slaves at all). According to Bentley, to make this Aristotelian move is to get the picture entirely wrong. Bentley contends that the existence of slavery in the social order tells us something fundamentally important about that social order, while not necessarily telling us anything at all about the essence of the human being (Bentley 1908: 12; Bentley 1935; see Kress 1970).

In the remainder of this section I will unpack this formulation; I use it to try to capture something very slippery, yet significant, in Truman's thinking about the group. Truman's position on the relation between group and individual proves far from straightforward, and it has led to widely divergent accounts. Given his obvious focus on *the group* and its role in politics, and taking into account some of his comments early on in the book about refusing to treat the individual as an isolated unit of analysis (Truman 1951: 16), it would be easy to take Truman for a critic of methodological individualism. Indeed, this is just how LaVaque-Manty reads Truman, suggesting that now might be a good time to return to Bentley and Truman for alternatives to the dominance of methodological individualism in today's political science. For LaVaque-Manty, this is what unites Bentley and Truman; it is the crucial point on which they agree, on which they share a fundamental understanding (*entente*). "The central commitment of Bentley and Truman's group interpretation of politics is that groups are irreducible. They cannot be reduced to the individuals who make them up. They cannot be reduced to the individuals' private interests or to their biological, psychological, or demographic attributes" (LaVaque-Manty 2006: 14). In striking contrast, Dean Mathiowetz sees Truman's emphasis on the group as serving ultimately only to obscure Truman's individualism. As Mathiowetz puts it, perhaps in implicit response to readings like LaVaque-Manty's, "Truman's individualism is covert" (Mathiowetz 2011: 185).

I aim not to reconcile these two divergent understandings of Truman; rather, with my formulation from above I mean to make some sense out of how such different readings can emerge in the first place. That is, while I side decisively with Mathiowetz in seeing Truman as committed to a type of individualism, I want to delineate Truman's understanding of group/individual interest in a way that sheds light on LaVaque-Manty's reading. Truman's account proves important for the way in which it seems to favour a group interpretation while still implicitly calling on an individualist ontology blinded to the politics of the social formation.

On my reading, for Truman the group matters to politics because it is the space *within which* interests are formed, and, for Truman, politics will always be a matter of interests. For this reason, Truman does want the initial focus for political analysis to lie on the group, not any isolated individual (such as those state-of-nature creatures produced by social contract theory). Yet when he turns to the task of telling his readers how to define a group, Truman remains quite comfortable doing so in terms of individuals. A group, therefore, is "any collection of individuals who have some characteristic in common" (Truman 1951: 23). Truman articulates the concept of a group in terms of individuals, even if he has already told us that we cannot study the politics of interest by looking at individuals who are isolated. In other words, on Truman's account, individuals never appear alone; they always become visible within groups. Already, one can see the slipperiness in Truman's account, since groups seem to matter for how they give us access to individuals.

And Truman highlights this dimension of his approach to interest groups when he adds one crucial addition/inflection to his above, basic definition of the group: we should study groups as the "basic social units" because groups create uniform behaviours *between and among the individuals* within them. Groups matter because of the internal relationships they contain: "These interactions . . . give the group its molding and guiding powers. In fact, they are the group" (Truman 1951: 24). When Truman says the group is "these interactions," he means that interactions, the "relationships" between and among individual members of the group, constitute the group precisely by constituting the shared interests of its individual members. A group, for Truman, is always a place where *individual* interest is formed and solidified. He goes on to specify the type and frequency of interactions among individuals required before a group can be said to exist, an argument that hinges on the process by which individual interest is consolidated. Truman writes: "The function of an association . . . is to *stabilize* the relations among their [individual] members" (Truman 1951: 56).

As LaVaque-Manty would emphasise in his reading, the group might be said to be the "fundamental unit of analysis" in the study of politics. However, as Mathiowetz might point out: this is precisely because within a specific group, *individual* interests are formed. More importantly, Truman himself emphasises that any methodological focus on the group should not serve to indicate that the group has a privileged ontological status. Truman responds to a potential critic/sceptic by making it clear that his account of interest groups does not hypostatise the group as metaphysically real. The clarification is crucial for understanding the "covert" individualism of Truman, and for enabling a productive contrast with Bentley. Truman says that "a group is 'real' in the sense that the interactions that are the group can be observed" (Truman 1951: 29). But since "group interactions" are always the interactions of *individuals within a group*, then we always observe individual actions, not "group actions." Truman's own political methodologies were not all that advanced from the perspective of today's social scientists, but his ontological account perfectly allows for—nay, encourages—the very sort of reduction to the individual that LaVaque-Manty wishes to resist (LaVaque-Manty 2006: 15).

Truman suggests that we should not make a false distinction between individual and society, but his reasoning shows that the distinction is false for the very reason that all group phenomena (including society itself) can be traced to individuals. If multiple individuals are members of a group and therefore have shared interests, then we are safe to talk about and analyse this group behaviour, but we are authorised to do so because, at base, group behaviour is the behaviour of individuals with common interests.[13] Truman refuses the isolated individual—"men exist only in society"—but he understands any group and any group activity as individual action—"society is the interaction of men" (Truman 1951: 29). For Truman, an interest group exists only on the basis of the "shared attitudes" of the members of that group, and as Mathiowetz shows, for Truman, "attitudes are fundamentally individualistic" (Mathiowetz 2011: 186). Truman contends that we do not find individuals anywhere except in groups, but he also insists that it is indeed individuals that we do find there (Truman 1951: 48). Perhaps, then, we might say that Truman refuses *methodological individualism*, since he tells the political analyst, practically, to look at groups, but he only does so while reinforcing a rather rigid *ontological individualism*, since the groups we are looking at are always and everywhere constituted by individuals. Truman thus insists on the status of individuals as the "elementary particle" for groups and society.

The picture of Truman's social ontology comes into relief: while we cannot isolate individuals, since their interests always form in relation to other individuals, we can isolate single groups, precisely as the locus in which those individual interests are shaped. Truman is therefore a pluralist in one sense, because, paraphrasing Hannah Arendt, we might say that for him, man does not exist in the singular, only men (in groups) exist in the plural. But his pluralism has a hard limit: since a group can exist in the singular, it remains the fundamental space for individual interaction. The idea of "relationality" in Truman centers almost exclusively on the relations among these individuals. If we were to construct a Trumanesque concept of the social whole, we would say that it is made up of discrete and bounded

13. LaVaque-Manty, in a move that shifts his account of Truman closer to both Mathiowetz's and my own, says that the "group approach" to politics can be compatible with the call for "microfoundations" work. In this way, he accepts the idea that Truman's focus on the group is not at odds with rational choice causal explanations of individual action, but he misses the way in which Bentley's approach is not just "incompatible" with microfoundations but explicitly developed in opposition to such an approach (*avant la lettre*, of course). As I show below, the account of the social formation that I develop out of Bentley's work rejects the entire idea that a social formation even has such "microfoundations."

units, interest groups—units that we can observe, count, and categorise and whose actions we can predict (Truman 1951: 63, 504).[14]

BENTLEY: GROUPS IN RELATION AS THE "RAW MATERIAL"

While Bentley's *The Process of Government* proves, by an absolutely enormous margin, to be his most well-known and impactful work, it is hardly the first or best place to begin to grasp his understanding of the group and the individual. Indeed, in many ways Bentley's once-canonised text actually presupposes familiarity with his earlier work while gesturing toward his own later clarifications and elaborations. For this reason, much in Bentley's understanding of the group, and especially of the individual's relation to the group, remains opaque in his one book ostensibly on politics. However, prior to *Process*, Bentley's work had already circled around the question of the individual, and immediately after publishing the book that would give him his only, if brief, fame, Bentley returned to clarify decisively his understanding of the individual in relation to the group.

After completing his undergraduate thesis in 1893, Bentley devoted his first serious piece of intellectual work to an essay titled "On the Relation of the Individual to Society." Written in late 1894, but never published, this essay sets out to answer the fundamental question of the best level of analysis for the social sciences broadly (Ward 1984: 34). In this and other early methodological essays written during the time of Bentley's dissertation

14. Truman's empiricism is thoroughgoing and genuine, and not, so far as I can tell, a subject of potential disputation among his readers. LaVaque-Manty, however, also attributes an empiricism to Bentley. He describes Bentley's famous book as requiring "a commitment to empiricism" (LaVaque-Manty 2006: 4). But the only way to support this claim is to quote *Process* out of context, in those places where Bentley emphasises the importance of observation and refers to the "raw material" of politics. These quotes notwithstanding, Bentley spent his career resolutely opposing all the central tenets of empiricism, and Ward painstakingly documents the ways in which Bentley's account of "observation" and references to science prove utterly incompatible with empiricist social science. He shows quite convincingly, as does a closer reading of Bentley's broader corpus, that Bentley's thought cannot be reconciled to the epistemological tenets of empiricism (Ward 1984: 80). Even the recent, newer edition of *Process* itself contains an introduction by the editor, Thelma Lavine, devoted mainly to underlining the fact that "the behavioralists' view of Bentley is now perceived to have been a misreading" (Lavine 2008: xv). Perhaps LaVaque-Manty tends to misrepresent Bentley here because his own (admittedly limited) approach to Bentley remains so bound up within the discourse of early twenty-first-century social science; thus he misreads Bentley's commitment to science and "observability" by seeing it through the lens of that much later, much different, paradigm.

research, he saw the answer to the "best level" of explanation to lie somewhere within individual volition, or "mind" (Ward 1984: 33–40). Bentley will later repudiate these early writings for their "psychologism," but it remains essential to emphasise that even in these very early days of Bentley's intellectual development, he never found himself at all sympathetic to an empiricist approach to social science. Ward stresses this point at both the specific level of this early essay, in which Ward says "Bentley is especially opposed to mechanistic causal explanations in social science" (Ward 1984: 34), and at the broadest level of Bentley's overall intellectual development, about which Ward writes forcefully (and, I think, convincingly):

> It is essential for students of Bentley to realize that he never agreed with "positivist" visions of social science. His exposure to the neo-Kantian currents of German social science [especially during his time studying in Germany in 1893–1894] immunized him against any version of the social science methodology that appeared mechanistic or reductionist. (Ward 1984: 33)

Ward's use of the word "immunized" is pejorative, but it also says something significant about Bentley's relation to positivism that can help illuminate later misreadings of Bentley—most famously, Truman's, but perhaps also LaVaque-Manty's—that would try to reconcile his thought with an emerging and then developed quantitative social science empiricism. For Bentley, the very idea of causal explanation of social and political action simply made no sense. When we look at the world, says Bentley, we find human meaning, we find complex human action, we find language forms (Bentley 1926; Bentley 1932; see Ward 1984: 28, 31, 36). We do not find mental processes, or any other sorts of sense-data. All of these are hypostatised "elementary particles" that only obscure our efforts to understand or explain a social formation that can simply never be reduced to such particles.

In this and other early essays, Bentley looks toward something like the individual, or what he calls "the individuality,"[15] as a potential answer to the

15. As Ward explains, this coinage of Bentley's refers more to the "properties" and less to the "experiences" of an individual (Ward 1984: 242). We might think of this as an early attempt by Bentley to move in the direction of something like "subject positions"—that is, an attempt to consider the location and status of "the individual" within a larger social formation. At the same time, we could take this notion as a gesture toward the idea that something like "individuality" might appear within or crystalise out of a social formation without that emergent shape being determined by or ultimately reducible to any fixed location within the social order from which it emerged. My thanks to Bill Connolly for helpful dialogue on this point.

question of how to explain or understand social phenomena.[16] Even here, Bentley's work remains incompatible with a present-day methodological individualism, but after his dissertation Bentley moves much further away from his own, early position—and from anything at all like an empiricist account. I would describe the development of Bentley's thought as follows: *Process of Government* marks the decisive break with "the individual," while the essay "Knowledge and Society" more directly and reflectively *declares* (post hoc) that break and works out its details. In other words, on my reading, in *Process* Bentley is already working with a radically non-individualist and non-foundationalist account of the social formation, but the text itself does not always make these points clear or elaborate on them; the lack of specificity about this point, in *Process*, makes the work opaque in places and opens the text to multiple (mis)readings. In important contrast, Bentley's essay "Knowledge and Society," written directly after the publication of *Process*, makes his position on the individual (in relation to society and the group) absolutely stark.

"Knowledge and Society" proves to be a crucial text in Bentley's overall body of work; written less than two years after the publication of his most-read work, this short essay elaborates in detail, and clarifies with much more precision, some of the central elements of Bentley's thought. These are dimensions of Bentley's thinking that prove fundamental to the arguments of *Process* yet remain murky there—elements that will prove central to Bentley over the course of four more decades of published work. In my own survey of Bentley's wide and deep body of writings, I have found "Knowledge and Society" to be one of, if not the most, important of his writings. I thus echo Ward's appraisal of this essay, when he writes:

> Bentley's seldom-read essay "Knowledge and Society" (1910) . . . is one of the most impressive statements of his agenda. Nearly forty years later he still considered it a suitable statement of a number of his views, an unusual judgement for a thinker who insisted almost obsessively on the inadequacy of his earlier writings. Bentley even considered reissuing *The Process of Government* in a revised version "coordinated" with "Knowledge and Society." (Ward 1984: 108)[17]

---

16. Ward suggests that Bentley's first answer, the one developed over the course of these early writings, is to propose "mind" as the explanatory variable for social science, especially in his 1895 essays. But Bentley means "mind" in the German *verstehen* sense, and not at all in the psychological (or psychologistic) sense; as an "answer" it searches for social meaning as the "basic unit of study," and "mind" has nothing to do with individual mental processes (Ward 1984: 31, 35).

17. Ward makes a strong case for the significance of many of Bentley's unpublished works to a deeper understanding of Bentley's project, many of which are now more

The last sentence in this quote may be the most important since it suggests the enduring significance of "Knowledge and Society" to those interested in Bentley's work vis-à-vis both the study of politics and the development of political science and the history of political thought as fields of knowledge. Given Ward's claims for the importance of this essay to an understanding of Bentley's project—and particularly to an understanding of his conception of the individual in relation to the group—it is striking that *none* of the recent literature on Bentley in the field of politics even includes the essay in its works cited list.[18]

I will read "Knowledge and Society" within the context of the much more famous arguments of *The Process of Government*, and thus, at the same time, I will use the more focused and more specific arguments about individuals in this essay to clarify and refine the terms of Bentley's better-known text. One way to state the fundamental thesis of Bentley's most-read work is as follows: groups and their actions are the very stuff of politics. The "raw material" of politics is, for Bentley, nothing more and nothing less than group action (Bentley 1908: 173).[19] The thesis seems simple enough on the face of it, but it obviously demands further elaboration of the idea or concept of a group. In response to this requirement of his own theory—to the definite need to account for the group—Bentley begins to make a series of intentionally circular responses. Hence, Bentley insists on conceptualising the group, offering a definition of it, *only through its actions*. A group "is" the pressure that the group applies. There is no "static" concept of the group, for the group is always in motion. A group "is always so many men, *acting, or tending toward action*—that is, in various stages

---

accessible thanks to Ward himself. "Knowledge and Society" was, in fact, published late in Bentley's lifetime (1954), but more than four decades after it was written (1910).

18. This claim extends from LaVaque-Manty's (2006) essay that focuses specifically on the question of individuals and groups, to Jordan's (2000) purported review of the literature, and even to Mathiowetz's (2011) otherwise insightful and sophisticated account of Bentley's understanding of individual/group. Writing well before Ward, Kress does cite "Knowledge and Society" (Kress 1970: 142), but only Ward places such great emphasis on this text, underscoring Bentley's own sense of the piece's significance to his thought.

19. Ward offers a thorough and persuasive argument for why Bentley's references to "raw material" for the study of politics in no way commits him to the tenets of twentieth-century social science empiricism. Quite the contrary, what Bentley actually means by "raw material" ties his thinking to the German *verstehen* tradition and furthers the cleavage between his approach to the study of society and that of the empiricists. On my reading, Ward's broad interpretation of Bentley's thought (and its development) takes the feet out from under LaVaque-Manty's casual references to Bentley's "commitment to empiricism" (Ward 1984: 81, and ff.; cf. LaVaque-Manty 2006: 7).

of action. *Group and group activity are equivalent terms*" (Bentley 1908: 210, emphasis added). What is a group? Action itself, the pressure exerted by the group so as to bring that group's very existence into view.[20]

But if we cannot freeze the group in place, prior to its action, this means that "group" must have a very specific relation to "interest." Thus, Bentley spins his hermeneutic circle yet again, by contending that just as group equals action, so, too, does group equal interest. "There is no group without its interest," and lest we misread this as a claim that a group is an entity definable apart from an interest that it might separately "have," Bentley clarifies that "an interest . . . is the equivalent of a group" (Bentley 1908: 210). Bentley himself spells out the logical conclusions here, showing that when we speak of an "interest group" or a "group interest" we are really speaking tautologically or redundantly, "merely for the sake of clearness in expression" (Bentley 1908: 210). In his overview, LaVaque-Manty suggests that interest for Bentley is something "reflected" by the group, or that the group can be understood with respect to an "underlying interest" (LaVaque-Manty 2006: 7, 8). In response, I want to stress that Bentley's very idea of "group" actually resists, at the definitional level, the notion of an "underlying interest." The interest cannot "underlie" or "reflect" the group, since the interest is the group; the interest and the group remain indistinguishable. I make this point as counter to LaVaque-Manty, but I certainly do not claim it as a unique interpretation of Bentley. Ward is emphatic here: "We cannot look beneath or behind the notion of 'group' in order to account for it. 'Group' for Bentley is a categorical term, for it is presented as an indispensable and irreducible part of our understanding of society" (Ward 1984: 78). And perhaps in a more subtle response to LaVaque-Manty than my direct one here, Mathiowetz argues similarly: "What lies behind interest group activity is contestation itself. Groups in conflict are the basic, fundamental unit of political analysis" (Mathiowetz 2011: 181). I would go so far as to say that Mathiowetz's second line here rewrites and alters his first: to say that the basic unit of political analysis is "groups-in-conflict" is to resist the idea that *anything* underlies the group.

20. Bentley thereby undercuts in advance, as it were, the possibility of appropriating his thinking of the group and group interests for any sort of "methodological groupism," which would simply invert the idea of "methodological individualism." Put differently, we would misread Bentley entirely if we took "the group" as *his* elementary particle; on the contrary, and as I show throughout this chapter, his theory of the group is designed to refute the possibility of any elementary particle. Importantly, this resistance to "groupism" also renders Bentley's thought incompatible with a narrow concept of "the party."

Indeed, Bentley's account refuses the sort of ontology that would propose groups as basic atoms that are then set into motion—that is, into conflict. Rather, there can be no single group; Bentley's "pluralism" goes so much further than Truman's. A group only has existence in relation to other groups, and that "relation" is always one of (some degree of) conflict. Bentley elaborates: "No group can be stated, or defined, or valued . . . except in terms of other groups. No group has meaning except in relation to other groups. No group can even be conceived of as a group—when we get right down to the facts—except as set off by itself, and, so to speak, *made a group by the other groups*" (Bentley 1908: 214, emphasis added).[21] Where for Truman the group mattered most as an area within which individual interest could be shaped and formed, for Bentley groups are entities always in motion with respect to other groups. Throughout *Process*, and throughout his career, Bentley consistently focuses on relations and relationality as primary. There can be no "primary particles" for Bentley for the very reason that only the motion, the action, the *relation* among so-called elements counts as "primary." Such relationality entails that there can be no closed framework; instead, we always find a porous and open social whole. Hence his refusal of any sort of quantum *unit*. The only unit is the group, but there is no such thing as a singular group, or a group in isolation from other groups.[22] This emphasis on a fundamental relationality helps explain Bentley's notion that groups and interests are "co-constitutive." This is my

21. On this point, LaVaque-Manty also reads Bentley quite oddly when he asserts that for Bentley interest proves to be "satisfactory as an explanation only when it is 'isolated' from other interests" (LaVaque-Manty 2006: 9). In a certain sort of way, this is true, in that Bentley rejects *both* the idea of causal explanation and isolated interests, so that, in order for causal explanation to be possible, interests would need to be isolable. Yet, for Bentley, both prove utterly impossible, and both are wrongheaded approaches to understanding interests within the social formation.

22. This account of Bentley's thinking vis-à-vis the group indicates why I resist LaVaque-Manty's description of "Truman's Bentleyan conception of a group as a collection of people engaged in an activity" (LaVaque-Manty 2006: 12). The definition seems straightforward, even banal: calling a group a "collection of people" is certainly not a technical or controversial definition. But Truman's definition cannot be called "Bentleyan" for the simple reason that Bentley himself refuses to identify the group as "a collection of individuals." For Bentley the group is an acting interest that only emerges in relation to other groups. We see "a group" in its conflict with other groups, which is to say that we *cannot see* a group as an aggregation or ensemble of individuals. I take Bentley quite seriously when he says that the "raw material" of politics is groups, not individuals. To do so means to draw out all of the ways in which Truman's approach to the group diverges quite radically from Bentley's. Again, they both say "group," but the worlds they describe when using this "same" word—these are different worlds.

word, but it captures Bentley's own sense that there can be no group with "its" interest, and no interest without the group that "expresses" that interest (Bentley 1908: 211–12).

Returning to Mathiowetz's line from above, we can see that "contestation" does not so much "lie behind" groups as it, too, proves to be co-constitutive of them. I see my reading of this line as a friendly amendment to Mathiowetz, since he himself offers just this sort of interpretation of Bentley when he goes on to develop the idea of interest as "the manifestation of politics, not its foundation" (Mathiowetz 2011: 182). In this context it seems to me worth the risk of anachronism to describe Bentley's account of politics as "postfoundationalist," since the resistance to stable, fixed, or elementary particles remains one of his abiding principles throughout his career. It proves tempting to reduce Bentley's account to the formula, interests = groups = action, but we can do so only while seeing the important *dynamic flow* across these equal signs, and Bentley's later work, especially with Dewey, elaborates on the "trans-actional" account of process and evolution (Dewey and Bentley 1949). But even here in *Process* (not to mention in its very title), we witness a powerful emphasis on the dynamics of group interaction; we see "group interest" as formed and emerging only within the "trans-actions" between and among groups. My account of Bentley's definitional work on the "group" has recurred to the idea of the hermeneutic circle, wherein the meaning of each particular element depends on not only other elements (groups always in relation to other groups) but also the broader structure as a whole. Yet most readers of Bentley's major book on politics feel a compulsion to ask not about that larger structure, but about what they see as a central element in any political account: the individual.

In *Process*, Bentley's remarks on the individual prove sparse. Most of the time, Bentley takes it as read that the "raw material" of society, of politics, simply is the group. Aside from his more focused and specific critique of the psychological language of "feelings" and "ideas" and "sentiments," Bentley sees little reason to elaborate on the "individual." Nonetheless, the rare comment he does make proves striking and significant, and such comments have not failed to provoke and even confuse readers over the years. Thus, at the end of the first long section of the book, Bentley sneaks in this claim: "The individual as the definite, firm, positive foundation for individualized feelings and ideas, is *a highly abstract social idea* himself, and in the way in which he is put to use, *fictitious*" (Bentley 1908: 168, emphasis added). This sentence emerges somewhat out of the blue, tucked into a paragraph that reiterates the main point of Bentley's first section of the book. And the grammatical structure of the sentence hides the counterintuitive punch at the end—a punch I have tried to draw out with my italics.[23] Harder to miss is the short shift to the individual that Bentley carries out at the heart of his conceptual work on the group. In the midst of pressing his claim that the only way to study the group is by observing its activity, which is nothing less than observing the interest itself in relation to other interests, Bentley asserts that the quality and status of a group's activity differs not at all from that of an individual. Groups *are* activity, as are individuals their activity; all that differs is the perspective from which such activity shall be observed. Here, however, Bentley again makes a stronger claim about the status of the individual in relation to understanding and explaining political and social action. Reprising his line from earlier, and even repeating its grammatical structure, Bentley writes: "The individual stated for himself, and invested with an extra-social unity of his own, is a fiction" (Bentley 1908: 213). Bentley does not linger on this striking claim; he quickly moves on to further elaboration of the concept of group.[24] Yet many readers might find themselves demanding clarification from Bentley, wondering if he means merely to eschew all tenets of methodological individualism, to deny the existence of the individual, or what.

The text of *Process* itself offers few *direct* answers. I would argue that any consistent reading of the book—from the detailed critique of psychologism and empiricism in the first part, to the development of the concept of the group and the insistence on the group (and the group alone) as the only "observable" "raw material" of politics, to Bentley's specific examples of

23. In teaching Bentley frequently over recent years I have found that both undergraduates and graduate students easily miss this sentence—miss it entirely in their reading of the book—and I did as well in my first few times through the text. In this context, Ward makes a very helpful observation when he argues that *Process* is Bentley's one and only text that tries (and, Ward implies, fails) to do "substantive social theory" while also offering "methodological reflections" (Ward 1984: 19). I am not prepared to condemn Bentley for this attempt, since the mixed genres of the book might also help to explain its wider appeal and greater longevity, but I do take Ward's point as providing a partial explanation for the opacity of this text. Here again, Bentley reminds the reader of Foucault, whose texts frequently combine concrete archival analysis with broad methodological generalisations (which remain broad, even when Foucault refers to them as "precautionary"). And just as these elements of Foucault's texts have served as the source for contentious interpretive disagreements, so have similar dimensions of Bentley's texts led readers to drastically different conclusions about his project.

24. We can see a certain development of Bentley's thinking on the individual in his theorisation of both leadership and despotism: even on those occasions when it looks most like we have one person whose actions prove most important, Bentley shows us that what matters in terms of politics still starts and ends with the group (Bentley 1908: 223, 314).

political activity—requires taking Bentley quite seriously about his refusal of the individual as any sort of explanatory concept. But rather than tease out subtle interpretations of ambiguous passages, why not turn to Bentley's own specific and detailed elaborations on the individual, all in a text written immediately following the publication of *Process* (and, one might imagine, designed to answer to specific confusions that arose in readings of that book)? "Knowledge and Society" has a general and vague title, but its opening heading, containing the very first words of the piece, removes any traces of ambiguity: "In What Sense Does an 'Individual Man' Have Existence for Science?" (Bentley 1954a [1910]: 3).

Bentley believed that one of the most serious obstacles standing in the way of developing a better understanding of social and political phenomena was the intuitive and commonly held conviction by which so many people "hold that their feeling for individual existence is fundamental as truth" (Bentley 1954a: 3; see Ward 1984: 11). As someone always committed to the idea that natural science and social science could mutually inform one another, Bentley turned here to the insights of other sciences, where he saw far more development away from the putative "definite reality" of the individual. The question, Bentley insists, need not concern metaphysical speculation on the status of the soul, but centers instead on whether we can properly understand social phenomena—whether we can make sense of and grasp the social formation—if we operate on the assumption of a definite, separate, and independent existence of "individuality." On this front Bentley makes a subtle yet important point: he argues that doing away with the individual for the purposes of understanding the world will not take away from that world (will not diminish it) but will rather augment it. He claims that, "The individual can be banished *only by showing a plus* of existence, *not by alleging a minus*. If the individual falls it will be because the real life of men, when it is widely enough investigated, proves too rich for him" (Bentley 1954a: 4, emphasis added). In other words, our grasp of the world and our explanation of social and political phenomena always prove too impoverished if we insist on explaining them through "the individual." To allow the individual to "fall" means to allow the richness of our explanations of society (of "men") to grow and flourish. We will be made richer through such explanations since we will then be able to understand the richness of the (social) world. The job of the social theorist or scientist is to try to "look at this richness directly," which means to look away from, to look through or past, the constricting frame of the individual (Bentley 1954a: 8).

Having set aside, he hopes, the fears of those who worry that the methodological risk of allowing the individual to fall would be too great, Bentley goes on to suggest that in many of the sciences, the individual has already been left behind—and not in any way to the detriment of society, of human beings. Here is Bentley describing insights of physiology from 1910, in a way that surely anticipates some of the best recent work on "new materialisms":

> However spatially isolated the individual appears at a crude glance, the more minutely he is examined, the more are his boundary lines found to melt into those of his environment, the more frequently are functions found which work through both individual and environment so that it cannot be told where the one ceases and the other begins, leaving by the way products near the limits which can hardly be said to be either the one or the other. (Bentley 1954a: 5)

From Bentley's perspective, the insights of physiology show that the idea of "the individual" turns out to be rather vague and inchoate. Bentley wants to press on this notion of "vagueness" and extend it to our thinking about the individual as a meaningful actor within the social formation.[25] Thus, he gives a series of examples designed to show that even in "everyday" life and action, the idea of the individual proves just as vague and unhelpful as it does for the physiologist. Looked at in terms of efforts to shore up the tidy outlines of the individual, we see only a history in which the individual completely disappears: from psychology, to epistemology, to metaphysics, "the sharply outlined individual which at first appears . . . proves promptly to be spectral" (Bentley 1954a: 7). Looked at in terms of the acquisition of knowledge, Bentley says—in a series of passages where a twenty-first-century reader can detect very audible echoes of the early Foucault—that we find the knowledge itself to have more distinctiveness, "greater

25. Bentley's point about "vagueness" proves subtle. On the one hand, he clearly wants to turn the empiricists' goal of precision against them, by showing that nothing is less precise, less definite than "the individual." To this extent, Bentley would certainly be one to question the general goal of quantitative precision as it appeared in early twentieth-century social science and as it now appears in early twenty-first-century social science. On the other hand, Bentley had read William James's *Principles of Psychology*, where James argues for the "the reinstatement of the vague" to its rightful place in human affairs (James 1890; see Gavin 1992). Bentley was always sympathetic to the Jamesian project: in 1943 he wrote a spirited defence of James, arguing that much of James's work had been misunderstood—all while focusing specific praise on James's 1890 text. Bentley saw James's concept of "datum" in the same light as Bentley's own, earlier idea of "raw materials" (Kress 1970: 176–77). For Bentley, the social formation is not constituted by "precise" elements, and is to that extent marked by "vagueness," and if "vagueness" is understood in Bentley's sense of a "rich materiality," then an account of the social formation must appreciate this very "vagueness." On this point, my deepest thanks go to Alex Livingston.

individuality" than the so-called individual himself (Bentley 1954a: 7). And finally, when we think of the individual in relation with other individuals, when we consider the individual in his or her dynamic *motion*, the importance of the outlines of a distinct individual always wanes.[26]

There is always so much more to the meaningful action of people than any account of "individuals" could possibly convey. For Bentley, the theorist has to study a social formation in its very *excess* of the individual: "The society, the group, the mob, even the isolated fact of formal knowledge, seem too rich to enclose in any one individual *or in any addition of such individuals*, one to another. Our task then becomes *to look at this richness directly*" (Bentley 1954a: 8, emphasis added). When Bentley speaks, repeatedly, in *The Process of Government* about the need to get to the "raw material" of politics, he is describing just this "richness" and expressing his call to analyse it directly. But as we see in such stark terms here, to look at the richness directly is to refuse to look for it in, or to see it through, the concept of the individual, and to refuse to consider it as a product of aggregated individual activity. Bentley's "raw material" is not the stuff of empiricism; it points to an account of the social order that definitively refuses the terms of empiricism[27] (see Bentley 1954a: 33).

In another passage that obviously develops the account in *Process*, Bentley gives his reader pointers as to what to look for, what to see when "looking at this richness directly." He writes:

---

26. In even simpler terms, Bentley explains in a later essay in this same volume that there is never a single individual in isolation, and an individual stated in terms of feelings, emotions, or psychological states always requires a relation to other individuals (and to a larger social whole). Hence: "We can never succeed in locating 'Jack-in-love'" other than as "Jack-in-love-with-Jill" (Bentley 1954b: 45–46).

27. Here and throughout this chapter my references to "empiricism" (and to Bentley's lifelong critique of empiricism) point specifically to both the twentieth-century behavioralist project in social science and the *empiricist* epistemology that undergirds that project. Therefore, while I myself do not pursue explicitly the connections between Bentley's thought and the enterprise of radical empiricism, I do not disavow those links nor discourage their development. If we understand radical empiricism as an endeavour that "plays up the temporal element in all connections, producing a kind of a protean connectionism that fits neither individualism, nor static versions of structuralism, nor the ideas of things fixed for too long," then we can plainly hear the resonance with Bentley's thought (W. Connolly, personal communication). As I see it, radical empiricism itself offers an utterly powerful critique of the logical empiricism that underwrites behavioralism. Therefore, if thought from the perspective of radical empiricism, behavioralism would amount to no empiricism at all. Nonetheless, my treatment of empiricism here remains confined to precisely those behavioralist notions that Bentley consistently challenged.

> Picture to yourself now the moving (i.e., acting) society in this state of reality. *There it is*. The hands of "one man" move, or his lips move, or his pen moves. The motion lies straight across "other men." This action "is" the action of the two or three thousand as one. *It is the real thing*. The actions are not "epiphenomena" to the "men, body or soul things" but are the living fact. (Bentley 1954a: 8–9, emphasis added)

Like empiricists, Bentley insists on observation. Like empiricists, Bentley sees "facts." But for Bentley, in utter opposition to many of the prime tenets of empiricism, "individuals" are not facts, are not even, for the purposes of understanding or explaining social and political action, real. The action is "the real thing." And this leads, for Bentley, to an utterly obvious conclusion, but one that needs to be repeated—and, I would add, one that Bentley may have needed to draw out and underline after *Process*, a text that, as I have shown, is far less direct, far less clear about this issue. In a line that nicely answers to confusions that arise on the reading of *Process*, Bentley writes in this later essay: "In order to study the phenomena of men in society we must take all stress off 'individuals'" (Bentley 1954a: 9). Any emphasis on, or beginning with, the "individual" (a term that Bentley conscientiously keeps in quotation marks throughout this essay) will always only prevent us from seeing, from grasping, society (the social formation).

Bentley's elaborated arguments in this essay prove essential to my broader project here (in this chapter, and in this book) because he consistently redirects our attention to the social formation itself, the very location of the "raw material" of politics, "the real thing" that is the social theorist's or scientist's task to understand/explain/interpret.[28] Bentley's "group theory," as it is so frequently referred to, must always be seen as radically pluralist and thoroughly anti-individualist. For these reasons, Bentley's project proves utterly irreconcilable with any empiricist work, including Truman's. But more than simply driving a wedge between Truman and Bentley, my interpretation here advances my broader account of the social formation by showing how Bentley's understanding of the group can play a central role in that account. Bentley's work gives a wide berth to the individualist/determinist impasse,

28. In my reading of Bentley and throughout my efforts to develop an account of the social formation, I refuse any formal or rigid distinctions between or among explanation, understanding, and interpretation. Much social science work does, of course, insist on a fundamental difference between understanding and explanation, but it seems to me that once one abandons or rejects the empiricist search for linear causality—as the ground for proper explanation and the mirror of the deeper goal of prediction—then stark differentiation of explanation, on the one hand, from understanding or interpretation, on the other, quickly becomes untenable.

since his thoroughgoing rejection of the individual is not made in the name of any sort of narrowly conceived structuralist account. In the next section I will elaborate on the implications of Bentley's understanding of groups for my own theory of the social formation.

GROUPS—THE STUFF OF THE SOCIAL FORMATION

In the preceding two sections I have underscored the irreconcilable difference between Bentley's and Truman's account of the social order. Their apparent agreement on the importance of the group to the study of politics only blocks from view their radical disagreement on what each author means when he says "group," and most importantly, on how that "group" is related to the "individual." All of this means that Bentley and Truman disagree fundamentally on how we understand the makeup of the social formation—the very "raw material," as Bentley would say, that constitutes it. Another way to begin shading in the outline of Bentley's theory of the social formation is to "zoom out" one or two levels. I want to leverage the specific dis-agreement over "the group," documented above, into a wider Bentleyan account—one consistent with the developing theory of the social formation throughout this project—of the social order. One way to carry out this shift in perspective is by making a rather unlikely comparison of Bentley to other thinkers of social order.

I contend that the best "cases" for close comparison are not liberal thinkers, nor other social science "pluralists" from the mid-twentieth century. Rather, Bentley's broader thinking of the social formation overlaps perhaps the most with conservative authors. Such a claim should not be surprising, despite Bentley's own progressive leanings (see Kress 1970 and Ward 1984) and despite his appropriation by disciplinary social science, since conservative thought has always provided a rich set of resources for understanding something like the social whole. Edmund Burke's metaphor of the "social fabric" is surely nothing less than an account of the social formation, and Burke's most trenchant criticisms of (what would become) liberal ideas, including the rights of man and the social contract, can be traced to his efforts to distinguish between a natural social order (one of distinction, and hence inequality) and an artificial construction of a rational and egalitarian order—which, from Burke's perspective, would itself only serve to undermine, weaken, or render chaotic that natural order.[29] Rooted

---

29. This claim proves consistent with Burke's writing as a whole, but it offers one specific way to interpret his first book, *A Vindication of Natural Society*, at least so long

as his thought always was in a German tradition, Bentley approaches the social formation much more like a conservative thinker would, in the specific sense that he identifies a broader social whole as the "given"; this is one of many reasons that Bentley's account of the social formation proves utterly inappropriable by empiricism. As Ward shows, Bentley remained committed, from the beginning to the end of his writings, to the idea that all individuals were part of a larger "whole," but a whole that had no direct empirical observability (Ward 1984: 28).[30] We can "observe" the action of groups, but they always occur within a larger context that, *en toto*, can never simply be seen; in these claims Bentley offers strong support for my 5th hypothesis that the social order cannot be depicted empirically or defined ostensively. Significantly, however—and in a way that underscores my 2nd and 3rd hypotheses—unlike conservatives such as Burke or Oakeshott, Bentley refuses any language of the "natural" (and conversely of "artificial") or of the logic of naturalisation. Bentley shares with Oakeshott an utterly anti-liberal approach to social order, but Bentley has no concomitant commitment to defending or upholding inequality (in a way that Oakeshott always, implicitly, does) (Oakeshott 1933; Oakeshott 1962; see Ward 1984: 70–71, 148).

I opened this chapter by borrowing an idea from Rancière to help delineate the relation between Truman and Bentley, and I would like to close it now by making a more substantive connection between Bentley and Rancière. In his own unique way, Rancière agrees with a conservative like Oakeshott when he (Rancière) asserts that the social order is a police order, one in which inequality and domination always rule (Rancière 1991; Rancière 1999). Rancière rejects the liberal idea of materialising a space of equality, of constructing an egalitarian social order; the social order is always and only a police order (3rd hypothesis). Yet Rancière makes

as we read that text, as Burke's later preface suggests, as satire (Burke 1999 [1757]; for the contrary reading of this early text as unironic, see Rothbard 1958).

30. In the text above I distinguish Bentley's account of the whole from that of both liberals and conservatives, and in the text below I draw both comparisons and contrasts with Rancière's account. Here I should also make clear that Bentley's understanding of the social formation differs from other varieties of Hegel-inspired "holism." Bentley would reject an account like T. H. Green's concentric-circles model of self-society-state, just as he would reject any general communitarian holism that too closely linked individual to society. For Bentley, such accounts fail because they hypostatise a concrete "individual" that is no more than a fiction, and because they *align* that individual with the social order. As he shows in his repeated criticisms of Aristotle, one cannot "read off" the individual from the social order (any more than one can derive the social order from the individual).

the most radical, most anti-conservative turn, when he points out that this social order of hierarchy and subjugation has its unexpected (and for conservatives, unspeakable) "foundation" in a kind of radical equality.[31] Every established relation of inequality depends on an immanent equality of intelligence of all speaking beings (8th hypothesis). Rancière asserts this principle, since it cannot literally be *argued* (Panagia 2001; Panagia 2014), as follows:

> There is order in society because some people command and others obey, but in order to obey an order you must understand that you must obey it. And to do that, you must already be the equal of the person who is ordering you. It is this equality that gnaws away at any natural order. (Rancière 1999: 16; cf. Dean 2009)

Implicitly, and in his own way, Rancière's account of the social order returns to and overturns Burke. In his satire of Bolingbroke, Burke rejects the idea of denaturalising the social order, of using legal constructs to render artificial that which, for Burke, is clearly most natural. Hence, contra Bolingbroke, Burke wants to "re-naturalise," or simply insist on the given naturalness of, the social order. Rancière, however, defends the following point: one of the things that any social order does is naturalise itself—that is, it passes off as natural the hierarchy and domination and inequality that constitutes it. A police order may be defended by conservatives who praise it for the order it maintains, but the social order hardly needs the work of conservatives since every social order always tries to naturalise its domination. Rancière's point is therefore a simple but important one. In the face of these naturalisation efforts, Rancière makes the polemical claim that such efforts at naturalisation are always the work of policing. But like it or not, ultimately the social order is *never* a natural order: "Convention alone can reign in the social order" (Rancière 1991: 78).

For his part, Bentley comes at the question of social order as a thinker concerned to advance social science. That is, unlike liberals, Bentley's project holds no commitments to constructing a theory of political legitimacy—that is, by producing an "artificial" or "rational" or "just" account of social order that then grounds political power (4th hypothesis). Unlike conservatives, then, Bentley is not concerned to re-naturalise the hierarchy or inequality of a given social order. And unlike Rancière, he is not intent

---

31. Foundation appears here in scare quotes because there is no substance to this apparent "ground" for the reason that Rancière's concept of equality refuses that very sort of substantialisation. I have expounded this point in detail elsewhere (Chambers 2013).

on polemicising the moment of "politics" that would disrupt a given social order. Bentley's "scientific" worldview means that his primary concern is a basic understanding of the social formation—what it is, how it is put together, and how it works. But as Ward points out, for Bentley this is a conceptual project, not a methodological one; Bentley criticises numerous epistemologies, but he is not an epistemologist for the very reason that he refuses the foundationalist idea that there can be any "rock bottom" for knowledge (Ward 1984: 9).[32] When we encounter the world, we encounter the social whole itself—here we see Bentley cross with Althusser—and we encounter it through language. Language is the "phenomenal form in which science and knowledge present themselves" (Bentley 1935: 5). From this quote Ward derives an obvious-yet-powerful conclusion, one that resonates with contemporary theory: "We cannot suppose that there is or can be any 'extralinguistic' access to reality" (Ward 1984: 10). Thus, despite the language he uses to express his own, very genuine, commitment to science, Bentley's approach to the world has much more in common with late twentieth-century postfoundational political theory than it does with late twentieth-century social science.

Yet his commitment to a disinterested scientific approach means that Bentley, unlike Rancière, offers neither formal arguments nor polemical interventions concerning equality. (Although he does consistently call out others for their naturalisation of inequality.[33]) And Bentley almost never invokes the language of artificial/natural; his references to the former term usually serve as synonyms for "specious" or "untenable" (Bentley 1908: 157, 162). However, the one place in *Process* where Bentley does engage with the "natural" proves very helpful in both drawing out his concept of the social formation and specifying the critical use to which his account of social order might be put. Bentley devotes an entire, and long, section of

32. Here one could locate another parallel between Rancière and Bentley: the former engages in a critique of ontology without doing ontology, while the latter challenges epistemological arguments without offering an epistemology of his own. Bentley, too, rejects ontology (see Ward 1984: 197).

33. One never gets anything like a clear sense of what Bentley thinks about equality, and that may be because he is more resolute than just about anyone (except maybe the early Foucault) in telling us that he does not care about the individual and his "inner" feelings/emotions/beliefs. Nonetheless, Bentley makes a series of apparently ad hoc claims that may add up to something more: against those who would assert a presumed inequality (such as Spencer), Bentley always responds in his harshest critical tone, and against those who believe they are enlightened egalitarians, Bentley always responds with his starkest scepticism designed to show up the hypocrisy of the putative egalitarians—his remarks on the treatment of animals provides a powerful example (Bentley 1908: 5, 46).

the first part of *Process* to a detailed summary and harsh critique of Herbert Spencer. Ward puts a fine point on Bentley's general position here: "The fusion of classical political economy and social evolutionism represented in the popular teachings of Herbert Spencer and William Graham Sumner had been repellent to Bentley from his first encounter with it" (Ward 1984: 23).

Generalising only a bit, we might say that Spencer's work represents, for Bentley and in his day, everything that is wrong with psychology and much of social science. Rather than try to account for the social order that he confronts, Spencer continually and consistently (Bentley damns Spencer with faint praise for the uniformity of his ideas) hypostatises "feeling things" that are meant to have some separate, causal effect on society.[34] But the so-called feelings and the so-called causality are never more than constructions, created at the hands of Spencer himself so that he can tie the given social facts to a theory he started with at the beginning. Spencer is always and continually "building up" sentiments and feelings so that he can then "fit them on to the social facts for which he needs them, according to the lights of his theory" (Bentley 1908: 45). But for all of his talk of feelings and their importance to the development of the individual, from Bentley's perspective none of this is ever anything more than "little puppets made by hand; little spooks miraculously appearing" (Bentley 1908: 46). In this context, and again paralleling Rancière, Bentley makes his own critique of conservative efforts at naturalisation, a move that proves central to the Spencerians. I quote Bentley's argument in full:

> A third difficulty that flows from Spencer's theory of feelings is that which involves the "natural" [placed immediately, and always, in quotation marks, by Bentley]. It is best exemplified in his views of government and government functions. His followers . . . can get anywhere in the whole range of social speculation by taking a good running start from Spencerian feelings. They can reach socialism or anarchy. They can reach anything they want. The "natural" is not what socially is, but what conforms to the "natural" feelings, as the individual upholder of the "natural" insists they must work out. All this is not science. It is an eighteenth-century distillation of a seventeenth-century deity, curiously garbed in nineteenth-century "knowable" force. (Bentley 1908: 52)

A Bentleyan theory of the social formation will thereby refuse the drive to naturalisation. Unlike Rancière, Bentley never explicitly says that "convention reigns" in the social order, and Bentley remained very much attentive to the way that ordinary or pre-scientific understandings were part and

34. One might say that in current-day empiricist social science these "feeling things" take the form of coded survey data.

parcel of the social formation itself (see Ward 1984: 11–13). Yet Bentley always contested naturalising moves, and he regularly refused to allow ordinary understandings to become reified or otherwise stand in as foundational facts. This is the sense in which I suggested above that Bentley's "group theory" of politics can augment other accounts of the social formation and also be put to some critical use.

Bentley's account of social order and my own developing theory of the social formation both eschew the idea of the theorist as constructing a "normative order" or building a model which would serve to measure the "legitimacy" of a given social order (cf. 3rd and 4th hypotheses). Ward—writing in a very different theoretical and political conjuncture, and taking on a far different set of debates than I—makes this point in a way that I can only reaffirm, when he writes, "For Bentley, 'order' is not a 'normative' term." Moreover, order is not opposed to "disorder," since there is an "order" to any social formation—one that we can see in the very raw material of politics—and this holds true despite the level of "chaos" in the world (Ward 1984: 89). We might say that even through the actions of the "anarchic" mob, and even at the moment of revolutionary upheaval, the social formation is still ordered in one way or another. Another way of putting this point is to declare that Bentley eschews the traditional "social order problem." For him, there is no *mechanism* that holds a society together. To call for such a mechanism is to presume the autonomous existence of discrete individuals who must then be, somehow, "held together," but Bentley rejects an account that would give primacy to individuals in this way. Groups are the raw material, and their actions, their process, is ordered.[35]

This logic leads to the following conclusion: to account for a social order is not to argue for or against its legitimacy but to come to terms with how it functions (that is, with how it works[36]). In this, very limited, sense, we can see again that Bentley shares something with contemporary social science empiricists, in that he distinguishes his project from so-called normative theory. Yet, Bentley understands, in a way that many contemporary empiricists and many contemporary "normative theorists" do not, that "order" does not come from the logic of public policy, nor from the prescriptions of philosophers. Bentley contends that "it is of the very definition of activity that it is systematized. Even the simplest motion with which the physicist

35. Thanks to Tripp Rebrovick for helpful clarification of this point.

36. To say *how* a society works means to respond to the primary questions of the social formation that I delineated in my Introduction: it means to say how a social order "hangs together," how it continues to exist by reproducing itself, and how the reproduction of its existence can change the structure and nature of its existence.

deals is part of a system of motion. When the geometrician gives position to a point, he admits system. In living beings there is no function that is not systematized" (Bentley 1908: 285; quoted in Ward 1984: 89). None of this amounts to a defence of the status quo. Such a formulation cannot be reduced to, or used to undergird, a conservatism since, as I have shown above, the conservative defence of the social order entails the very naturalisation that Bentley (like Rancière) adamantly refuses. To say that order exists, and in a sense, must exist, is not to say that it should exist; nor is it to say that *this particular order* must exist.

The politics of any given social order depend upon how we engage with Bentley's raw materials: groups in relation, in conflict, forming and reshaping "their" interests. It matters a great deal that Bentley's raw material is not an elementary particle, and that his understanding of the social formation cuts against any effort to find, locate, or construct such an elementary particle. Thus, no account of interests and groups can successfully be carried out in abstraction or isolation from the larger social order. Groups and their interests cannot form spontaneously, but only ever within the social formation. Reformulating Bentley's ideas in the context of the social formation gives a sharper edge to a related point, one that Mathiowetz nicely draws out when he argues that Bentley's idea of an "interested group" renders untenable the distinction between subject/objective interests. Any such dichotomy only ever "preserves rather than deflects the presumption that interests are individual and psychological" (Mathiowetz 2011: 192).

As I have shown previously, the move to distinguish subjective and objective interests always leads to a critical theory of unmasking and demystification—in general, to a logic of inversion, one that tries to pierce the cloud of ideology and find the truth beneath the lies (Chambers 2013). Bentley's account of social order offers a way to reject this logic. For him, the groups are the interests, the interests are the groups, and the groups are only ever activity.[37] The task of the Bentleyan social scientist is therefore

---

37. My refusal of the category of the normative, coupled with Bentley's own distance from "objective" interests, will surely, for some, raise the specter of historicism, which in the Straussian formula always devolves to relativism. But there is no "danger" of relativism in Bentley's project (or my own). Bentley believed in the scientific principles that some explanations or understandings were better than others; some conceptualisations grasp the whole, in its very richness, better than others. The fact that we cannot construct an a priori model that predicts in advance which interpretation will prove to be the better one, only tells us that the social formation can only be "grasped" (i.e., conceptualised) in particular historical instances.

not to establish the objective interest underlying group action, but to come to terms with, to grasp, the dynamic relations among the groups themselves—the interests as the "raw materials" that manifest in the world. I would therefore suggest that Bentley's understanding of groups, when incorporated into the wider set of theories of the social formation that I have been developing here, opens the door to a different sort of critical theory: not the project of demystification but the effort at transforming a given social formation.

Let me expand on this point by taking my distance from Ward, who ends his rich work on Bentley with a critique of Bentley's "formalism." In rejecting any correspondence theory of knowledge, Bentley eschewed as well any correspondence theory of language. Science's task was not to model an external world but to produce a grammar that better helped us grasp a world that was itself expressed in our own language. In an uncharacteristically aphoristic form, Bentley puts it this way: "Man is a bit of the cosmos inspecting *itself* [not, significantly, *himself*]" (Bentley, quoted in Ward 1984: 232, emphasis added). Ward worries about the status of the grammar that would be needed to support such a formalist project: if the practice of science is nothing other than the practice of scientists (since there can be no a priori epistemological establishment of what is or is not science), then, Ward asks, how do we really know when we are doing science? If the fact/value distinction cannot be resolved—Bentley thought it could not—then "the task of science [becomes] so immense and its development . . . so tentative that questions of its application virtually disappear" (Ward 1984: 232). Despite patiently refuting the social science appropriation of Bentley, and despite carefully criticising the empiricist epistemology, with these, his concluding criticisms, Ward echoes today's social science empiricism both in its repeated demand for the "application" of "theory" and in its frequent calling out of reinforcements for the fact/value distinction. In response, I suggest that in searching for the significance of Bentley's now-century-old project, Ward is looking in the wrong place. Bentley's group theory has less to offer to a social *science*, committed both to the idea of science and to the notion that theory must be "applied," than it has to give, as I have shown here, to a project on the theories and politics of social formations. Ward's unease with formalism is alleviated if we refuse the project of *completing* a pure formalism, and turn our attention instead to the possibility of grasping (and perhaps transforming) the social formation.

I would even go so far as to suggest that a theory of the social formation, such as Bentley's, might have the capacity to breathe new life into a critical theory beyond inversion, a critical theory that understands critique not as unmasking or moral grounding but as the actualisation of an alternative—an alternative that the current social formation can only deem "impossible." To specify or elaborate these claims, however, is to go well beyond the terms of Bentley's writings. It is, rather, to say something much broader about theories and politics of the social formation; it is to connect and tie together a number of key threads of this book as a whole, a task I now turn to in the Coda.

Coda

No social order is *constituted by* individuals. This claim holds in the sense both that society is not the product of the free will and consent of sovereign individuals and that the social totality is not formed by individuals as its elementary particles. In this way, Bentley's understanding of "group interests" as formative of the social order brings my account full circle: it both illuminates my first two hypotheses and provides the ultimate counterpoint to Butler's hollowed-out understanding of "the social" as no more than an aggregative term—a reference to the "more than one." To refuse all aggregative models of the social order means to turn to a sense of "the whole" as an object of knowledge beyond the reach of empiricism (5th hypothesis); it means that the only way to grasp the social order, to bear society in mind, is to give an account of the social formation.

All such accounts will have to grapple with the fact that any social formation is structured in and by domination. I indicated in my 3rd hypothesis a point that I have developed throughout the book: social orders are constituted by vertical relations of power; a social order is by definition hierarchical, and the social formation is a structure that supports and maintains domination. Perhaps more significantly, as I indicated in the previous chapter, any social formation naturalises the very order of inequality that it supports and sustains; this makes the social formation a location for both the production and legitimation (through that very naturalisation) of domination and inequality. As I have also shown, moreover, the alternative to all this cannot be "reform" of the social order, or the production of a substantive realm of equality either inside (e.g., liberal egalitarianism) or outside (e.g., anarchist equality) the social formation. The social order cannot be "normatively redeemed" (4th hypothesis).

Despite all this, I maintain that my exploration of theories and politics of the social formation does not in any sense lead logically to cynical or nihilistic conclusions. Here I wish to indicate some of the reasons why. First of all, as I hinted in the last chapter, to give a robust and rigorous account of the social formation is always already to offer a particular sort of challenge to the domination and inequality that is constitutive of any given social order. This is the case because an account of the social formation will have to include a delineation of the logic by which the social order *passes off as natural* the very domination that it produces. At a certain level, then, to give an account of the social formation is always already to *denaturalise* the social formation; it is always to make, and to stress, Rancière's point (which is also a rather Gramscian point) that the *order* of any social formation is radically contingent (though surely not random)—that convention, not nature, rules (Rancière 1991; Gramsci 1971). Derrida formulates the point most aphoristically, and perhaps therefore most polemically: "Naturalism is no more natural than conventionalism" (Derrida 1995: 231). Naturalism and conventionalism, in other words, are different names given to similar mechanisms of policing. Of course, this is the very claim that would be denied by a logic internal to the social order, a logic that always tries to render natural and legitimate the domination inherent to any social order. The assertion that "convention rules" is therefore much more than a "neutral observation": it proves to be a rhetorical, a polemical, a political act. Examples here abound, but one can start and end with the concept of "the free market"—to give a theoretical and historical account of the actual functioning of markets is to denaturalise the concept and to "reshoot the scene" of inequality (to see it and hear it differently, anew) that is produced in and through the naturalising logic of this concept.[1]

I emphasise the theoretical and political importance of this logic of denaturalisation, a logic that proves inherent to the work of giving an account of social formations, but I do not limit the significance of theories of the social formation to a narrow or restricted understanding of denaturalisation. Taking this position calls for further exploration of a more precise and more robust understanding of denaturalisation, a point I take up below. At the same time, and as I show here, my position above must be linked to the further claim that politico-theoretical work on the social formation exceeds

1. Here I use the cinematic metaphor of "reshooting" in an effort to bring together visual and aural dimensions—to capture both a "becoming legible" and a "becoming audible" of the partition/distribution of the sensible.

(and must be always be made to exceed) mere historicisation or simplistic genealogy. Theories of the social formation go beyond simple contextualism for the very reason that to give an account of the social formation is always to consider the possibility of radical change. I stated at the outset of this book that to study the social formation is to raise a fundamental concern about how a social order holds together, but it is also, therefore, to pose the question of what happens when a particular social order can no longer be sustained. (In many ways, this is the question of capitalism, according to Marx.) To grasp the historical development of social formations means to rethink the possibilities of social and political change. The question of change, of how a social formation transforms, returns me here at the end to just where I began the book—with new objects of the social formation.

When, in early 2005, Michael Burry envisioned a new object, the credit default swap on mortgage-backed securities, he also gained a perspicacious vision of the social formation, and above all, Burry saw that the social formation was going to *change*, that it simply had to change. Indeed, Burry understood that the social order would need to transform so radically that it might become something altogether new: the change to come might not occur *within* the given social order, but might well alter the social order itself (a possibility that still remains alive, yet certainly not guaranteed, at the time of my writing). However, Burry's was not a divine vision of predestination; he was not prescient in the sense of foretelling an inevitable future. Althusser would reject the idea of a determining fate, and we can use his words to describe Burry's location within his social formation and his capacity to see the new object: Burry's vision was "a reflection of immanent necessity that ties an object . . . to its conditions of existence" (Althusser 2009: 26). Of course, Burry's own actions, his efforts to bring the CDS on MBS into existence by lobbying Wall Street investment banks to sell them to him, proved to be much more than a mere reflection of structural necessity. New objects are also not divinely created or brought into being; they do not emerge out of the ether but are produced by the actions of groups.[2] Thus we might draw out a number of conclusions about

2. Burry did not act alone, even if Lewis's individual-centered narrative might tempt the reader to see his actions as isolated. Lewis himself shows that there were a variety of other actors, themselves linked to powerful and expansive groups and networks, who also saw and agitated for the emergence of new objects (Lewis 2010). Bentley's insights about the formation of a social order might allow us to focus on the interest (i.e., group) concerned to bet against the housing market and the economy as a whole; that group (i.e., that interest) appears through its actions—that is, by buying CDS on MBS, by shorting stocks, by purchasing gold, by lobbying for legislation designed to make sure that in the event of a crash, holders of financial "insurance policies" get paid off first, and so on.

the relation between the object and the social order: a new object requires a new social formation; at the same time, a new object helps bring about a new social formation; and finally, the production of new objects depends upon both broad structural conditions and meaningful political action within that frame.

It is in this context that I wish to expand briefly upon the claims with which I wound up my last chapter. First, the theories of the social formation that I have advanced over the chapters of this book serve to undermine the possibility, and to eschew the strategy, of taking critique as the "unveiling" of "hidden" mastery or subjugation. Althusser states directly that "Marx never believed that an ideology might be dissipated by the knowledge of it," and his explanation for this claim proves even more important: "for the knowledge of this ideology, as the knowledge of its conditions of possibility, of its structure, of its specific logic and its practical role, within a given society, is simultaneously knowledge of the conditions of its necessity" (Althusser 1969: 230). To give an account of the social formation may well be to analyse the way in which a particular social order produces and then naturalises hierarchical relations, but there is no secret or mystery to be exposed, and there are no guarantees that denaturalising the logic of domination will somehow, all on its own, alter that logic.

This is why I read Marx as a very specific sort of "denaturaliser" of capitalism, which means, on the one hand, distinguishing his project from the naive sort of "ideology critique" with which it is so often associated and, on the other, enriching our overall idea of denaturalisation. Because he was always bearing the social order in mind, Marx resisted the idea of an essential truth underlying false appearances. In his discussion of commodities as fetishes, Marx states that things "appear as what they are," and he makes plain that "the categories of bourgeois economics . . . are forms of thought which are socially valid, and therefore objective, for the relations of production" of this particular social formation (Marx 1990: 166, 167). When he calls a process of capitalism mysterious (or even magical), rather than pointing to a falsehood or an error, *Marx is in fact identifying the very process of naturalisation* that I have described above. Marx's writings articulate the mode by which a particular capitalist social order passes itself off as natural. The mystery, in other words, is itself a result of the process of naturalisation: we take as a "given," as "natural," that which the social order naturalises. The mistake (of the political economists, for example) lies not in taking the categories of the social formation as real categories; the mistake lies in taking those categories as natural, in taking them not only as "socially valid" for this historical conjuncture (which they are) but also as given in nature, as universally true for all time and place (which they are not, since they are only made possible by this particular social formation). At every turn, Marx staunchly criticises this kind of naturalisation, and in exploring the mysteries of capitalism he rearticulates the contingency of the social order.

This leads to the second claim with which I ended the previous chapter: giving an account of the social formation means refusing the temptation toward moral denunciation of apparent wrongs. Marx underscored this point repeatedly, especially in his frequent takedowns of the utopian socialists who, in their rush to ethical condemnation, so often failed to grasp the actual functioning of a capitalist system (Marx 1955). Today, we can take a rather banal, but for that reason perhaps quite important, example of this phenomenon: as I mentioned in my Introduction, a theory of the social formation rejects the idea that the "problem" with a capitalist social formation is the so-called greed of individual capitalists (McElwee 2013). Doubtless there are greedy capitalists, but there are also greedy communists, greedy farmers, and non-greedy capitalists. The critique of "capitalist greed" fails from the outset in that it offers no more than "non-greedy capitalism," which is either a contradiction in terms or simply another (longer) name for "capitalism." I should also note here that "ideology critique" and "ethical censure" intersect in the space of certain types of conspiracy theory, wherein the secret mechanisms take the form of a group of hidden actors (in dark rooms) who pull the levers of society. An account of the social formation surely has space to analyse and understand oligarchical structures and corruption. After all, every social order is in some sense "oligarchical" (as Rancière says, we do not live in democracies but in oligarchic orders). Yet one of the cautionary methodological prescriptions (as Foucault might have put it) of a theory of the social formation consists in assuming that the problems or faults with any given social order always far exceed the corruption of that order; the "answer" is never to render the social order transparent to itself or simply to eliminate "distortions" or corruption. For these reasons, this project centered on exploring theories and politics of the social formation must point toward a different concept of critique.

When reconsidered through the concept of the social formation, critique must become something quite different than the above, standard accounts. To see what a critical political theory of the social formation might look like requires one first to lay stress on the point that every social formation constitutes its own domain of "the impossible"—those subjects and objects that cannot exist in *this* social order, because if they did exist, if they were possible, then this would have to be some *other* social order. Critique therefore must be thought as the actualisation—in the sense of the bringing into existence—of a new, "impossible" object or subject. To rethink critique within the terms of the theory of the social formation means to invent or develop a novel notion of critique that links it to the *new objects* of a social formation.[3] What if critique turned not on making the invisible visible, not on ethical condemnation—what if critique hinged upon developing the vision to *see new objects*? This form of critique would then need to be linked to an idea of politics as bringing about those objects, calling them into existence and *producing* them.[4]

This last logical move makes it clear that critique cannot be the sole project or primary possession of political theory. The actual transformations wrought by critique manifest not in theory but in the world. Another way of putting this is to say that in a certain sense it simply is not the job of a theory of the social formation, or of *any* political theory, to change the world in some sort of direct, linear-causal way. Yet to say that each and every political theory ought not bear the burden of directly effecting change is neither to deprecate the status or value of political theory nor to claim that political theory has nothing to do with struggle, with politics, with the transformation of social orders, nor to suggest that political theory might not wind up changing the world. After all, an understanding of social formations indicates the futility of *any* linear, monocausal account of political change, so at the same time that we resist the tendency to measure the significance of political theory by the metric of immediate political change, we must also remain open to the possibility that theory may indeed bring about or help contribute to (unanticipated) change—change that no one predicted, perhaps that no one thought possible. A theory of the social formation may or may not produce new objects, since the actual constitution of new objects of the social formation is a process under no one's direct control. Nonetheless, to give an account of the social formation is most certainly to develop the perspicacious view necessary to envision such objects in the first place—and this remains a necessary precondition of any change in, or to, the social formation. Furthermore, as I see it, one of the important tasks of political theory is to *ask the question* of how change comes about,

3. In this sense, then, the "new object" is the "impossible object"—that which cannot appear in this social formation but which, in appearing, transforms the social formation.

4. This Coda is surely not the place to introduce entirely new thinkers and repertoires of thought; nevertheless, some readers might want to consider my concluding turn here in relation to Deleuze and Guattari's (1987) notion of the creation of concepts as the proper project of thought.

and on this front a theory of the social formation has much to offer because it places the temporal, historical development and transformation of social orders front and center in its analysis. While no political theory leads *directly* to political action or structural transformation, an account of the social formation has the capacity to conceptualise change by grasping the social order, to effect critique by envisioning new objects, and therefore to mobilise a politics that would bring those objects into being. No more can we ask of any political theory.

Works Cited

Albergotti, Reed, and Vanessa O'Connell (2013). *Wheelmen: Lance Armstrong, The Tour de France, and the Greatest Sports Conspiracy Ever*. New York: Gotham Books.

Althusser, Louis (1969). *For Marx*. Translated by Ben Brewster. New York: Pantheon Books.

Althusser, Louis (1970). "Idéologie et appareils idéologiques d'État. (Notes pour une recherche)." (Online). Available from http://classiques.uqac.ca/contemporains/althusser_louis/ideologie_et_AIE/ideologie_et_AIE_texte.html (accessed December 20, 2012).

Althusser, Louis (1971). "Ideology and Ideological State Apparatuses (Notes Towards an Investigation)," in *Lenin and Philosophy, and Other Essays*, 23–173. New York and London: Monthly Review Press.

Althusser, Louis (1976). *Essays in Self-Criticism*. Translated by Grahame Lock. London: New Left Books.

Althusser, Louis (1999). *Machiavelli and Us*. Translated by Gregory Elliott. London: Verso.

Althusser, Louis (2006). *Philosophy of the Encounter: Later Writings, 1978–1987*. Translated by G. M. Goshgarian. London: Verso.

Althusser, Louis (2009). *Reading Capital*. Translated by Ben Brewster. London: Verso.

Anderson, C. D. (1961). "Early Work on the Positron and Muon." *American Journal of Physics* 29.12: 825–30.

Apostolidis, Paul (2015). "Migrant Day Laborers, Neoliberalism, and the Politics of Time." Forthcoming in Anna Agathangelou and Kyle Killian (eds.), *Time and Violence: Defatalizing the Present*. New York: Routledge.

Arendt, Hannah (1958). *The Human Condition.* Chicago: University of Chicago Press.

Armstrong, Lance (2013). "Lance Armstrong Exclusive Interview." By Daniel Benson, *Cycling News.* (Online). Available from http://www.cyclingnews.com/news/lance-armstrong-exclusive-interview (accessed June 10, 2013).

Armstrong, Lance, and Sally Jenkins (2001). *It's Not About the Bike: My Journey Back to Life*. New York: Berkley Books.

Arthur, Christopher (2006). "A Guide to Marx's *Grundrisse* in English." (Online). Unpublished manuscript, available from http://chrisarthur.net/grundrisse.doc (accessed January 10, 2009).

Bachelard, Gaston (1984). *The New Scientific Spirit.* Translated by Arthur Goldhammer. Boston: Beacon Press.

Balibar, Étienne (1994). "Althusser's Object." Translated by Margaret Cohen and Bruce Robbins. *Social Text* 39: 157–88.

Benhabib, Seyla (1995). "Feminism and Postmodernism: An Uneasy Alliance," in *Feminist Contentions: A Philosophical Exchange*, 17–34. New York: Routledge.

Bennett, Jane (2010). *Vibrant Matter: A Political Ecology of Things.* Durham: Duke University Press.

Bennett, Jane, and Michael Shapiro, eds. (2002). *The Politics of Moralizing*. New York and London: Routledge.

Bentley, Arthur (1908). *The Process of Government: A Study of Social Pressures.* Chicago: University of Chicago Press.

Bentley, Arthur (1926). *Relativity in Man and Society*. New York: Putnam.

Bentley, Arthur (1932). *Linguistic Analysis of Mathematics*. Bloomington, IN: The Principia Press.

Bentley, Arthur (1935). *Behavior, Knowledge, Fact*. Bloomington, IN: The Principia Press.

Bentley, Arthur (1954a). "Knowledge and Society," in Sidney Ratner (ed.), *Inquiry into Inquiries: Essays in Social Theory*, 3–26. Boston: Beacon Press.

Bentley, Arthur (1954b). "New Ways and Old to Talk About Men," in Sidney Ratner (ed.), *Inquiry into Inquiries: Essays in Social Theory*, 37–52. Boston: Beacon Press.

Bergson, Henri (2009). *Matter and Memory*. New York: Forgotten Books.

Bloch, Joseph (1938). *Revolution der Weltpolitik*. Karlsbad: Druck von J. Müller.

Blokland, Hans (2011). *Pluralism, Democracy, and Political Knowledge: Robert A. Dahl and His Critics on Modern Politics*. Burlington, VT: Ashgate.

Boland, Tom (2007). "Critique as a Technique of the Self: A Butlerian Analysis of Judith Butler's Prefaces." *History of the Human Sciences* 20.3: 105–22.

Bowman, Paul (2006). "Review of *Interrogating the Real*." *Culture Machine*. (Online). Available from http://www.culturemachine.net/index.php/cm/article/view/175/156 (accessed March 2, 2014).

Bowman, Paul (2010). *Theorizing Bruce Lee: Film-Fantasy-Fighting-Philosophy. Contemporary Cinema*, Vol. 5. Amsterdam: Rodopi.

Bowman, Paul (2013). *Beyond Bruce Lee: Chasing the Dragon through Film, Philosophy and Popular Culture*. New York: Wallflower Press.
Boyd, Roddy (2011). *Fatal Risk: A Cautionary Tale of AIG's Corporate Suicide*. Hoboken: Wiley & Sons.
Brown, Wendy (2001). *Politics Out of History*. Princeton: Princeton University Press.
Brown, Wendy (2005). *Edgework: Critical Essays on Knowledge and Politics*. Princeton: Princeton University Press.
Burke, Edmund (1999). "A Vindication of Natural Society," in Isaac Kramnick (ed.), *The Portable Edmund Burke*, 29–62. New York: Penguin.
Butler, Judith (1987). *Subjects of Desire*. New York: Columbia University Press.
Butler, Judith (1993). *Bodies That Matter: On the Discursive Limits of "Sex."* New York: Routledge.
Butler, Judith (1995). "Conscience Doth Make Subjects of Us All." *Yale French Studies* 88: 6–26.
Butler, Judith (1997a). *Excitable Speech: A Politics of the Performative*. New York: Routledge.
Butler, Judith (1997b). *The Psychic Life of Power: Theories in Subjection*. Stanford: Stanford University Press.
Butler, Judith (1999). *Gender Trouble: Feminism and the Subversion of Identity*. London and New York: Routledge.
Butler, Judith (2000). *Antigone's Claim: Kinship Between Life and Death*. New York: Columbia University Press.
Butler, Judith (2004a). *Precarious Life: The Powers of Mourning and Violence*. London: Verso.
Butler, Judith (2004b). *Undoing Gender*. New York: Routledge.
Butler, Judith (2005). *Giving an Account of Oneself*. New York: Fordham University Press.
Butler, Judith (2009). *Frames of War: When Is Life Grievable?* London: Verso.
Butler, Judith (2012). "Judith Butler Responds to Attack." (Online). Available from http://mondoweiss.net/2012/08/judith-butler-responds-to-attack-i-affirm-a-judaism-that-is-not-associated-with-state-violence.html (accessed September 10, 2012).
Butler, Judith, and William Connolly (2000). "Politics, Power and Ethics: A Discussion Between Judith Butler and William Connolly." *Theory & Event* 4.2.
Butler, Judith, Ernesto Laclau, and Slavoj Žižek (2000). *Contingency, Hegemony, Universality: Contemporary Dialogues on the Left*. London: Verso.
Canguilhem, Georges (2000). *A Vital Rationalist: Selected Writings from Georges Canguilhem*. Edited by François Delaporte. Translated by Arthur Goldhammer. New York: Zone Books.
Carver, Terrell (1975). *Karl Marx: Texts on Method*. Oxford: Basil Blackwell.
Carver, Terrell (1982). *Marx's Social Theory*. Oxford: Oxford University Press.
Carver, Terrell (1996a). Introduction to *Marx: Later Political Writings*, ix–xx. Translated and edited by Terrell Carver. Cambridge: Cambridge University Press.

Carver, Terrell, trans. (1996b). *Marx: Later Political Writings*. Cambridge: Cambridge University Press.

Carver, Terrell (2008). "Marx's Conception of Alienation in the *Grundrisse*," in Marcello Musto (ed.), *Karl Marx's* Grundrisse*: Foundations of the Critique of Political Economy 150 Years Later*, 48–66. New York: Routledge.

Carver, Terrell (2010). "The *German Ideology* Never Took Place." *History of Political Thought* 31.1: 107–27.

Carver, Terrell (2014). "'Roughing It': The 'German Ideology' 'Main Manuscript'." Unpublished manuscript.

Cavarero, Adriana (2000). *Relating Narratives: Storytelling and Selfhood*. Translated by Paul A. Kottman. New York: Routledge.

Chambers, Samuel (2003). *Untimely Politics*. Edinburgh: Edinburgh University Press.

Chambers, Samuel (2007). "'Sex' and the Problem of the Body: Reconstructing Judith Butler's Theory of Sex/Gender." *Body & Society* 13.4: 47–75.

Chambers, Samuel (2009a). "A Queer Politics of the Democratic Miscount." *Borderlands* 8.2.

Chambers, Samuel (2009b). *The Queer Politics of Television*. London and New York: I. B. Tauris.

Chambers, Samuel (2011). "Untimely Politics *avant la lettre*: The Temporality of Social Formations." *Time and Society* 20.2: 199–225.

Chambers, Samuel (2013). *The Lessons of Rancière*. Oxford: Oxford University Press.

Chambers, Samuel, and Terrell Carver (2008). *Judith Butler and Political Theory: Troubling Politics*. London: Routledge.

Cohen, G. A. (2000). *Karl Marx's Theory of History: A Defence*. Princeton: Princeton University Press.

Connolly, William (1981). *Appearance and Reality in Politics*. New York: Cambridge University Press.

Connolly, William (1993). *The Terms of Political Discourse*. Oxford: Blackwell.

Connolly, William (2002). *Neuropolitics: Thinking, Culture, Speed*. Minneapolis: University of Minnesota Press.

Connolly, William (2005). *Pluralism*. Durham: Duke University Press.

Connolly, William (2008). *Capitalism and Christianity, American Style*. Durham: Duke University Press.

Connolly, William (2012). "Steps toward an Ecology of Late Capitalism." *Theory & Event* 15.1.

Connolly, William (2013). *The Fragility of Things: Self-Organizing Processes, Neoliberal Fantasies, and Democratic Activism*. Durham: Duke University Press.

Corlett, William (1996). "Containing Indeterminacy: Problems of Representation and Determination in Marx and Althusser." *Political Theory* 24.3: 464–92.

Coyle, Daniel (2012). "How Lance Armstrong Is Like Lehman Bros." *Slate*. (Online). Available from http://www.slate.com/articles/sports/sports/2012/10/lance_armstrong_doping_how_the_cyclist_is_like_lehman_bros.html (accessed February 3, 2014).

Dahl, Robert (1956). *A Preface to Democratic Theory*. Chicago: University of Chicago Press.

Dean, Jodi (2009). "Politics without Politics." *Parallax* 15.3: 20–36.

Deleuze, Gilles (1988). *Bergsonism*. Translated by Hugh Tomlinson and Barbara Habberjam. New York: Zone Books.

Deleuze, Gilles (2004). "How Do We Recognize Structuralism?" in David Lapoujade (ed.), *Desert Islands and Other Texts, 1953–1974*, 170–92. Translated by Michael Taormina. Los Angeles and New York: Semiotext(e).

Deleuze, Gilles, and Félix Guattari (1987). *A Thousand Plateaus: Capitalism and Schizophrenia*. Translated by Brian Massumi. Minneapolis: University of Minnesota Press.

Derrida, Jacques (1981a). *Dissemination*. Translated by Barbara Johnson. Chicago: University of Chicago Press.

Derrida, Jacques (1981b). *Positions*. Translated by Alan Bass. Chicago: University of Chicago Press.

Derrida, Jacques (1992). *Given Time: I. Counterfeit Money*. Translated by Peggy Kamuf. Chicago: University of Chicago Press.

Derrida, Jacques (1994). *Specters of Marx: The State of the Debt, The Work of Mourning & the New International*. Translated by Peggy Kamuf. New York: Routledge.

Derrida, Jacques (1995). "The Rhetoric of Drugs," in Peggy Kamuf (ed.), *Points . . . Interviews, 1974–1994*, 228–54. Translated by Michael Israel. Stanford: Stanford University Press.

Derrida, Jacques (1998). *Of Grammatology*. Translated by Gayatri Spivak. Baltimore: The Johns Hopkins University Press.

Dewey, John, and Arthur Bentley (1949). *Knowing and the Known*. Boston: Beacon Press.

Dinan, Matthew (2010). "Traces of Plato: Derrida and Plato on Philosophy and the City." Paper given at the Annual Meeting of the American Political Science Association, Washington, DC, September 2010.

Dolar, Mladen (1993). "Beyond Interpellation." *Qui Parle* 6.2: 75–96.

Edelman, Lee (2004). *No Future: Queer Theory and the Death Drive*. Durham: Duke University Press.

Engels, Friedrich (1968). "Letter to Conrad Schmidt, 27 October 1890." (Online). Translated by Donna Torr. Available from http://www.marxists.org/archive/marx/works/1890/letters/90_10_27.htm (accessed December 28, 2012).

Engels, Friedrich (1972). "Letter to J. Bloch, 21 September 1890." (Online). Translated by Brian Baggins. Available from http://www.marxists.org/archive/marx/works/1890/letters/90_09_21.htm (accessed December 28, 2012).

Engels, Friedrich (2000). "Letter to Conrad Schmidt, 12 March 1895." (Online). Translated by Donna Torr. Available from https://www.marxists.org/archive/marx/works/1895/letters/95_03_12.htm (accessed February 4, 2014).

Faigley, Lester (2002). *Fragments of Rationality: Postmodernity and the Subject of Composition*. Pittsburgh: University of Pittsburgh Press.

Finlayson, Alan (2003). Introduction to *Contemporary Political Thought: A Reader and Guide*, 1–28. Edited by Alan Finlayson. New York: New York University Press.

Foucault, Michel (1972). *The Archaeology of Knowledge*. Translated by A. M. Sheridan Smith. New York: Pantheon Books.

Foucault, Michel (1977). *Language, Counter-Memory, Practice: Selected Essays and Interviews by Michel Foucault*. Edited by Donald Bouchard. Translated by Donald Bouchard and Sherry Simon. Ithaca, NY: Cornell University Press.

Foucault, Michel (2005). *The Hermeneutics of the Subject: Lectures at the Collège de France, 1981–1982*. Translated by Graham Burchell. New York: Palgrave-Macmillan.

Foucault, Michel (2009). *History of Madness*. Edited by Jean Khalfa. Translated by Jonathan Murphy and Jean Khalfa. London: Routledge.

Gavin, William (1992). *William James and the Reinstatement of the Vague*. Philadelphia: Temple University Press.

Graeber, David (2011). *Debt: The First 5,000 Years*. New York: Melville House.

Gramsci, Antonio (1971). *Selections from the Prison Notebooks*. New York: International Publishers.

Grosz, Elizabeth (2004). *The Nick of Time: Politics, Evolution, and the Untimely*. Durham: Duke University Press.

Gunnell, John (1993). *The Descent of Political Theory: The Genealogy of an American Vocation*. Chicago: University of Chicago Press.

Gunnell, John (1996). "The Genealogy of American Pluralism: From Madison to Behavioralism." *International Political Science Review* 17.3: 253–65.

Hall, Stuart (1977). "Culture, the Media, and the 'Ideological Effect'," in James Curran, Michael Gurevitch, and Janet Woollacott (eds.), *Mass Communication and Society*, 315–48. Beverly Hills: Sage.

Hall, Stuart (1985). "Signification, Representation, Ideology: Althusser and the Post-Structuralist Debates." *Critical Studies in Mass Communication* 2.2: 91–114.

Hall, Stuart (2003). "Marx's Notes on Method: A 'Reading' of the '1857 Introduction'." *Cultural Studies* 17.2: 113–49.

Hamilton, Tyler, and Daniel Coyle (2012). *The Secret Race: Inside the Hidden World of the Tour de France*. New York: Bantam Books.

Hartsock, Nancy, and Neil Smith (1979). "On Althusser's Misreading of Marx's 1857 'Introduction'." *Science and Society* 43: 486–89.

Harvey, David (1981). "The Spatial Fix: Hegel, Von Thunen, and Marx." *Antipode* 13.3: 1–12.

Harvey, David (2001). "Globalization and the 'Spatial Fix'." *geographische revue* 2: 23–30.

Harvey, David (2006). *A Brief History of Neoliberalism*. New York: Oxford University Press.

Harvey, David (2007). *The Limits to Capital*. New York: Verso.

Harvey, David (2010a). *A Companion to Marx's* Capital. London: Verso.

Harvey, David (2010b). *The Enigma of Capital and the Crises of Capitalism*. New York: Oxford University Press.

Hegel, G. W. F. (2009). *The Phenomenology of Spirit*. Translated by J. B. Baillie. New York: Digireads.

Hegel, G. W. F. (2010). *The Science of Logic*. Translated by George di Giovanni. Cambridge: Cambridge University Press.

Heuberger, Jules, et al. (2013). "Erythropoietin Doping in Cycling: Lack of Evidence for Efficacy and a Negative Risk-Benefit." *British Journal of Clinical Pharmacology* 75.6: 1406–21.

Hobsbawm, Eric (1987). *The Age of Empire: 1875–1914*. New York: Pantheon Books.

Hollingdale, R. J., trans. (1990). *Twilight of the Idols and The Anti-Christ*. London: Penguin Books.

Honig, Bonnie (2010). "Antigone's Two Laws: Greek Tragedy and the Politics of Humanism." *New Literary History* 41.1: 1–33.

Honig, Bonnie (2013). *Antigone, Interrupted*. Cambridge: Cambridge University Press.

Hutchings, Kimberly (2008). *Time and World Politics: Thinking the Present*. Manchester: Manchester University Press.

Ignatiev, Noel (1995). *How the Irish Became White*. New York: Routledge.

James, William (1890). *The Principles of Psychology*. New York: Henry Holt.

Jameson, Fredric (2002). *The Political Unconscious: Narrative as a Socially Symbolic Act*. New York: Routledge.

Johnson, Barbara (1981). Translator's Introduction to *Dissemination*, by Jacques Derrida, vii–xxxv. Chicago: University of Chicago Press.

Jordan, Grant (2000). "*The Process of Government* and *The Governmental Process*." *Political Studies* 48.4: 788–801.

Judt, Tony (2008). *Reappraisals: Reflections on the Forgotten Twentieth Century*. New York: Penguin Press.

Kaufmann, Walter, trans. (1977). *The Portable Nietzsche*. New York: Penguin Books.

Kress, Paul (1970). *Social Science and the Idea of Process: The Ambiguous Legacy of Arthur F. Bentley*. Urbana, IL: University of Illinois Press.

Laclau, Ernesto, and Chantal Mouffe (1985). *Hegemony and Socialist Strategy: Toward a Radical Democratic Politics*. London: Verso.

Latour, Bruno (2004). *Politics of Nature: How to Bring the Sciences into Democracy*. Translated by Catherine Porter. Cambridge, MA: Harvard University Press.

Latour, Bruno (2005). *Reassembling the Social: An Introduction to Actor-Network Theory*. Oxford: Oxford University Press.

LaVaque-Manty, Mika (2006). "Bentley, Truman, and the Study of Groups." *Annual Review of Political Science* 9: 1–18.

Lavine, Thelma (2008). Introduction to *The Process of Government: A Study of Social Pressures*, by Arthur Bentley, xii–xxvii. New Brunswick, NJ: Transaction.

Lévi-Strauss, Claude (1966). *The Savage Mind*. Chicago: University of Chicago Press.

Lewis, Michael (2010). *The Big Short: Inside the Doomsday Machine*. New York: W. W. Norton.

Lloyd, Moya (2007). *Judith Butler: From Norms to Politics.* Cambridge: Polity.

Luxon, Nancy (2013). *Crisis of Authority: Politics, Trust, and Truth-Telling in Freud and Foucault.* New York: Cambridge University Press.

Lyotard, Jean-François (1988). *The Differend: Phrases in Dispute.* Translated by Georges Van Den Abbeele. Minneapolis: University of Minnesota Press.

Madison, James (2012). "No. 10," in *Federalist.* Chicago: Acheron Press.

Mann, Geoff, and Joel Wainwright (2008). "Marx without Guardrails: Geographies of the *Grundrisse.*" *Antipode* 40.5: 848–56.

Marx, Karl (1897). *Zur Kritik der Politischen Ökonomie.* Edited by Karl Kautsky. Stuttgart: Dietz Verlag.

Marx, Karl (1903). *Einleitung.* Edited by Karl Kautsky. In *Die Neue Zeit.* 21 Jahrgang, I Band. Stuttgart. No. 23: 710–18; No. 24: 741–45; No. 25: 772–81.

Marx, Karl (1904). *A Contribution to the Critique of Political Economy.* Translated by N. I. Stone. Chicago: Charles H. Kerr.

Marx, Karl (1953). *Grundrisse der Kritik der Politischen Ökonomie.* Reprint of 1939 and 1941 originals. Berlin: Dietz Verlag.

Marx, Karl (1955). "The Poverty of Philosophy." (Online). Translated by the Institute of Marxism Leninism. Available from http://www.marxists.org/archive/marx/works/1847/poverty-philosophy/index.htm (accessed February 13, 2014).

Marx, Karl (1959). *Economic and Philosophic Manuscripts of 1844.* (Online). Translated by Martin Mulligan. Available from https://www.marxists.org/archive/marx/works/1844/manuscripts/preface.htm (accessed March 8, 2014).

Marx, Karl (1973). *Grundrisse: Foundations of the Critique of Political Economy.* Translated and edited by Martin Nicolaus. London: Penguin Books.

Marx, Karl (1990). *Capital: Volume 1: A Critique of Political Economy.* Translated by Ben Fowkes. London: Penguin Classics.

Marx, Karl (1996a). "'Introduction' to the *Grundrisse,*" in Terrell Carver (ed.), *Marx: Later Political Writings,* 128–57. New York: Cambridge University Press.

Marx, Karl (1996b). "'Preface' to *A Contribution to the Critique of Political Economy,*" in Terrell Carver (ed. and trans.), *Marx: Later Political Writings,* 158–62. New York: Cambridge University Press.

Marx, Karl, and Friedrich Engels (1963). *Werke, Vol. 29.* Berlin: Dietz Verlag.

Marx, Karl, and Friedrich Engels (1974). *Werke, Vol. 37.* Berlin: Dietz Verlag.

Marx, Karl, and Friedrich Engels (1983). *Marx and Engels Collected Works, Vol. 40.* London: Lawrence and Wishart.

Marx, Karl, and Friedrich Engels (2000). *The German Ideology.* (Online). Translated by Tim Delaney, Bob Schwartz, and Brian Baggins. Available from http://www.marxists.org/archive/marx/works/1845/german-ideology/ (accessed February 12, 2010).

Marx, Karl, and Friedrich Engels (2002). *Marx and Engels Collected Works, Vol. 48.* London: Lawrence and Wishart.

Mathiowetz, Dean (2011). *Appeals to Interest: Language, Contestation, and the Shaping of Political Agency.* University Park, PA: The Pennsylvania State University Press.

Mayhew, Robert (1997). *Aristotle's Criticism of Plato's* Republic. Lanham, MD: Rowman & Littlefield.

McElwee, Sean (2013). "Sorry Neoliberals: Inequality Is Driven by Greed, not Technology." *Salon.* (Online). Available from http://www.salon.com/2013/11/30/sorry_neoliberals_inequality_is_driven_by_greed_not_technology/ (accessed: December 10, 2013).

McInerney, David (2005). "Althusser's Underground Railroad: From Dialectical Materialism to the Non-Philosophy of the Non-State." *Borderlands* 4.2.

McLellan, David, trans. (1971a). *Karl Marx: Early Texts*. Oxford: Blackwell.

McLellan, David (1971b). *The Thought of Karl Marx: An Introduction.* New York: Harper & Row.

Milchman, Alan, and Alan Rosenberg (2007). "The Aesthetic and Ascetic Dimensions of an Ethics of Self-Fashioning: Nietzsche and Foucault." *Parrhesia* 2: 44–65.

Mitchell, Timothy (2011). *Carbon Democracy: Political Power in the Age of Oil.* London: Verso.

Montag, Warren (1998). "Althusser's Nominalism: Structure and Singularity 1962–1966." *Rethinking Marxism* 10.3: 64–73.

Montag, Warren (2005). "'Foucault and the Problematic of Origins': Althusser's Reading of *Folie et déraison*." *Borderlands* 4.2.

Montag, Warren (2013). *Althusser and His Contemporaries: Philosophy's Perpetual War*. Durham: Duke University Press.

Morgenson, Gretchen, and Robert Gebeloff (2013). "Wall St. Exploits Ethanol Credits, and Prices Spike." *New York Times.* (Online). Available from http://www.nytimes.com/2013/09/15/business/wall-st-exploits-ethanol-credits-and-prices-spike.html?_r=0 (accessed February 2, 2014).

Nicolaus, Martin (1973). Foreword to *Grundrisse: Foundations of the Critique of Political Economy*. Translated and edited by Martin Nicolaus. London: Penguin Books.

Nietzsche, Friedrich (1889). *Götzen-Dämmerung; oder, Wie man mit dem Hammer philosophiert.* Frankfurt: Insel Verlag.

Nietzsche, Friedrich (1968). *The Will to Power*. Translated by Walter Kaufmann and R. J. Hollingdale. Edited by Walter Kaufmann. New York: Vintage Books.

Nietzsche, Friedrich (1996). *Human, All Too Human: A Book for Free Spirits*. Translated by R. J. Hollingdale. Cambridge: Cambridge University Press.

Nietzsche, Friedrich (1998). *Twilight of the Idols*. Translated by Duncan Large. New York: Oxford University Press.

Nietzsche, Friedrich (2006). *On the Genealogy of Morality*. Translated by Carol Diethe. New York: Cambridge University Press.

Norton, Anne (2004). *95 Theses on Politics, Culture, and Method*. New Haven: Yale University Press.

Oakeshott, Michael (1933). *Experience and Its Modes*. Cambridge: Cambridge University Press.

Oakeshott, Michael (1962). *Rationalism in Politics and Other Essays*. New York: Basic Books.

Oxford University Press (2010). *New Oxford American Dictionary*. Third Edition. New York: Oxford University Press. Available from http://www.oxfordamericandictionary.com (accessed February 6, 2010).

Oxford University Press (2011). *Oxford English Dictionary*. Third Edition. Oxford: Oxford University Press. Available from http://dictionary.oed.com/entrance.dtl (accessed February 6, 2010).

Panagia, Davide (2001). "*Ceci n'est pas un argument*: An Introduction to the Ten Theses." *Theory & Event* 5.3.

Panagia, Davide (2006). *The Poetics of Political Thinking*. Durham: Duke University Press.

Panagia, Davide (2010). "Partage du sensible," in Jean-Philippe Deranty (ed.), *Jacques Rancière: Key Concepts*, 95–103. London: Acumen.

Panagia, Davide (2014). "Jacques Rancière's Style." *Novel* 47.2: 284–300.

Postone, Moishe (1993). *Time, Labor, and Social Domination: A Reinterpretation of Marx's Critical Theory*. New York: Cambridge University Press.

Rahman, Smita (2009). "Secularism and Modernity: Alienation and the Renewal of Values in Political Islam." *Journal of Islamic Law and Culture* 11.1: 38–51.

Rancière, Jacques (1991). *The Ignorant Schoolmaster: Five Lessons in Intellectual Emancipation.* Translated by Kristin Ross. Stanford: Stanford University Press.

Rancière, Jacques (1995). *La mésentente: politique et philosophie.* Paris: Galilée.

Rancière, Jacques (1999). *Disagreement: Politics and Philosophy.* Translated by Julie Rose. Minneapolis: University of Minnesota Press.

Rancière, Jacques (2001). "Ten Theses on Politics." Translated by Rachel Bowlby and Davide Panagia. *Theory & Event* 5.3.

Rancière, Jacques (2006). *The Politics of Aesthetics: The Distribution of the Sensible.* Translated by Gabriel Rockhill. London: Continuum.

Rancière, Jacques (2009). "A Few Remarks on the Method of Jacques Rancière." *Parallax* 15.3: 114–23.

Read, Jason (2005). "The Althusser Effect: Philosophy, History, and Temporality." *Borderlands* 4.2.

Rohrhuber, Julian (2007). "Intuitions/Anschauungen." (Online). Available from http://wertlos.org/faits_divers/files/faits_divers_01.pdf (accessed February 3, 2014).

Ross, Andrew (2013). "The Politics of Debt Resistance." *New Labor Forum* 22.3: 12–15.

Rothbard, Murray (1958). "A Note on Burke's *Vindication of Natural Society*." *Journal of the History of Ideas* 19.1: 114–18.

Rushing, Sara (2009). "Preparing for Politics: Judith Butler's Ethical Dispositions." *Contemporary Political Theory* 9.3: 284–303.

Sartre, Jean-Paul (1991). *Critique of Dialectical Reason.* New York: Verso.

Shamir, Haim (1997). *France and Germany in an Age of Crisis, 1900–1960: Studies in Memory of Charles Bloch.* Leiden: E. J. Brill.

Sheingate, Adam (2013). "Creating Political Strategy, Controlling Political Work: Edward Bernays and the Emergence of the Political Consultant," in Gerald Berk, Dennis Galvan, and Victoria Hattam (eds.), *Political Creativity: Reconfiguring*

Institutional Order and Change, 146–66. Philadelphia: University of Pennsylvania Press.

Shulman, George (2011a). "Acknowledgment and Disavowal as an Idiom for Theorizing Politics." *Theory & Event* 14.1.

Shulman, George (2011b). "On Vulnerability as Judith Butler's Language of Politics: From *Excitable Speech* to *Precarious Life*." *WSQ: Women's Studies Quarterly* 39.1–2: 227–35.

Smith, Steven (1984a). *Reading Althusser: An Essay on Structural Marxism*. Ithaca, NY: Cornell University Press.

Smith, Steven (1984b). "Althusser and the Overdetermined Self." *The Review of Politics* 46.4: 516–38.

Smith, Steven (1985). "Althusser's Marxism without a Knowing Subject." *American Political Science Review* 79.3: 641–55.

Stolze, Ted (1998). "Deleuze and Althusser: Flirting with Structuralism." *Rethinking Marxism* 10.3: 51–63.

Strickland, Bill (2013). "Injustice for All." *Bicycling*. (Online). Available from http://www.bicycling.com/news/featured-stories/injustice-all?page=0,2 (accessed September 15, 2013).

Taylor, Charles (1985). *Human Agency and Language*. Cambridge: Cambridge University Press.

Taylor, Richard (1957). *Life, Language, Law: Essays in Honor of Arthur F. Bentley*. Yellow Springs, OH: The Antioch Press.

Thomas, Paul (1991). "Critical Reception: Marx Then and Now," in Terrell Carver (ed.), *The Cambridge Companion to Marx*, 23–54. Cambridge: Cambridge University Press.

Thompson, Edward (1978). *The Poverty of Theory: An Orrery of Errors*. New York: Monthly Review Press.

Truman, David (1951). *The Governmental Process: Political Interests and Public Opinion*. New York: Knopf.

Tucker, Robert, ed. (1978). *The Marx-Engels Reader*. New York: Norton.

Vilar, Pierre (1973). "Marxist History, a History in the Making: Towards a Dialogue with Althusser." *New Left Review* 80: 65–106.

Walker, Drew (2010). "Getting Beyond Repressive Subjection." Paper presented at the Annual Meeting of the American Political Science Association, Washington D.C., September 2010.

Walker, Drew (2013). "Humanism at the Limits: Alienation, Difference, Critique." PhD dissertation, Johns Hopkins University.

Walsh, David (2007). *From Lance to Landis: Inside the American Doping Controversy at the Tour de France*. New York: Ballantine Books.

Ward, James (1984). *Language, Form, and Inquiry: Arthur F. Bentley's Philosophy of Social Science*. Amherst, MA: University of Massachusetts Press.

Weiss, Richard, ed. (1999). *The Discovery of Anti-Matter: The Autobiography of Carl David Anderson, the Youngest Man to Win the Nobel Prize*. River Edge, NJ: World Scientific.

Wenman, Mark (2013). "William E. Connolly: Resuming the Pluralist Tradition in American Political Science." *Political Theory.* (Online). Available from http://ptx.sagepub.com/content/early/2013/10/18/0090591713507932.abstract (accessed January 15, 2014).

West, Cornel (2011). "Prophetic Religion and the Future of Capitalist Civilization," in Eduardo Mendieta and Jonathan VanAntwerpen (eds.), *The Power of Religion in the Public Sphere*, 92–100. New York: Columbia University Press.

Widder, Nathan (2008). *Reflections on Time and Politics*. State College, PA: Pennsylvania State University Press.

Wikipedia (2013). "Doping at the Tour de France." Available from http://en.wikipedia.org/wiki/Doping_at_the_Tour_de_France#cite_ref-3 (accessed February 11, 2014).

Williams, Caroline (2001). *Contemporary French Philosophy: Modernity and the Persistence of the Subject*. London: The Athlone Press.

Wise, J. Macgregor (2003). "Reading Hall Reading Marx." *Cultural Studies* 17.2: 105–12.

Wittgenstein, Ludwig (1953). *Philosophical Investigations*. Translated by G. E. M. Anscombe. Oxford: Blackwell.

Wolin, Sheldon (1969). "Political Theory as a Vocation." *American Political Science Review* 63.4: 1062–82.

Young, Robert (1990). *White Mythologies: Writing History and the West.* New York: Routledge.

Žižek, Slavoj (1990). "Beyond Discourse-Analysis." Appendix to Ernesto Laclau, *New Reflections on the Revolution of Our Time*, 249–60. London: Verso.

Index

www.ingramcontent.com/pod-product-compliance
Ingram Content Group UK Ltd.
Pitfield, Milton Keynes, MK11 3LW, UK
UKHW040153091026
15587UKWH00018B/59

9 781783 480227